Country Music and Philosophy

Back to the Future *and Philosophy: Essays
on Traveling Through the Space-Time Continuum*
(edited by Joshua Heter and Richard Greene, 2026)

'90s Alternative and Philosophy: Modern Rock Meditations (edited
by Joshua Heter and Richard Greene, forthcoming)

*Skateboarding and Philosophy:
Essays Concerning the Life of the Grind* (edited by
Joshua Heter and Josef Thomas Simpson, 2025)

Country Music and Philosophy

Honky Tonk Meditations

Edited by
JOSHUA HETER *and* BRETT COPPENGER

McFarland & Company, Inc., Publishers
Jefferson, North Carolina

This book has undergone peer review.

ISBN (print) 978-1-4766-9675-1
ISBN (ebook) 979-8-3686-0004-8

Library of Congress cataloging data are available

© 2026 Joshua Heter and Brett Coppenger. All rights reserved

Front cover image © Joshua Heter.

Printed in the United States of America

*McFarland & Company, Inc., Publishers
Box 611, Jefferson, North Carolina 28640
www.mcfarlandpub.com*

Acknowledgments

Working on this book has very much been a pleasure. We'd like to thank everyone at McFarland for their help in making this volume a reality. We are also indebted to the School of Humanities at Jefferson College and the Department of Philosophy at Tuskegee University as well as all of our families, friends, and colleagues for their support during our work on this project. We'd also like to thank the innumerable, gifted country artists whose music inspired this volume. And, of course, we would very much like to thank the talented authors whose work makes up this book.

Table of Contents

Country Strong

Joshua Heter *and* Brett Coppenger

The origin of country music has somewhat surprising similarities to the origin of philosophy. Those who composed and played what would eventually lead to the creation of country music weren't setting out to do anything world-changing. They were simply making *folk* music in the original and most literal sense of the term: music for and of the people.

Beginning almost from the moment they started settling in the New World and continuing through the next three centuries, immigrants (many of whom would make their home in the American South and throughout Appalachia) of course brought with them their culture which importantly included their musical traditions. Artists and performers playing the West African banjo, the Irish fiddle, the Italian mandolin, the Spanish guitar, and a host of other instruments would all find a new creative flourish in America as they made music together and among one another. As such, what they created owed its existence to the world at large, which, at least in that important regard, made it particularly American.

Crucially, it was the collection of so many eclectic voices, backgrounds, and styles which proved to be one of the greatest strengths for the newly American music-makers as their diversity led to so much innovation and creativity. Throughout this period, the music of the relatively new and burgeoning nation would take a variety of forms and be given a number of labels. Appalachian music, mountain music, African American spirituals, Cajun music, blues, and folk music (of various sorts) all gave a unique and distinct flavor to great swaths of the United States as the country began to form its own cultural identity.

By the early 1920s, country music as a unified cultural entity began to solidify. Before the end of the decade, the first country music records would be produced, many of the first recognizably country stars began performing (e.g., the Carter Family, Jimmie Rodgers, etc.), and the new medium of broadcast radio would carry the developing, homegrown sound throughout the regions with which it would become inextricably linked. Eventually, (Tennessee and) Nashville in particular would emerge as something of a hub and capital for country music, unofficial designations which the area maintains today.

Initially thought of by many as something of an unsustainable novelty, country music would only grow in popularity over the subsequent generations as it cemented itself as a permanent cultural fixture not only in America but across the globe. Today, country artists aren't limited as they once were, touring from town to town in the deep South, scratching out a respectable but mostly unimpressive living. Country artists—many of whom are the biggest stars in entertainment—now tour the world, playing to countless fans and raking in millions.

With all of this in mind and as we've alluded, the origin of philosophy is not entirely dissimilar from that of country music. Those who first engaged in and composed philosophy weren't setting out to do anything world-changing. They were simply trying to understand one another and the grand, bemusing universe in which they found themselves.

As history tells us, what we now recognize as (Western) philosophy arose in the 7th century BCE in Asia Minor, the area that is now modern-day Turkey. There, the intersection of well-worn trade routes led to the inevitable convergence of travelers from disparate parts of the map where their unique and conflicting worldviews clashed with one another. Because of this, many of those with incompatible beliefs and values would try to resolve their ideological disagreements with reason and argumentation. Thus, not unlike the emergence of country music, philosophy was born out of the unplanned intersection of a vast array of modes of thought and expression. As philosophers will still tell you, the ability to develop and defend one's ideas will only be strengthened when one is exposed to and challenged by a variety of differing perspectives.

Nevertheless, not long after its inception, philosophy quickly spread throughout the Ancient world. Importantly, (Greece and) Athens in particular became something of a capital and hub for the burgeoning discipline. Coincidentally, Nashville—again, a primary hub for country music—has been called "The Athens of the South," due to its large number of well-regarded institutions of higher learning.

During philosophy's earliest period, philosophers began to raise questions about the nature of reality, what it means to live a good life, the definition of justice, and the very existence and nature of the gods. Philosophy's influence on the world would steadily grow, and the discipline would eventually become the backbone of the most prestigious and important universities in the world. And long before they would bear the fruit for which they are better known, the geneses of disciplines like cosmology, evolutionary biology, and even computer science were set in motion by philosophers asking challenging questions about the world around them. What started as the attempts of a handful of folks seeking understanding of one another and the universe in general led to the reshaping of the world into the modern marvel of which we are all beneficiaries.

With all they have in common, it should perhaps be of little surprise that country music raises so many intriguing questions relevant to philosophy. And this book was put together to raise, clarify, and perhaps even answer some of those very questions. What exactly is country music; is it the type of thing that can be defined? Why do we listen to such sad country songs? What is authenticity, and does good country music have to be *authentically* country? What is the relationship between country music and patriotism; is patriotism always a good thing? Is country music's celebration of outlaws in any way morally problematic? Why do so many people claim to dislike country music? Is the simplicity that is often found in country music an aesthetic virtue or vice?

The authors of this book (and the all-too-fortunate editors who were able to bring them together) come to this project with a deep admiration for country music; they also hold a variety of differing worldviews and perspectives. Much like the artists whose work led to the creation of country music, as well as the thinkers who came before us, we take the diversity of our backgrounds, interests, and intellectual proclivities to be perhaps our greatest strength. So, we'd invite you to saddle up and ride along with us as we attempt to think deeply about, better understand, and more fully appreciate country music.

I

Getting to the Heart
of Country

On What Makes It Country

Jeannie DePoe *and* John M. DePoe

Whether or not you're a fan of country music, there seems to be an undeniable quality of "truth" within the lyrics of some of the greatest songs of the genre. Famed country songwriter Harlan Howard (along with a handful of others) went so far as to describe country music as "three chords and the truth," an idea which can be illustrated by seemingly countless examples. Hank Williams's song "I'm So Lonesome I Could Cry"[1] has some of the most poetic and moving words that have stood the test of time. Moreover, many country songs capture the emotional ecstasy and sorrow of human relationships, such as George Jones's "He Stopped Loving Her Today,"[2] Patsy Cline's "I Fall to Pieces,"[3] and Reba McEntire's "Does He Love You?"[4] And much of country music has eulogized the virtues of family life for the rural and the poor. "Workin' Man Blues" by Merle Haggard[5] and "Coal Miner's Daughter" by Loretta Lynn[6] are archetypes of this country music trope.

But just how important are these timeless, universal ideas to country music? More broadly, we might ask, what makes country music *country*? Johnny Cash is perhaps the most famous country artist of all time who, toward the twilight of his career, covered the Nine Inch Nails song "Hurt."[7] No one has ever accused Trent Reznor of writing country music. Yet, here is a song which, when sung by Johnny Cash, sounds authentically country. It sounds as if Cash himself wrote the song. Is that enough to make it country? All of these considerations again lead us to consider the question, what is it that makes a song count as country music? To state the question in slightly more philosophical terms, what is the essence of country music?

What Makes Something What It Is?

Before taking a stab at determining what makes country music "country," we need to say something about how philosophers go about defining things. In philosophy, a good definition will attempt to capture the essence or necessary character of whatever is being defined. If someone defined country music as "the music produced by George Strait and Garth Brooks," the definition would fall well short of philosophy's goal. While songs by George Strait and Garth Brooks represent clear *examples* of country music, as a matter of definition, they exclude much of what country music is. Most obviously, if country music is defined only as the music produced by George Strait and Garth Brooks, it would exclude all other music (produced by any other artist!), even other music that is obviously country. Sure, examples can be helpful for discovering the essence of a thing, but examples by themselves do not identify the essential characteristics of a thing.

An ideal definition of a thing will state the necessary and sufficient conditions that characterize that thing.[8] A necessary condition is one that—in all possible circumstances—must be met for the thing to be. A necessary condition for something to be a boat, for example, is that it floats in water. Another way to think about a necessary condition is that without it, the thing doesn't exist. Thus, if something doesn't float, then it ain't a boat! A sufficient condition is a circumstance that always describes when the thing exists. For instance, being a fishing boat is a sufficient condition for being a boat. Philosophers typically try to define a thing with a series of individually necessary conditions (i.e., each one is needed for a thing to be that kind of thing) that are jointly sufficient (i.e., when all such conditions are met together, they always ensure that the thing in question is that kind of thing).

We can illustrate this with Aristotle's definition of a human being as a rational animal. This might be understood as saying that there are two necessary conditions for being a human: (1) having rationality and (2) being an animal. Each condition is required to be human,[9] and anything that has both conditions at the same time must be a human. If it were possible, for example, to revivify a dead body so that it continued to have bodily life but lacked rationality (like a zombie, perhaps), then such a creature wouldn't be human. Having a rational nature, likewise, isn't sufficient on its own to ensure that a thing is human since angelic beings are rational. But because they are not animals, they wouldn't count as human.

So, when we try to give a definition of country music, what we are trying to do is to capture the essence of country music with a set of conditions or characteristics that are individually necessary and jointly sufficient to pick out all but only those songs that are country music. To put it another way, we want to identify the attributes that any music must have in order to be country and what features—when taken together—make a song a country song.

Failed Country Music Definitions

The final verse of David Allan Coe's song "You Never Even Called Me by My Name"[10] features an interesting commentary about the essence of country music. Right before the final verse, Coe tells his fans that after declaring his song to be a "perfect country and western song," Steve Goodman (the song's writer) objected on the grounds that "he hadn't said anything at all about Mama, or trains, or trucks, or prison, or gettin' drunk." He then wrote a fourth verse to the song to make it a "perfect" country and western song.

That final verse famously contains all of the important elements outlined by Coe: mama, trains, trucks, prison, and gettin' drunk. If taken literally—which almost certainly was not Coe's intent—he could be understood as claiming that the individually necessary and jointly sufficient conditions for a perfect country and western song are that the song be about Mama, trucks, prison, and gettin' drunk. By this criterion, however, some classic country songs wouldn't really be country songs at all. "It's a Great Day to Be Alive" by Travis Tritt[11] is nearly a perfect country song, even though it doesn't include any of the topics that Coe identified as necessary for a perfect country song to include. The same is true of George Strait's "Amarillo by Morning,"[12] The Carter Family's "Keep on the Sunny Side,"[13] Johnny and June's "I Walk the Line,"[14] and dozens of other classic country songs. So, the conditions laid out for a country song given by Coe are not necessary after all. Lots of great country songs don't include them.

Furthermore, the conditions stated by Coe aren't jointly sufficient for identifying a country song either. Consider the possibility of a rap artist creating a song about Mama, trucks, prison, and gettin' drunk, but the song is recorded using the music, beats, style, etc., of rap music. This shows that satisfying all of Coe's conditions doesn't make a song a country song. So, these conditions also fail to tell us what the sufficient conditions are for a country song.

The Family Resemblance Concept of Country Music

It turns out that some concepts can be defined using necessary and sufficient conditions, while others simply cannot. For example, take the concept of a game. Somewhat famously, no one seems to be able to provide a feature that necessarily characterizes every game.[15] Does every game require two people? No, there are solitary games. Do games require keeping score and having a winner? No, some games have no score and no winners or losers. For seemingly any proposed necessary condition for a game, one can find a game that doesn't need it. Likewise, there seems to be no universal set of characteristics that necessarily are included in every country song.[16] We'll leave this as an exercise for the reader, but for any characteristic that might be a plausible candidate for being necessary to country music, there are great country songs that don't have it.

For concepts like a game or country music, philosophers have often said that their essential character is best captured with a cluster of concepts or a *family resemblance* of characteristics. The idea here is that these concepts can be grasped by providing a series of characteristics (none of which are necessary), which give the overall look and feel of the concept or the family resemblance of the concept. Perhaps it is possible to give a list of characteristics where instances of the concept have at least one of them. If it is possible to state the essence of country music, we believe that the cluster concept or family resemblance approach is the most promising way to do so.

We would like to propose the following characteristics as constituting the paradigmatic cluster that characterizes the essence of country music, that is to say that these are the traits that constitute the "family resemblance" of country music:

1. … can be danced to as a waltz, two-step, or half-step.
2. … features the fiddle, steel guitar, or harmonica.
3. … lauds iconic music or musicians.
4. … authentically conveys observations about life from the experiences of the artist.
5. … has humorous lyrics.
6. … extols the virtues of blue-collar, working life.
7. … is about rural culture, including farming, ranching, and rodeoing.
8. … is about family (both broken and healthy ones).
9. … is about romantic relationships, including marital infidelity.
10. … is about the values of faith or patriotism.

This list is probably incomplete, but we found that our favorite country songs from various decades typically satisfy two or more of these conditions. David Allan Coe's song "If That Ain't Country"[17] contains themes of adversity and the truth of a boy growing up in a poor family. It also contains some lyrics that might be offensive. One line sticks out: "Mama she's old far beyond her time / From choppin' tobacco and I've seen her crying / When blood started flowin' from her calloused hand and it hurt me." The image of seeing a mother work hard to help her family and the pain it causes her son to see the effects of her physical labor strike at the heart of the listener. That's a truth that speaks to many people. The song continues as it describes the son in jail as his mother prays for him night after night. The theme of a mother's love is a near constant in country music. "Mama Tried" by Merle Haggard is one of the greatest reminders of this: "She tried to raise me better, but her pleading I denied."[18]

Top hits from Roger Miller and Joe Diffie meet criteria 1, 5, and (depending on the song) 6–10. Randy Travis's golden hits satisfy 1, 4, and 6–10 (depending on the song). The music of the Carter family is typically characterized by 1, 2, 4, and 10. Even Garth Brooks's songs (that some older readers may not care to accept as country) satisfy 2, 5, 7, 8, and 9. We don't see any problem with paradigmatic country artists, like Hank Williams (Sr. or Jr.), Merle Haggard, June Carter, George Jones, Charley Pride, Emmylou Harris, Dolly Parton, Keith Whitley, Dwight Yoakam, Brooks & Dunn, and any others being able to satisfy this account easily.

The problem for our family resemblance view is how to *exclude* songs that clearly aren't supposed to be classified as country music. For instance, Cat Stevens's song "The First Cut Is the Deepest"[19] meets at least two criteria from our list (4 and 9). But it clearly isn't a country song. How can we amend this account of country music to exclude such examples?

One idea is to provide clear ways to exclude a song from being classified as country music. For this litmus test, we have two characteristics that should exclude a song from counting as country music. First, a song can be excluded from the genre of country if it isn't causally influenced by previous country music.[20] Second, and perhaps more controversially, songs that lack an authentic connection between the song and the artist shouldn't be included in the genre of country music.

In the case of Cat Stevens's "The First Cut Is the Deepest," it can be excluded from country music because it was not produced by the causal influences of prior country music. Indeed, this may also explain why fans of country music disapprove of established artists in other genres who decide to produce a country album even though they have no deep connection to the roots of the movement (e.g., Aerosmith, Bon Jovi, Lady Gaga, etc.). It feels inauthentic and as if the artists lack understanding of those who have gone before them. The second exclusionary principle seems to explain why we want to reject generic, commercially produced music from Nashville that often gets played on country radio but seems out of step with the honesty and integrity conveyed by artists like Johnny Cash, Patsy Cline, or Willie Nelson. Much of the newer country music also seems to betray a stronger causal influence from hip-hop and pop music (thereby constituting a second reason to exclude it as being genuinely country). As Waylon Jennings put it, "But I don't think Hank done it this way, no, I don't think Hank done it this way, okay."[21]

Resemblance and the Global Family

There is a sound, a culture, and a tradition that we believe makes country music country. Early country music had a recognizable sound. It borrowed from all different genres and cultures to create this sound. The banjo comes from West Africa. The guitar comes from Spain. The fiddle (or violin, as fancy folk call it) is from the British Isles. Many of the early songs were folk songs from various countries or the mountains of Appalachia with African American spirituals constituting a large part of the country music songbook. These disparate influences came together to create the sound of country music.

More than a sound, country music also addresses specific themes in life. Country music sprang from the needs of Americans, especially those who felt left out, to tell their story. That is what is at the heart of country music: the story. From "Jolene" by Dolly Parton[22] to "Fist City" by Loretta Lynn,[23] we see that two women can have very different opinions about other women seeking the attention of their men. Women can have very strong opinions in both of these songs based on how they feel that they themselves would respond. Every woman can identify with one or both of them.

In the end, what makes country music "country" cannot be pinned down by a single instrument, theme, or even the voice behind the lyrics. Country music, like the stories it tells, is more than the sum of its parts. It owes its existence to a long history of cultural fusion, borrowing from a variety of musical traditions from around the globe. Yet, as we alluded to at the opening of this essay, there does seem to be something which holds it all together: an authenticity rooted in human experience. It doesn't matter if the song is about heartbreak, hard work, or small-town life; what defines country music is its ability to communicate truths that resonate across generations authentically. It's music that gives people a voice and allows them to be heard.

Notes

1. Williams, Hank. 1949. "I'm So Lonesome I Could Cry." B-side to "My Bucket's Got a Hole in It." Williams, Clarence (prod.) MGM Records.

2. Braddock, Bobby; Putnam, Curly. 1979. "He Stopped Loving Her Today." *I Am What I Am.* Jones, George (rec. artist). Sherrill, Billy (prod.) Epic.

3. Cochran, Hank; Harlan, Howard. 1961. "I Fall to Pieces." *Showcase.* Cline, Patsy (rec. artist). Bradley, Owen (prod.) Decca Records.

4. Knox, Sandy; Stritch, Billy. 1993. "Does He Love You?" *Greatest Hits: Volume Two.* McEntire, Reba (rec. artist). Brown, Tony; McEntire, Reba (prods.) MCA Nashville.

5. Haggard, Merle. 1969. "Workin' Man Blues." *A Portrait of Merle Haggard.* Haggard, Merle (rec. artist). Nelson, Ken (prod.) Capitol Records.

6. Lynn, Loretta. 1969. "Coal Miner's Daughter." *Coal Miner's Daughter.* Lynn, Loretta (rec. artist). Bradley, Owen (prod.) Decca Records.

7. Reznor, Trent. 1995. "Hurt." *American IV: The Man Comes Around.* Cash, Johnny (rec. artist). Rubin, Rick; Cash, June Carter (prods.) Universal Records.

8. For a helpful resource on necessary and sufficient conditions, see Brennan, Andrew. 2024. "Necessary and Sufficient Conditions," *The Stanford Encyclopedia of Philosophy,* Edward N. Zalta & Uri Nodelman (eds.).

9. Some might think that the first condition isn't required because small children and mentally incapacitated individuals may lack rationality, yet they are still human. Those in the Aristotelian tradition would say that these people have a rational nature, even if it is impaired or in a state of potency. Thus, these cases where it appears that individuals lack rationality still have a rational nature (not fully realized), which satisfies this condition.

10. Goodman, Steve. 1971. "You Never Even Called Me by My Name." *Once Upon a Rhyme.* Coe, David Allan (rec. artist). Bledsoe, Ron (prod.) Columbia Records.

11. Scott, Darrell. 2000. "It's a Great Day to Be Alive." *Down the Road I Go.* Tritt, Travis (rec. artist). Tritt, Travis; Walker, Billy Joe, Jr. (prods.) Columbia Nashville.

12. Fraser, Paul; Stafford, Terry. 1973. "Amarillo by Morning." *Strait from the Heart.* Strait, George (rec. artist). Blake, Mevis (prod.) Atlantic Records.

13. Blenkhorn, Ada; Entwisle, J. Howard. 1928. "Keep on the Sunny Side." *Keep on the Sunny Side.* The Carter Family (rec. artist). Various producers. Bluebird Records.

14. Cash, Johnny. 1956. "I Walk the Line." *Johnny Cash with His Hot and Blue Guitar!* Cash, Johnny (rec. artist). Phillips, Sam (prod.) Sun Records.

15. Wittgenstein, Ludwig. 1953. *Philosophical Investigations.* Anscombe, G.E.M. (trans.) The MacMillan Company.

16. *Ibid.*

17. Coe, David Allan; Coe, Deborah; Spears, Fred. 1977. "If That Ain't Country." *Rides Again.* Coe, David Allan (rec. artist). Bledsoe, Ron (prod.) Columbia Records.

18. Haggard, Merle. 1968. *Mama Tried.* Haggard, Merle (rec. artist). Nelson, Ken (prod.) Capitol Records.

19. Stevens, Cat. 1967. "The First Cut Is the Deepest." *New Masters.* Stevens, Cat (rec. artist). Hurst, Mike (prod.) Deram.

20. We will have to ask for a special exception to be made for "foundational" country music, that is, the first canonical country songs that were created before prior country music existed

21. Jennings, Waylan. 1975. "Are You Sure Hank Done It This Way." *Dreaming My Dreams.* Jennings, Waylan (rec. artist). Clement, Jack (prod.) RCA Nashville.

22. Parton, Dolly. 1973. "Jolene." *Jolene.* Parton, Dolly (rec. artist). Ferguson, Bob (prod.) RCA Victor.

23. Lynn Loretta. 1968. "Fist City." *Fist City.* Bradley, Owen (prod.) Decca Records.

Heaps, Barbecue, and Country Music

Zack Garrett

Country music is a lot like barbecue (or "bbq"). Of course, I don't just mean that there is a fair amount of overlap between those who listen to country music and those who enjoy bbq. What I have in mind here is that the way the concept of country music works is a lot like the way the concept of bbq works. There are many different factors that go into making something bbq. It ought to include meat, but the kind of meat, the way it's cooked, and the sides which often accompany that meat can vary. Bbq must have a special combination of seasoning, but that seasoning can be delivered through a dry rub or a sauce. Country music, in a similar fashion, has many dimensions on which it can vary. Country music seems to need string instruments, but that role could be fulfilled by a fiddle, a guitar, or a mandolin. Country music also seems to need something like a theme that ties it to the past, but the theme could be anything from small-town romances to the gospel message.

However, for both bbq as well as country music, all of these varying dimensions lead to borderline cases. There are meals that straddle the line between bbq and non-bbq. There are songs that are a bit country but not enough to clearly or unquestionably categorize them as such. This is because both bbq and country music are *vague* concepts; neither has a precise or rigid definition.

In this essay, we'll explore the kind of philosophical analysis that applies to both bbq and country music. To do this, we'll focus heavily on artists who have transitioned or straddled genres. From Taylor Swift's transformation from country to pop star to Post Malone's album *F-1 Trillion*, we'll closely examine the grilled chickens and impossible meats of the country music world. We'll then explore the many philosophical theories of vague concepts and what light they might shed on country music.

Heaps of Sand

The concept of country music and the concept of bbq share one important quality: they are vague. In this way, they are also similar to concepts like "heap (of sand)," "bald," and "rich." Vague terms or concepts famously lead to a particularly thorny paradox known as the *sorites* paradox. "Sorites" comes from the ancient Greek word "σωρός" for "heap," but I will present the paradox here in terms of the concept, "rich." After all, I doubt many people nowadays care what a heap is, but most of us care about the meaning of the word "rich." This is evidenced at least in part by the fact that it made at least some news that Taylor Swift recently crossed the threshold of being a billionaire. To understand the paradox, consider the following two principles:

> (Base) A person with $1 in net worth is not rich.
> (Tolerance) Adding or taking away $1 in net worth will never make the difference between someone being rich and them being not rich.

Both of these principles seem true. For (Base), surely $1 is not enough to be rich. If it were, then the word "rich" would lose its meaning; almost everyone would be rich. If (Tolerance) were false, then someone could fluctuate from being not rich to rich (and vice versa) by buying a cup of coffee in the morning and then finding a dollar bill on the ground later that afternoon. This doesn't seem to track with the way we use the word "rich." The status of being rich seems a little more stable than this. Note, however, that if you think (Tolerance) is false, and that a single dollar can determine whether or not someone is rich, then why couldn't we say the same thing about a single penny or even $0.000001? We can make the change in net worth in (Tolerance) arbitrarily small, but doing so will only make the principle harder to reject.

But accepting both (Base) and (Tolerance) leads to a problem. Take someone with a net worth of $1, then give them one additional dollar at a time. Since, according to (Tolerance), $1 never changes them from non-rich to rich, they would never become rich. Note that this is the case no matter how many dollars they are given. If the giving is continued long enough and done incrementally enough, then they will eventually have as much money as Taylor Swift and still not be rich. So, if we accept both (Base) and (Tolerance), we reach a clearly absurd conclusion. Both (Base) and (Tolerance) seem true, but from them, we reach what seems to be an absurd conclusion. A person with more money than Taylor Swift isn't rich! Something must have gone wrong here. Either the logic we used to get from (Base) and (Tolerance) to the conclusion is flawed, or one of the two principles is false. At the end of this essay, we'll explore some attempts at solving this paradox. For now, though, we need to show how bbq and country music relate to all of this.

Country Music Scores

Let's start by analyzing bbq and use what we learn from this analysis to perform a similar study of country music. Suppose we wanted to know whether or not a particular meal counted as bbq. One way we could decide this is by creating a point system to judge meals for their bbq-ness. Bbq-like properties earn the meal points and non-bbq-like properties lose it points. The point system may look something like this:

Meat	Seasoning	Sides
Beef +1	Vinegar +0.2	Cornbread +1
Pork +1	Tomato Paste +0.2	Mac and Cheese +1
Chicken +0.5	Cumin +0.2	Pasta -1
Lamb -0.5	Curry -0.5	
No Meat -5		

To judge whether a meal counts as bbq, add up the points the meal gets from the list. Call the score that a meal receives its bbq-score. The higher a meal's bbq-score, the more bbq it is. For example, a pulled pork sandwich with a side of mac and cheese may get a score of 2.4 or more (depending on the seasoning used). Note that the point system above is woefully inadequate for the task. It is missing, for example, a way of evaluating the proportions of the spices that make up the sauce. Too much tomato paste and not enough cumin and you start to get something more akin to tomato sauce as opposed to bbq sauce. So, the amount of points garnered by the seasoning combinations will depend on their proportions. Many other aspects of bbq are missing as well, but giving a full analysis would take this essay too far afield (and make me too hungry!).

Nevertheless, we are now in a position to make sense of the vagueness of the concept of bbq. If we line up a number of meals such that the first ones are clearly not bbq and the last ones clearly are, then we can generate the sorites paradox for the concept of bbq. On one side, we start with Caesar salads, say, and move eventually to charcoal-grilled hamburgers. Continuing from hamburgers, we make it to pulled pork sandwiches and eventually to brisket and ribs. Somewhere along the line from meals that do not receive enough points to those that do, we have a point at which we can draw a (figurative or literal) line: non-bbq meals on one side; bbq meals on the other. The point, however, is that it seems impossible to draw a *non-arbitrary* line for exactly how many points are needed. If we choose a meal with a score of 1.6 as being bbq, then why not treat a meal with a score of 1.599 as bbq? After all, the difference between the two meals may be imperceptible in regard to the amount of cumin or chili powder that's used. But then, if a 1.599 meal counts as bbq, why not a 1.598 meal? Why not a 1.597 meal (and so on)?

Again, a similar analysis can be given for the concept of country music. There are a variety of dimensions on which we can judge whether or not a song is country, and we can assign values to those different dimensions. Here is another (potentially inadequate) example of how this might be done.

Instrumentation	Lyrical Themes	Artist's Background
Has Strings +1	The old days +1	As Hank Williams put it, "has looked at the backside of a mule" +2[1]
Electric Instruments -1	Religious themes +1	From NYC -2
No Strings -2	Heartbreak +1	
	Partying in the club -1	

We can now arrange songs on a scale from those that have particularly high country scores to those with low scores. The songs that score highly are clearly country songs. Those that score lower are not. The problem posed by the sorites paradox is drawing a satisfying line between the country songs and the non-country songs. To better understand the sorites paradox of country music, we can treat Taylor Swift's transition from a country star at the beginning of her career to a pop star more recently as a starting place.

A Sorites Paradox for Country

Swift's early discography is almost entirely full of paradigm examples of the modern conception of country music. The instrumentation on her early records primarily focused on the guitar, and Swift's voice was accented by the quintessential twang of a country singer. Though her early songs focus heavily on the experiences of young girls, they often involve elements of heartbreak. These early songs will score highly using the kind of point system described in the previous section.

Many purists about the genre might question the authenticity of her music. This controversy reveals an interesting aspect of the kinds of point systems we're using and of the genre of country music in general. The concept of country music has changed drastically over the century of its existence. From Ralph Peer's search for old-timey sounding music to the guitar playing of Maybelle Carter. From the yodeling of Jimmie Rodgers to the singing cowboys of the late '30s, country music started as an incredibly malleable genre and has only continued to change over the decades. Compare, for example, the songs of Hank Williams, Sr., to those of Randy Travis. Philosopher Emmie Malone argues that country music is a dual-character concept. Its growth is born from a conflict between traditionalists (who wish to keep country music the way it is) and progressives (who seek to build on the genre and move it forward).[2] But, as country music does move forward, the point system must adapt. As guitars have become more common, an increasing number of songs will have higher country scores.

Though Swift may have started country, her music evolved faster than the genre, and so her later albums move too far for country music to keep up and would almost certainly be better classified as pop. Swift's transition from country to pop was not immediate. Her songs went through the blurry gray area between the two genres. In terms of the point system, some of the songs in that middle period had point values that did not put them squarely with the country songs or with the pop songs. That is to say, some of her songs were analogous to bbq cheeseburgers or vegan short ribs on the bbq-scale; they're borderline cases. So, Swift's discography gives us a good starting example of a sorites paradox for country music.

Imagine we went through the process of assigning country scores to each of Swift's songs from her first album through *Red*. These country scores will not necessarily be arranged chronologically. Some of her later songs may have higher values than earlier songs. Still, we could arrange all of the songs from those that are the most country to those that are the least so. We won't take on such a herculean task here, but we can at least consider the beginning of such a list.

"Picture to Burn,"[3] "Teardrops on My Guitar,"[4] and "Our Song"[5] all rate as highly country. All of them are reminiscent of innocent small-town relationships. All of them keep a twangy guitar as the central focus of the instrumentation. Even the so-called "Pop Version" of "Our Song" maintains a number of features of modern country music.

Similar themes continue into *Fearless* with the songs "Fifteen"[6] and "You Belong with Me."[7] Things begin to evolve with the aptly titled "Change."[8] Unlike many of the other songs on the album, "Change" gives off the feeling of a pop/rock song. An electric guitar provides a strong backing to lyrics about revolution and change—lyrical themes uncommon in a genre that sells itself on nostalgia for a simpler time. This makes "Change" less country than the other songs on the album and less country than some of the songs from *Speak Now* and *Red*.

The song "Speak Now"[9] slides along the scale from country to pop. Swift's singing takes on a more singsong feeling akin to many pop songs. But, in "Speak Now," the chorus brings the song back to the kind of country music that Swift started her career with. The song likely falls in the blurry area where drawing lines will become difficult.

"Enchanted"[10] presents another interesting example of a borderline case. Bits of Swift's older sound can still be heard in the song, but it received mixed reviews. From pop to rock to country, it was given different classifications by different critics. Music critic Brittany McKenna describes it like this: "The power balladry of 'Enchanted' is one of several tracks on *Speak Now* that find Swift venturing outside of the boundaries of country music."[11] *The Telegraph*, on the other hand, describes the song as "one of Swift's more old school country tracks."[12] One of the best indicators of a borderline case of a vague concept is intractable disagreement. When two sides disagree about the classification of something and they both seem reasonable, it may be the case that they *are* both reasonable. The thing they are trying to classify is simply vague and within the blurry boundary.

From this point on, Swift's songs move to being on the pop side of the scale from country to pop. A few songs on the album *Red* will still receive a high country-score. "All Too Well,"[13] for example, scores higher than many of the songs on *Speak Now*. "22"[14] and "Shake It Off,"[15] on the other hand, fall squarely within the pop genre with few of the country music elements remaining.

If we lined up all of Swift's songs and tried to find the line between country and pop/rock, would we be able to do so? We can, of course, find the clear and obvious cases, but drawing a line between any two songs in the blurry boundary between country and pop will feel unsatisfying. If "Enchanted" counts as country, then why not "Story of Us"?[16] Swift is only human, and she can only release so many songs. But we could imagine Swift making substantially more songs that fill in the gaps on our scale from country to pop. If all of those gaps were filled in, then we would have a genuine sorites series just like the one about the concept, "rich." Drawing a line between country and pop would feel as unsatisfying as drawing a line between rich and non-rich.

Of course, we don't need Swift to fill in the gaps in her discography. Countless songs fall in all of the spots on the scale from country to pop. For instance, Post Malone recently released his own potential country album, *F-1 Trillion*. Malone, a New York-born, face-tattooed musician, has been melding genres for some time. *F-1 Trillion* contains some mostly paradigm cases of country music—some even recorded with established country music stars such as Tim McGraw, Brad Paisley, and Dolly Parton. Despite the country trappings of his songs, they receive lower country scores because of the artist's non-rural background. In addition, Malone and Hank Williams, Jr., sing the lines "platinum on my teeth, wagyu on my grill" and "my lambo and my ammo's all camo green."[17] They mix the bravado and urban trappings of many rap songs with the rural and nostalgic themes of country music.

Songs run the gamut from country to pop. For most any value we could imagine on the scale of country scores, there is a song that gets that value. So, we can create a genuinely difficult sorites paradox out of country music songs. But remember that the sorites paradox is problematic. In the case of the concept, "rich," it seems to entail that no one is rich. In the context of country music, if we start from a country song and move down the scale, we can get to the conclusion that every song is a country song. This can't be right. Surely, "Baby Shark" is not a country song. So, if we wish to define country music, we will have to deal with the sorites paradox.

Solutions to the Paradox

One of the most popular solutions to the sorites paradox is called *epistemicism*.[18] According to epistemicists, every vague concept we use has a precise meaning; the epistemicist would say that there is (for instance) an exact ratio of seasonings down to the molecular level for a sauce to count as a bbq sauce. One extra molecule of tomato paste could render the sauce a non-bbq sauce. Epistemicists simply believe that we are ignorant of the precise meanings of our words. So, they would say that there is an exact country-score that, once exceeded, would determine that a song is in fact country. In the debate about which songs on Swift's album *Speak Now* are country and which are not, some people are right and others are wrong; we simply aren't in a position to know who is who. Epistemicism strikes many as counterintuitive because it entails that we do not know the meanings of many of the words we seem to be competently using. According to epistemicism, a person really can be rich one second, lose a penny, and no longer be rich.

Another theory of vagueness that attempts to solve the paradox is called contextualism.[19] What we think of as country music changes with context. If you've been listening to a lot of old-school country—think the Carter Family or Hank Williams, Sr.—then Swift's early country albums may not seem to be country music at all. On the other hand, if you've been listening to Miranda Lambert or Tim McGraw, then Swift's music will strike you as more country. Contextualists believe that when we move along a sorites series like the one we can create out of country songs, the line between country and pop seems to move along with us. The line stays just out of reach. Each song in the series is a little less country, but because it is similar to the previous song in the series, it still feels country. The fact that each song is compared with the previous song means that we are unwilling to say that it is the first pop song in the series, and so the line between country and pop moves down the series ahead of us.

According to both epistemicism and contextualism, there is a fact of the matter about which songs are country and which are not. Contextualists just believe that these facts change from context to context. However, contextualists run into a problem when they are presented with a borderline case of a country song out of the blue, with no prior context. Imagine you haven't listened to any music in years and suddenly hear Post Malone's "Finer Things." Without nearby songs in your context, you cannot determine which side of the line the song is on.

Many philosophers find both epistemicism and contextualism problematic and argue that there actually isn't a fact of the matter about which songs are country and which are pop. Of course, there are clear examples of country songs and clear examples of pop songs, but the ones that fall between the clear cases are neither country nor non-country, they fall through the gap between the concepts. We can think of these theories as "gappy" theories. They treat vague concepts as being ill-defined and failing to completely draw boundaries between the things that fall within the concept and the things that don't.[20]

Of course, another option in responding to the issue is to simply give up on the whole idea of grouping songs into country and pop in the first place. Instead of drawing some cutoff in country scores and saying anything with a value higher than the cutoff is country, we might just stop at the country scores themselves. That is to say, we treat any particular song as country *to a degree* but never country full-stop. For example, "Teardrops on My Guitar" might have a country-score of 4 and "Enchanted" a score of 2, but neither of them is country full-stop—they are each just country to varying degrees.[21] Of course, this seems to go against the way we actually use the label "country music." When we attach the genre to a song on our playlists, we do so in a binary way. It's either country, or it ain't.

Higher-Order Vagueness

It's also worth pointing out that you may have any number of problems with the values we assigned to the country scores or to the way we've evaluated songs throughout this essay, as you should (or at the very least, as is to be expected). But this is indicative of a further problem associated with vague concepts. Sometimes vagueness itself is vague. I weighted the dimensions of country music according to *my* assessment, but you may weight them differently. Doing so will lead to a different ordering of the songs in our sorites series. This can lead to a song being clearly country on one approach to the scale and borderline country on another. Like most disagreements about vague concepts, our disagreement about the country scores seems unresolvable. So, it too may be vague. This would mean that a song could be a borderline borderline country song. It could fall in the blurry boundary between the songs that are clearly country and those that are in the blurry boundary between country and pop.

Vagueness is present in many concepts we use, but concepts corresponding to genres of music are particularly vague. If you've taken anything from this essay, it very well may be that there is no satisfying answer to be found here. Epistemicism and contextualism both tell us that there is a line between country and other genres, but it is elusive. So-called "gappy" theories tell us that there is no line to be found at all, and so no answer about whether the borderline country songs are country or not. The degree theory is nice, but it doesn't really match the way we use words, and it relies on a scale that, because of higher-order vagueness, is up for much debate. If there is any satisfying takeaway here, it is probably that we should embrace the borderline cases of country music for what they are … music. Listen to the songs you enjoy, and don't worry too much about their classification.

NOTES

1. Peterson, Richard A. 1997. *Creating Country Music: Fabricating Authenticity*. University of Chicago Press, 217.
2. Malone, Emmie. 2023. "Country Music and the Problem of Authenticity." *British Journal of Aesthetics*, 63, no. 1, 75–90.
3. Swift, Taylor; Rose, Liz. 2006. "Picture to Burn." *Taylor Swift*. Chapman, Nathan (prod.) Big Machine Records.
4. Swift, Taylor; Rose, Liz. 2006. "Teardrops on My Guitar." *Taylor Swift*. Chapman, Nathan (prod.) Big Machine Records.
5. Swift, Taylor. 2006. "Out Song." *Taylor Swift*. Chapman, Nathan (prod.) Big Machine Records.
6. Swift, Taylor. 2008. "Fifteen." *Fearless*. Chapman, Nathan (prod.) Big Machine Records.
7. Swift, Taylor; Rose, Liz. "You Belong with Me." *Fearless*. Chapman, Nathan (prod.) Big Machine Records.
8. Swift, Taylor. 2008. "Change." *Fearless*. Chapman, Nathan (prod.) Big Machine Records.
9. Swift, Taylor. 2010. "Speak Now." *Speak Now*. Chapman, Nathan. Big Machine Records.

10. Swift, Taylor. 2010. "Enchanted." *Enchanted*. Chapman, Nathan (prod.) Big Machine Records.

11. McKenna, Brittany. 2017. "Why Taylor Swift's 'Speak Now' Is Her Best Album." *Billboard*.

12. Moloshok, Danny. 2024. "10 of the Best Taylor Swift Songs." *The Telegraph*.

13. Swift, Taylor; Rose, Liz. 2012. "All Too Well." *Red*. Chapman, Nathan (prod.) Big Machine Records.

14. Swift, Taylor; Martin, Max; Shellback. 2013. "22." *Red*. Martin, Max; Shellback (prod.) Big Machine Records.

15. Swift, Taylor; Martin, Max; Shellback. 2014. "Shake It Off." *1989*. Martin, Max; Shellback (prods.) Big Machine Records.

16. Swift, Taylor. 2011. "The Story of Us." *Speak Now*. Chapman, Nathan (prod.) Big Machine Records.

17. Malone, Post; Bell, Louis; Vojtesak, Ryan; Combs, Luke; Smith, Ernest Keith; McNair, James. 2024. "Finer Things." *F-1 Trillion*. Bell, Louis; Handsome, Charlie; Hoskins (prods.) Mercury Records; Republic Records.

18. For more on epistemicicsm, see Williamson, Timothy. 2022. *Vagueness*. Routledge.

19. For a succinct and clear exposition of contextualism, see Raffman, Diana. 2005. "How to Understand Contextualism about Vagueness: Reply to Stanely." *Analysis*, 65, no. 3, 244–248.

20. For this kind of analysis of Sorites paradoxes, see Tye, Michael. 1994. "Sorites Paradoxes and the Semantics of Vagueness." *Philosophical Perspectives*, 8, 189–206.

21. For this kind of degree approach to Sorites paradoxes, see Smith, Nicholas J.J. 2008. *Vagueness and Degrees of Truth*. Oxford University Press.

The Essence of Country

Catherine Villanueva Gardner

In many ways, the summer of 2024 was a watershed moment for Black country artists. Shaboozey tore up the *Billboard* Top 100 with "A Bar Song (Tipsy),"[1] the theme of which is pretty self-explanatory, while Beyoncé held court on the album charts with *Cowboy Carter*, a sophisticated musical ode to her country roots which debuted at #1 on the *Billboard* album chart. Indeed, Beyoncé was the first Black woman to achieve such a status since the Top Country Albums list began in 1964, and "Texas Hold 'Em," the introductory single from the album, was the first success in the genre for Beyoncé.[2]

Despite their commercial success, the country authenticity of certain Black American artists, such as Beyoncé and Lil Nas X, has been questioned by both music critics and country fans alike. Even though established country star Billy Ray Cyrus participated in the music video and on a remix, Lil Nas X's "Old Town Road" (originally released in 2018) was not considered by many to be *truly* country.[3] The song reached #19 on the *Billboard* Hot Country Songs Chart in early 2019 until the magazine disqualified the song, claiming it did not fit the country genre, stating that while the song "incorporates references to country and cowboy imagery, it does not embrace enough elements of today's country music to chart in its current version."[4]

Moreover, the saga of "Daddy Lessons," from Beyoncé's *Lemonade* (2016), points to the tensions over genre-crossing by artists, tensions that may be racially coded.[5] Apparently, Beyoncé submitted the song to the Grammy nominating committee for inclusion in the country category but was rejected.[6] As stated in *Rolling Stone*, this rejection is particularly puzzling considering that another track from the same album, "Don't Hurt Yourself"[7] (a fierce Janis Joplin–style fusion of soul and blues), was nominated for Best *Rock* Performance.[8] Even when Beyoncé performed "Daddy Lessons" with The Chicks at the 50th Annual Country Music Association

Awards to acclaim from critics, winning two Golden Boot awards in 2017, there was still some pushback from other country artists. Indeed, music critics have interpreted lyrics in "Ameriican Requiem," the opening song of *Cowboy Carter*, as addressing this exclusion: "Said I wouldn't saddle up, but / If that ain't country, tell me, what is?"[9]

Thus, now seems to be an opportune moment to explore what is perhaps the fundamental, underlying issue here. What exactly *is* country music? Is there some essence or cultural touchstone that makes a song authentically country? Some of the resistance to categorizing these Black artists as "country" may be rooted in racial bias, but it is also rooted in cherished definitions of country music *itself*. Rather than engaging in excavating racism, therefore, perhaps we should focus on an examination of identifying the very essence of country music. And here we can turn to the discipline of philosophy as it will be able to guide us to ask the *right questions* about what the essence of country actually is. Taking my lead from Beyoncé, I shall argue that the essence of country music is not simply about regional accents or particular musical instruments; it's also about a certain attitude of resistance, and it's about the speaking of unvarnished social truths.

Significantly, country music traditions are often seen as identical to "American traditions." On the one hand, and problematically, this has sometimes led to a racial coding that accompanies these claims to "Americanness." But, on the other hand, the issue runs far deeper than this racial coding. Part of the conundrum with country music is that, unlike other genres of popular music, *its very essence* is defined by its *being a traditional music*.[10] In other words, there is an important genre issue at play. Thus, if we hope to truly understand its essence, we need to investigate these traditional elements of country music.

Country Music as Traditional Music

It is initially tempting to believe that the essence of country music is composed solely of sartorial signifiers (e.g., hats, boots, jeans), particular themes (e.g., horses, religion, drinking, trucks, etc.), and a design aimed at accompanying the distinctly American leisure hour (which is why so many country songs are centered around barbecues, bars, line dancing, etc.). Even when one hears country music in the workplace, its role is often to remind employees and customers that the weekend is just around the corner. But country music is not just associated with a specific form of American entertainment; it has always had a private and serious side, with songs about relationships, heartache, and death. But does this serious side also have a public or political facet?

Initially, it may seem that the forays of country music into the political world tend to be infrequent. Alan Jackson's song about the tragedy of 9/11, "Where Were You (When the World Stopped Turning)," is an interesting counterexample where Jackson asks his audience what they were doing during the attack on the Twin Towers: "Did you stand there in shock at the sight of that black smoke / Risin' against that blue sky? / Did you shout out in anger in fear for your neighbor?"[11] Even though the song may be considered trite and sentimental by critics, there is little doubt that Jackson was able to capture the almost impossible-to-articulate feelings of Americans experiencing large-scale terrorism on their home soil. What is significant about the song is that Jackson deliberately frames himself as just an average Joe who has little need of knowledge outside of religion or the Bible, and he describes himself as particularly nonpolitical (e.g., by not watching CNN or even being able to tell the difference between Iraq and Iran).

Importantly, Jackson's song focuses on the pain and shock of 9/11, albeit through very patriotic eyes, and he avoids anti–Muslim sentiments or criticism of others. Unfortunately, the same cannot be said of a version of the subgenre of "Country Protest" that has recently emerged, a subgenre that is quite distinct from the original country protest of musicians like Woody Guthrie. In 2024, three songs exemplified this new country protest subgenre, with Jason Aldean's "Try That in a Small Town" and Oliver Anthony's "Rich Men North of Richmond," containing racialized undertones, along with Austin Moody's "I'm Just Sayin'" functioning as a class-baiting anti-woke anthem. All three songs are overtly populist, and thus, it may be tempting to believe that country songs can offer little sophisticated political content.

However, there is reason to conclude that, on the contrary, there have *always* been country songs offering incisive social commentary, criticizing class oppression and resisting the indignities of poverty, songs about the micro-politics of our everyday lives, our choices (or lack thereof), and our sense of identity and place. These songs, I would argue, are also part of the deeper essence of American country music. They constitute a small subset of the genre, perhaps, but one large enough to be identifiable as part of the country tradition, and I now want to explore this part of the tradition and discuss its distinct "Americanness." I can then show its shared roots with the country music of the Black artists whose country authenticity has been questioned.

Dolly Parton's "Coat of Many Colors"[12] is a classic example of what I am going to call "country at the margins," a subgenre that also incorporates social truth-telling and admiration of ordinary heroism.[13] The song references many standard country themes—divine love and the love of a mother, the Bible, family, etc.—but it also speaks of the poverty and class alienation experienced by a poor rural child from Tennessee. In the song, Parton describes going to school with worn and tattered clothing that made her the object of ridicule among her classmates. Though the song is musically upbeat, and the message is about valuing family and God over material possessions, we should not ignore the realities of Southern poverty it's based upon.

Loretta Lynn's "Coal Miner's Daughter" explores similar themes to Parton's "Coat of Many Colors." Lynn sings of the struggles and joys of her poor rural family as they try to make ends meet. And though the family was poor in regard to their material possessions, they were rich in love.[14] Like Parton, Lynn is singing about her own true memories, but the details of her memories contain much more of a sting in their tail. In an interview, Lynn recounted that "the song says Mommy's fingers were bleeding. I'd seen them bleed many times. In the wintertime, we had these old clotheslines made out of wire. It would be so cold that her fingers would stick to that wire. She'd pull them loose, and I'd see the hide come off of those fingers. I would hide and cry."[15] The song describes the hard work her father did to provide for the family, as a subsistence farmer by day while "he shoveled coal [at night] to make a poor man's dollar." Here, in one simple phrase, Lynn reminds us of the often dangerous, back-breaking work done by the poor for survival wages (which can be contrasted with the relatively comfortable, reasonably compensated work to which many of us are accustomed).

Later in the interview, Lynn states, "You know, you hear about poor people in other countries. There are a lot of poor people in our country if you go to the right places." Neither Lynn nor Parton is depicting some fantasy of country life; rather, they are talking about the rawness of rural poverty and the oppression of living at the social margins. Moreover, and unfortunately, there is a particularly American type of poverty—the poverty of the marginalized within a nation of excessive riches—that both these women are singing about, a deep-rooted poverty that is as much a part of American tradition as the self-made millionaire, and, as such, makes this poverty part of the American country tradition. But here we are not just talking of poverty in regard to a mere lack of money but the accompanying classism and "othering" of the poor. In her essay "A Question of Class," Dorothy Allison discusses how her poor white family was seen as part of a dehumanized group that was somehow—almost ontologically—different from the white middle-class, because they were supposed to hold a different set of values, to somehow value their own lives and the lives of their children less.[16] And intentionally or otherwise, both Parton and Lynn address this type of dehumanizing classist view by demonstrating the real love their parents had for their children.

Even the commercially successful Blake Shelton offers a song in a similar vein to Parton and Lynn: "Come Back as a Country Boy." The song does not invoke some fantasy of rural life, but instead speaks of the hard labor and poverty associated with being a country boy: "My back is always breakin' / my dogs are always barkin' / My money has trouble makin', and my truck has trouble startin'." Despite these difficulties, he insists that he would not want any other life because being a country boy is all he's known, and it's all he ever wants to be. Note the difference of Shelton's song with Alan Jackson's "Country Boy," which is essentially just a boast about the power of his truck, or it may simply be a metaphor he's floating to a woman he's just met: "'Cause I'm a country boy, I've got a four-wheel drive / Climb in my bed, I'll take you for a ride."[17] In contrast, Shelton isn't singing about material goods or sex; rather, he is praising a country life, one that is authentically lived.

Perhaps the most poignant of songs about human life at the margins is Guy Clark's "Desperados Waiting for a Train," a song that initially begins with a description of the hero-worship of a young boy for a grandfather figure (Guy Clark wrote this song in honor of Jack Prigg, a man he considered his grandfather).[18] As a young boy, the narrator imagines the two of them living life on the edge, "like some old Western movie," and he's proud that the old man taught him to drive so that he could give the old man a ride when he was too drunk to get home. As the boy begins to grow up, he now sees the older man differently: "Well to me he's one of the heroes of this country / So why's he all dressed up like them old men?" The narrator now begins to see the man as the listener sees him: a broken-down, old alcoholic. And this insight provides an important narrative jolt for the listener. Rather than dismiss those at the margins and frame their existence in terms of their "use" to society (with use understood in terms of social status and as workers for the capitalist system) we need to understand that they may be heroes for others and that they have existential significance for those others. Similarly, we should recognize the ordinary heroism of the parents of those like Parton and Lynn and the heroism of the daily life depicted by Shelton as they resist life at the margins.

Interestingly, despite its apparent resistance to marginalization and its call for a recognition of humanity, David Allan Coe's "Take This Job and Shove It," a song popularized by Johnny Paycheck, is in fact a narrative of disempowerment and disappointment.[19] The song begins with an empowering chorus, "Take this job and shove it / I ain't workin' here no more." However, as the song progresses, we realize that the narrator is only *imagining* saying this as he makes plans to confront his boss at some point in the future. Coe is describing urban, rather than rural, poverty, working in a factory that has taken its physical toll on him, while a life of barely scraping by has taken an emotional toll and ended his marriage. More than any of the other songs I've discussed thus far, Coe is writing about alienation in capitalist America, where its workers can expect a life of dehumanization that has no escape.

Converging Traditions

Thus far, I have described "country at the margins," a category that depicts marginalized American life, both rural and urban, a life of poverty and disempowerment. Despite this marginalization, the singers discussed above resist dehumanization, aim to live authentic lives, and admire the ordinary heroes who help them with this resistance and authenticity. And it is at the location of this subgenre of "country at the margins" that Black country music joins its white counterpart, with both sharing in this particularly American musical tradition. Obviously, marginalization and poverty are not exclusive to America, but they take a particular form in this country, as they occur within a country of such extremes of wealth, freedoms, and injustices. I would argue that these *specifically American* problems actively need to utilize the *specifically American musical genre* of country music, as it is this musical tradition that can best express life at the margins in a nation of excesses of wealth and status. And it is here that there can be a convergence of Black and white American musical traditions, traditions of oppression and resistance that are best expressed in the quintessentially American musical genre: country music.

Contemporary Black American country music both looks to established country traditions *and* also to its own Black musical and political traditions: traditions of resistance, such as the anthems of the Civil Rights movement. An example of this type of contemporary Black country music is Mickey Guyton's 2020 single "Black Like Me," which received a nomination for Best Country Solo Performance at the 63rd Annual Grammy Awards, making Guyton the first Black woman to receive a Grammy nomination in that category.[20] Like Parton, Lynn, and Coe, Guyton offers tropes of life at the margins and admiration of the ordinary heroism of her parents who worked hard, struggling at times to provide. Where she differs from Parton, Lynn, and Coe is that Guyton describes how race intersects with this life as she recounts instances on the playground in which she was teased for being different and asks us to consider, "If you think we live in the land of the free / You should try to be black like me." Notably, Guyton is explaining how race also intensifies both this marginalization and this admiration, as her parents had to work twice as hard to achieve the same basic standard of living as white folks.

Another central example of this type of politicized contemporary Black country is Willie Jones's Civil Rights anthem, "American Dream," which addresses the realities of Black-lived lives in America.[21] Speaking directly to a young Black man, Jones begins by praising the young man's courage and drive, while simultaneously warning him of the dangers he will face in white America. As the song progresses, Jones begins to specify these dangers, from the distant echoes of Jim Crow to the state-sanctioned violence in today's America. These warnings are all held together by the seemingly optimistic chorus: "Proud to be a Black man / Livin' in the land of the brave and the free." But Jones is reminding us that the American dream is altogether different for Black men; even though this young man is American, he lives in a different world from white Americans. The white American dream is home ownership, possession of material goods, etc., which stands in contrast to the Black American dream of achieving equality and freedom, a fundamental prerequisite to life itself.

Finally, Black American artists have used the established country tradition to critique dominant cultural narratives about Black folks. Dolly Parton's "Jolene" has been covered by both Lil Nas X and Beyoncé, with each bringing their own interpretation to this quintessential country song.[22] In the original version, Parton begs the beautiful Jolene not to take her man. Lil Nas X offers a lyrically faithful rendition, maintaining the original genders of the song's characters, singing in a deep voice into a flower-bedecked microphone, in such a way that the song becomes a resistance to expectations for American Black masculinity and a simultaneous call for the humanization of the queer Black community. Beyoncé's revised version of the song is a further refashioning of the expectations of Black American masculinity, explicitly resisting the controlling cultural narratives of Black American men as unfaithful partners and irresponsible parents as Beyoncé admonishes Jolene that it will take more than her looks and seductive stares to lure away a happy family man.[23]

A Final Refrain

Significantly, these Black American artists have deliberately chosen country music as the most appropriate genre to express their emotions and frustrations. Yes, their songs *could* have been written and performed as the blues or as political anthems, but ultimately, these songs are not just racialized; rather, at their heart lies a protest at being marginalized in America. Even if their narrators find joy and love in their lives (and it is important to understand that they *do*), we can see that country music provides the appropriate *American musical tradition* to express this protest.

Thus, returning to the initial question that prompted this discussion, we can see that focusing too much on the race of the singer may simply be a distraction from understanding the true essence of country and its place in American life.

NOTES

1. Chibueze, Collins; Sastry, Nevin; Cook, Sean. Jones, Jerrell; Williams, Mark. 2024. "A Bar Song (Tipsy)." *Where I've Been, Isn't Where I'm Going.* Shaboozey (rec. artist). Sastry, Nevin; Cook, Sean (prods.) American Dogwood.

2. Beyoncé; Bates, Brian; Boland, Elizabeth Lowell; Boggs, Atia; Bulow, Megan; Ferraro, Nathan; Saadiq, Raphael. 2024. "Texas Hold 'Em." *Cowboy Carter.* Beyoncé (rec. artist). B, Killah; Ferraro, Nathan (prods.) Parkwood; Columbia Records.

3. Hill, Montero; Reznor, Trent; Ross, Atticus; Roukema, Kiowa. 2018. "Old Town Road." (EP) 7. Lil Naz X (rec artist). YoungKio; Reznor, Trent; Atticus, Ross (prods.) Columbia Records.

4. Leight, Elias. 2019. "Lil Nas X's 'Old Town Road' Was a Country Hit. Then Country Changed Its Mind." *Rolling Stone.*

5. Beyoncé; Gordon, Wynter; Cossom, Kevin; Delicata, Alex; Scott, Darrell. 2016. "Daddy Lessons." *Lemonade.* Beyoncé (rec. artist). Dixie, Derek; Delicata, Alex (prods.) Parkwood; Columbia Records.

6. Fekadu, Mesfin. 2016. "AP Source: Grammy country committee rejects Beyoncé song." *The Associated Press.*

7. Beyoncé; White, Jack; Gordon, Diana; Plant, Robert; Page, James; Jones, John Paul; Bonham, John. 2016. "Don't Hurt Yourself." *Lemonade.* Beyoncé (rec. artist). White, Jack; Dixie, Derek (prods.) Parkwood; Columbia Records.

8. Hudak, Joseph. 2016. "Beyoncé's Country Song 'Daddy Lessons' Rejected by Grammys." *Rolling Stone.*

9. Beyoncé; Boggs, Atia; Ochs, Camaron; Scott, Darius; Carter, Shawn; Dixie, Derek; Johnson, Tyler; Wilson, Ernest; Batiste, Jon; Saadiq, Raphael; Price, Michael; Walsh, Dan; Stills, Stephen. 2024. "Ameriican Requiem." *Cowboy Carter.* Beyoncé (rec. artist). No I.D.; Johnson, Batiste T.; Tyler, Khirye; Harrell, Kuk (prods.) Parkwood; Columbia Records.

10. For an interesting discussion of country music as an American tradition, one that both "emphasizes and celebrates tradition in its lyric content" (243), see Sartwell, Crispin. 1993. "Confucius and Country Music." *Philosophy East and West.* Vol. 43. No. 2: 243–254.

11. Jackson, Alan. 2002. "Where Were You (When the World Stopped Turning)." *Drive.* Stegall, Keith (prod.) Arista Nashville.

12. Parton, Dolly. 1971. "Coat of Many Colors." *Coat of Many Colors.* Ferguson, Bob (prod.) RCA Victor.

13. There are a surprising amount of different types of country genres and subgenres. See Coroneos, Kyle "Trigger." 2022. "Compendium of Country Music Definitions, Subgenres, Terms, & Eras." *savecountrymusic.com.*

14. Lynn, Loretta. 1970. "Coal Miner's Daughter." *Coal Miner's Daughter.* Bradley, Owen (prod.) Decca Records.

15. Zollo, Paul. 2022. "Behind the Song: Coal Miner's Daughter by Loretta Lynn." *American Songwriter.*

16. Allison, Dorothy. 2024. "A Question of Class." *History as a Weapon.*

17. Jackson, Alan. 2008. "Country Boy." *Good Time.* Stegall, Keith (prod.) Arista Nashville.

18. Clark, Guy. 1975. "Desperados Waiting for a Train." *Old No. 1.* Moman, Chips (prod.) RCA Records.

19. Coe, David Allan. 1978. "Take This Job and Shove It." *Family Album.* Sherrill, Billy (prod.) Colombia Records.

20. Guyton, Mickey. Chapman, Nathan; Churchill, Fraser; Dillon, Emma Davidson. 2020. "Black Like Me." (EP). *Bridges*. Chapman, Nathan; Whitehead; Forest (prods.) Capitol Nashville Records.

21. Jones, Willie. 2021. "American Dream." *Right Now*. Addix, Dream; Essancy, Jason (prods.) Sony Music; Nashville Records.

22. Parton, Dolly. 1973. "Jolene." *Jolene*. Ferguson, Bob (prod.) RCA Victor.

23. Parton, Dolly; Beyoncé; Andrews, Denisia; Coney, Brittany; Gesteelde-Diamant, Terius. 2024. "Jolene." *Cowboy Carter*. Beyoncé (rec. artist). Vickery, Alex; Rochon, Jack; Tyler, Khirye (prods.) Parkwood; Columbia Records.

II

Country Music Aesthetics

Simply Country

Joshua Heter

When a work of art (e.g., a song, a film, a painting, or some other creation) is said to have *aesthetic value*, it is often the case that the complexity of the piece seems to be an important part of what makes it aesthetically valuable. To say that an artwork has aesthetic value is simply to say that it is beautiful in some way or (more broadly) that it has the capacity to bring about a pleasurable or gratifying aesthetic experience. For instance, it seems like it should be uncontroversial to suggest that Don Brown's "I Can't Stop Loving You"[1] has considerably more aesthetic value than the sound of a banjo being thrown down a flight of stairs. But this is just to say that "I Can't Stop Loving You" is much more beautiful or has a much greater capacity to bring about a pleasurable experience for the listener than the sound of a banjo clanging down the stairs.

There are many examples which seem to illustrate that an artwork's complexity counts as a point in favor of its aesthetic value. For instance, we can all think of a beloved movie or TV show that rewards multiple viewings, not merely because of our own sentimentality for revisiting a story we've already enjoyed but because the piece is so rich with detail in its performances, plot points, and thematic flourishes that hardly anyone would be able to fully appreciate with only a single viewing. Likewise, any number of pieces of classical music from masters such as Bach and Beethoven can be thought of, not merely as works of art, but as works of mathematics as they can be admired for their quantitative intricacies as much as their broad qualitative appeal. And any well-trained sommelier will tell you that judging the quality of wine will often involve assessing a wine's complexity. Great wines are often described as "multidimensional" with various harmonizing notes and flavors.

So, it seems as if complexity can be an important component of an artwork's aesthetic value. Clearly, all of the preceding examples would be aesthetically *worse* had they been created without the level of complexity they in fact have. But just how important is complexity for aesthetic value? In answering this question, some philosophers have gone so far as to make the case that complexity is a *necessary condition* for aesthetic value.[2] Perhaps, one might even attempt to argue, given the important role that complexity seems to play in judging so many works of art as aesthetically valuable, that the aesthetic value of an artwork is directly proportional to its level of complexity.

What we've said thus far is, of course, relevant to the subject matter of this book because country music is often described as being *simple* in a variety of different ways.[3] Not only do country artists sing about embracing the simplicity of a certain type of life, but (perhaps more germane to the point) they sing about simple matters generally. Many of the most beloved country songs are about easy-to-understand and relatable concerns such as lost love, regret, faith, fun, admiration for one's country, nostalgia, etc. And, beyond the simple themes that are common to country music, the musical artistry on display—while frequently lovely and inventive—is likewise often noted for its simplicity. In contrast to elaborate, complicated works of classical music, country songs are often composed with simple chord progressions and straightforward, uncomplicated melodies and structured with a familiar verse, chorus, verse arrangement.[4]

All of this seems to raise a plainly straightforward problem for country music (or at least, country music defenders). If complexity in art seems to be a virtue and if the simplicity of country music is one of its more identifiable characteristics, could all those country music critics be right; is country music just a lesser art form? Does country music's simplicity just make it ... *bad*?

Objectivity and Aesthetic Judgment

Does country music's simplicity entail that it has lesser (or hardly any) aesthetic value? Before attempting to tackle this question, we should address a potential objection to the project as a whole: isn't aesthetic value simply subjective? Whether any piece of art is aesthetically valuable, one might argue, depends entirely upon the perspective or tastes of the person experiencing it. Some people enjoy classic country ballads like Merle Haggard's "My Favorite Memory,"[5] while others prefer more upbeat anthems such as Brooks & Dunn's "Boot Scootin' Boogie."[6] But neither (type of) song has more aesthetic value *objectively* or *in reality*. All that exists is what's aesthetically valuable "for me," "for you," or "for an individual." So, as the reasoning goes, trying to give or defend any sort of objective criteria (such as complexity or the lack thereof) for what's aesthetically valuable is inherently misguided.

For better or worse, we are well short of the space needed in this essay (or even this book!) to give a full treatment of the objection here. Philosophers (perhaps unsurprisingly) are torn on the matter of whether aesthetic value is purely subjective. But many aren't merely satisfied to lament that "beauty is in the eye of the beholder," so there isn't really anything to say about what's beautiful (or more broadly, what's aesthetically valuable) beyond surveying what people tell us they *find* aesthetically valuable. On the contrary, at least some philosophers argue that there are likely at least *some* objective elements for what constitutes aesthetic value.

Recall that to say that an artwork has aesthetic value is simply to say that it has the capacity to bring about a pleasurable or gratifying aesthetic experience. Whether or not an individual actually *has* a pleasurable or gratifying aesthetic experience, of course, depends at least in part upon subjective elements that are unique to that individual and their predispositions. But, insofar as works of art do have *capacities* to bring about such experiences, it is those capacities we are attempting to investigate when we raise questions about country music, its alleged lack of complexity, and its aesthetic value. Put differently, we can identify and analyze aspects of works of art which tend to lead to pleasurable aesthetic experiences, and that is simply what we are doing here. So, while aesthetic value may be "subjective" in *some* sense, that does not preclude the possibility of identifying aesthetic strengths and weaknesses of various works of art (such as those found in or allegedly missing from country music).

Complicating Simplicity

Again, the question at hand is whether country music's simplicity entails that it has lesser (or hardly any) aesthetic value. But what exactly *is* simplicity? For our purposes, we needn't give any sort of rigid definition of the concept, but we can be at least a bit more precise about what we mean when we say that country music is simple. As we previously alluded, country music is simple in at least two important ways. Country music (often enough) contains what we might call *thematic simplicity* as well as *aesthetic simplicity.*[7]

Thematic simplicity is the simplicity of country music's lyrical content; it is found in the uncomplicated subjects and themes about which country artists so frequently compose their lyrics. Country artists sing about fairly straightforward and accessible subjects such as relationship troubles, lost love, appreciation for family, adherence to faith, and having fun. And the way in which country artists most often expound upon these topics is not with any sort of heady, academic analysis. They're typically presented in an easy-to-understand, accessible manner.

Consider "Move It on Over"[8] by Hank Williams. The song recounts the story of a man who upsets his wife by returning home late one night, so much so that she locks him out of the house. Forced to sleep in the literal doghouse, he tells the beloved family pet, with whom he must now share sleeping quarters, to "move it on over." It's not exactly Shakespeare (nor is it intended to be). It's a humorous, silly tale; a style of comedy that is nothing if not broad and uncomplicated. And, while this is just one example, it is hardly an aberration. There are countless such country songs which attempt to entertain with an uncomplicated novelty, a transparently sentimental reflection, or an easily digestible moral lesson.

The second type of simplicity which is often found in country music is again aesthetic simplicity: the simplicity of country music's purely musical or presentative features. It's the simplicity of country's chord progressions, melodies, harmonies, and rhyming structures. These too, often enough, tend to be fairly uncomplicated for and easily absorbed by a wide range of audiences.[9]

For instance, Johnny Cash's hit single "Cry! Cry! Cry!"[10] was recorded—at a trim two minutes and 29 seconds—with Cash as the sole vocalist playing acoustic guitar with his signature style, at points making it little more than a percussion instrument. Backed solely by The Tennessee Two—Luther Perkins on electric guitar and Marshall Grant on bass—the song consists most notably of a meandering but memorable melody and lacks any dramatic flourishes such as backing vocals, key changes, etc. No matter what one thinks of the song, it is undoubtedly simple in regard to its purely musical or aesthetic qualities, especially contrasted with the pieces of classical music mentioned near the opening of this essay. And this is, of course, only one example of many such country songs which exhibit aesthetic simplicity.

With all of this in mind, if country music is simple in a number of different, fundamental ways, and *if* complexity is substantively important to aesthetic value, then this all counts as a reason to question the aesthetic value of country music.

The Value of Thematic Simplicity

It's true. Country music does tend to be simple in at least two important ways; it often contains both thematic as well as aesthetic simplicity. But now, the point is this. The degree to which country music may be simple can be at least somewhat overstated, and there is a case to be made that though complexity may contribute substantially to the aesthetic value of plenty of works of art, it does not therefore follow that simplicity *per se* counts against aesthetic value.

In regard to this latter point, we should mention that there is at least *some* empirical evidence that audiences don't necessarily find aesthetic value to be directly correlated with complexity. In other words, it seems as if it is not the case that for those enjoying art, the more complexity, the better. Rather, often enough, audiences enjoy complexity in art to a point, but their enjoyment then begins to decrease at a certain threshold as complexity continues to increase.[11] Thus, if complexity isn't an inherent virtue in regard to aesthetic value, perhaps simplicity, one could argue, isn't an inherent aesthetic vice. Regardless, our defense of country music can proceed by addressing both its thematic as well as its aesthetic simplicity.

Again, the lyrical content of a great many country songs is straightforward and uncomplicated. But it is far from obvious that these songs are therefore devoid of or lacking in aesthetic value. To be sure, a complex, intricately woven story or piece of prose may have plenty of fine qualities which would be diminished the degree to which they were made more simple. But this does not preclude the possibility that works of art with simple, easy-to-grasp thematic content have aesthetic strengths of their own. Take for example the famous six-word story (often dubiously attributed to Ernest Hemingway): "For sale: baby shoes, never worn." The story packs a punch and stays with us (at least in part) *because* it is so uncomplicated. Adding even a single detail would only take away from its aesthetic value in a way that's exactly converse to complex works whose aesthetic value would be lessened by removing details. In a similar way, the aesthetic value of haiku and certain simple jokes can be thought to rely on brevity and a *lack* of complexity.

In addition, it's also relevant that many country songs carry with them a moral lesson, but sometimes broad, simple moral lessons—like so many contained in country music—can be the most weighty and are best suited to help shape us into the people we want to be. As the philosopher John Dyck puts it: "it seems clear that generic moral advice is important: love your friends and family; be loyal; enjoy the little things. It may be trite advice, but it's true nevertheless … [and, therefore] It's just not clear that simplicity makes a work morally deficient."[12] And it does seem as if broad, easily digestible morals—such as those mentioned by Dyck—often serve as important guiding principles in our ethical journey in a way that much more detailed, minutia-focused moral principles do not. Thus, insofar as country music tends to focus on these more broad moral ideas, its simplicity in this regard may in fact count as a point in favor of its value. Thus, it doesn't seem as if country music's thematic simplicity gives us any special reason to question its aesthetic value.

The Value of Aesthetic Simplicity

Even if the defense of country music's aesthetic value—in light of its thematic simplicity—can ultimately win the day, country music is also *aesthetically* simple, and perhaps it is this type of simplicity which counts against the genre's value as a form of art. However, it's worth pointing out that not all country songs are aesthetically simple. For instance, the Charlie Daniels Band's "Devil Went Down to Georgia"[13] contains a pair of blistering, technically impressive fiddle solos which could be described as anything but simple. Similarly, "Wichita Lineman"[14] by Glen Campbell contains a dramatic, sweeping orchestral arrangement, recorded by members of the Wrecking Crew (the Los Angeles–based studio musicians who contributed to much of the grand and complex popular music of the mid–20th century). And the song contains a striking key change from F major to the (relative minor) D major without fully resolving, putting the listener in a similar headspace as the song's central character, a lonely, reflective county line worker thinking of love while dutifully working his mostly mundane job.[15]

Nevertheless, songs such as these are an exception to the norm of country music's more common aesthetic simplicity. As such, any defense of country music's aesthetic value (in the face of the charge that its simplicity counts against it) based primarily on such examples should be less than persuasive. That said, it's also perhaps noteworthy that most (if not all) country songs do have at least a modicum of complexity. A chord (made with a guitar, with a piano, or by a collection of different instruments or vocalists) is—almost by definition—a complex musical structure consisting of three or more notes working in literal harmony to produce a sum more (aesthetically valuable) than its parts. And there can be a fair amount of musical theory just below the surface of even some of the simplest melodies.

Insofar as country songs contain these very basic elements found in essentially all popular music, they have a degree of complexity which presumably can help us account for the aesthetic value millions of country fans seem to find in them. Again, this all serves as a reminder that we shouldn't overstate the degree to or the manner in which country music is simple. Still, the country music defender should say a bit more here. Perhaps country music isn't perfectly or totally simple, and perhaps this entails that country music is not *totally* without aesthetic value. But it may still contain a relatively significant amount of simplicity when compared to other forms of (even popular) music and may therefore hold a lower status relative to other pieces of music (popular or otherwise).

I'd like to therefore consider an imperfect but potentially useful analogy involving an activity not completely unrelated to country music: football (as there are dozens of country songs about the sport).[16] Different types of football plays can vary widely in regard to their complexity. A run up the middle typically consists primarily of the quarterback handing the ball off to a running back who then runs through a hole in the defense created by the offensive line, all of which is relatively uncomplicated. In contrast to this, a double-reverse flea-flicker begins with the quarterback handing the ball off typically to a running back or receiver who then hands off or laterals to yet another offensive player who then laterals back to the quarterback who then attempts a forward pass (most often well) downfield. And, of course, a double-reverse flea-flicker is much more complicated than most football plays, so much so that it is typically considered to be a trick play. Yet, whether an individual play is simple or complex, it has the same end: to advance the ball down the field, ultimately culminating with an offensive player in possession of the ball in the end zone.

Similarly, whether a piece of music is simple or complex, it arguably has the same end: to bring about a pleasurable or gratifying aesthetic experience in the listener. And, just as a football play (such as a run up the middle) can be successful—and therefore can have (what we might call) football value despite its simplicity—so too can a piece of music be successful—and can therefore have *aesthetic* value despite its simplicity. For any particularly simple football play to have success, certain players may need to have a role of outsized importance (e.g., a successful run up the middle may require an especially adept offensive line or running back), but what ultimately matters is that the play *works*. Similarly, for any particularly simple country song to have success, certain musical elements may need to have a role of outsized importance (e.g., the song may require an especially lovely melody or winsome chord progression), but what ultimately matters is that the song works. Thus, insofar as simplicity isn't an inherent vice for football plays, neither is it an inherent vice for country songs.

To be sure, there are a number of disanalogies between the success of a football play and the success of a piece of music. For instance, a particular musical performance can be successful in creating a gratifying aesthetic experience for one listener but not another. However, though fans may disagree on the proper ruling of a play, it's not literally the case that a particular play can be successful in the sense that the play resulted in a first down from the perspective of one fan but not another. However, it's not entirely obvious that disanalogies such as this undercut the intended defense of the aesthetic value of simple pieces of country music. That a piece of music successfully produces the intended effect in some listeners but not others is simply a fact about music in general, regardless of the issue of simplicity and complexity.

All things considered, country music does contain relative amounts of simplicity (of various kinds). But, though some may attempt to argue that this entails that country music is of lesser value, it's hard to see why this should be the case. It seems as if the issue may not be that simple.

Notes

1. Gibson, Don. 1958. "I Can't Stop Loving You." *Oh Lonesome Me*. Atkins, Chet (prod.) RCA Records.

2. Beardsley, Monroe. 1981. *Aesthetics: Problem in the Philosophy of Criticism*, 2nd Edition. Hackett Publishing Company.

3. John Dyck is the philosopher to first make this point and to truly take seriously the issue of country music's simplicity and the philosophical issues it raises. See Dyck, John. 2021. "The Aesthetic of Country Music." *Philosophy Compass*.

4. *Ibid*.

5. Haggard, Merle. 1981. "My Favorite Memory." *Big City*. Haggard, Merle (prod.) Epic Records.

6. Dunn, Ronnie. 1992. "Boot Scootin' Boogie." *Brand New Man*. Cook, Don; Hendricks, Scott (prods.) Arista Nashville.

7. Dyck. As Dyck puts it, "country music is simple not just in its content—the things it is about—but also in its form—its melodies and patterns are easy to identify."

8. Williams, Hank. 1947. "Move It on Over." Rose, Fred (prod.) MGM Records.

9. Dyck.

10. Cash, Johnny. 1955. "Cry! Cry! Cry!" Phillips, Sam (prod.) Sun Records.

11. On the origin of this idea, see Berlyne, D.E. 1971. *Aesthetics and Psychobiology*. Appleton-Century-Crofts.

12. Dyck.

13. Daniels, Charlie; Crain, Tom; DiGregorio, Joel; Edwards, Fred; Hayward, Charles; Marshall, James W. 1979. "The Devil Went Down to Georgia." *Million Mile Reflections*. Charlie Daniels Band (rec. artist). Boylan, John (prod.) Epic Records.

14. Webb, Jimmy. 1968. "Wichita Lineman." *Wichita Lineman*. Campbell, Glen (rec. artist). Capitol Records.

15. Savage, Mark. 2017. "Glen Campbell's 'Wichita Lineman': The Unfinished Song That Became a Classic." BBC Music.

16. For instance, see Beathard, Casey; Turnbull, Dave. 2010. "The Boys of Fall." *Hemingway's Whiskey*. Kenny Chesney (rec. artist). BNA Records. Green, Drew; Philips, Hunter; Starr, Lee; Columbia, Nick. 2021. "I Hate Alabama." *Smoky Mountains*. Conner Smith (rec. artist). Valory Music Co. Elkins, Elizabeth; Henningsen, Aaron; Henningsen, Brian; Henningsen, Clara; Olivarez, Vanessa. 2015. "Drinkin' Town with a Football Problem." *Summer Forever*. Billy Currington (rec. artist). Mercury Nashville.

Wittgenstein Plays the Pedal Steel

Jeffrey Patrick Colgan

In Townes Van Zandt's beautiful and tragic song "Tecumseh Valley," he offers the story of a young woman who, during an especially trying winter, must travel from her hometown to seek work in a nearby valley and supplement her struggling father's income.[1] The song begins with an image of this hopeful and alluring young woman through the eyes of the narrator: "The name she gave was Caroline, the daughter of a miner / And her ways were free, and it seemed to me the sunshine walked beside her."[2]

With this opening, the listener might well expect the track to be a love song, with this first stanza being a passionate description of a woman by a lover enthralled. However, we soon come to find that the song is, in fact, an elegy. The protagonist—whose name may or may not be Caroline—eventually comes to ruin and an early death in her adopted Tecumseh Valley. Yet as this heartbreaking song comes to a close, the listener finds something surprising. After following the protagonist through her travails and descent, we are met not with a final verse that offers an editorialized moral, nor are we offered a chorus, as this song has no chorus. Rather, Van Zandt repeats the opening verse again, word for word. Careful listeners will note that this verse is heard very differently than its previous iteration. It is no longer ambiguous in its intent; it is undeniably a lamentation for the deceased.

Not quite anaphora nor a refrain, this framing device—wherein the song is *framed* by a repeated verse—is distinctive to the traditions of country, folk, and blues. When done successfully, the intervening verses and choruses complicate and enrich the images, turns of phrase, and themes of the first verse, adding profundity and often poignancy to the song's final words. For the philosopher, the framing device offers what appears to be a paradox: the last verse is the *same* as the first, in that it repeats the exact same words with the same musical accompaniment, and often even with almost the same vocal delivery; yet it is at the same time importantly *different*, as its reception by the listener has drastically changed over the course of the song. How can this be? How can these verses be at once the same and different?

Successful song structures in the country music tradition often utilize the interplay between specific lines and the context in which those lines appear to compelling effect, creating a dialogue within the song itself. This essay explores this transmutation that songs can affect upon themselves, investigating how this device works and what it illustrates about country, folk, and blues traditions specifically as well as language generally. Something profound is at work in this apparent paradox—with profound here meaning both of great importance as well as concerning something so deep and ordinary as to escape our notice. Such repetition exemplifies the *profound* importance of context and embeddedness for both aesthetic form and semantics in language. The thought of Ludwig Wittgenstein (1889–1951) has much to offer this exploration, as he was a philosopher who rigorously investigated the role of context in linguistic meaning and whose own writings on aspect perception share much with the apparent paradox of the framing device in country music. With Wittgenstein's help, country songs that make use of this device can be shown to be particularly illuminating examples of the contextual way that meaning is conveyed.

Confronting the Paradox of the Framing Device

Before turning to Wittgenstein and context-dependent meaning, it is important to first clarify what the framing device is and why it takes the form of a paradox. Framing, in the context of this essay, is a rhetorical device used in country, folk, and blues song structures, wherein the first verse is repeated at the end of the song. Such a device can come in many different forms. It could be a song in which the only element repeated is the framing verse: schematized as A B C D A, where A denotes the repeated verse. Van Zandt's "Tecumseh Valley" follows a similar structure. Alternatively, the song could have a traditional verse-verse-chorus structure that is framed by the repeated verse: A B C D E C A, where C denotes the chorus and A the repeated framing verse. Guy Clark's "Dublin Blues" follows such a structure.[3] The structure could be even simpler, where only one stanza separates the framing verses: A B A. "Fame" by Billy Joe Shaver is an example of this simplest version of the device.[4] The framing device requires only that the first and last verse are the same in regard to their lyrical content and musical accompaniment.

In the songwriter's terminology, the framing device is distinct from refrains, choruses, and reprises. A refrain is most often a lyrical line that is repeated throughout a song, such as Hank Williams' insistence that "I'm so lonesome I could cry."[5] Chorus can be traced back to Ancient Greek χορός (khorós), and like the choruses of Hellenic tragedy that called for the group to come together and offer a collaborative commentary on the plot of the play, the choruses of popular music often feature an ensemble quality with all the instruments playing in unison and additional harmony parts added. Further, they often feature key lines of the song that are repeated throughout and that can serve as a comment on or response to the content of the verses. Reprise, in the musical context, usually refers to a repeated musical passage or theme in music, where what is repeated is of a much larger scale than a single lyrical line or even a stanza. It is worth acknowledging that not all of these terms must refer to repeated *lyrical* content. A chorus need not have lyrics at all; if it does, the lyrics do not need to be the same for each iteration of the chorus. So too with reprise. Since what is repeated are entire musical passages or themes, these usually refer to more than just lyrical content and can be applied to music that lacks any lyrical content—consider the use of reprise in the sonata form of 18th-century European art music, such as Joseph Haydn's 8th symphony.

The framing device is not ubiquitous in country music (or folk or blues for that matter). More common is the unframed verse-verse-chorus structure, with the oft-repeated chorus serving as a sort of earworm. But for certain strands of country music that aspire to a literary sophistication and perhaps resist certain commercial pressures, framing is a frequently employed device. Beyond Van Zandt's "Tecumseh Valley" and the other aforementioned examples, some paradigmatic cases are Van Zandt's "Snow Don't Fall," Guy Clark's "L.A. Freeway," Billy Joe Shaver's "Omaha" (famously recorded by Waylon Jennings), the traditional "Lonesome Valley" in its arrangement by Woody Guthrie, and Blaze Foley's "Rainbows and Ridges," as well as "Louisiana Man" by Lucinda Williams.[6]

Why does the framing device present itself as a paradox? A philosophical paradox is, in its most relevant sense, a self-contradictory statement. For example, "the wiener schnitzel both has mustard on it and does not have mustard on it" (with the general form here being "*A* is both *X* and *not-X*"). How can the wiener schnitzel both have mustard on it and yet not have mustard on it? How can any *A* both be an X and be a *not-X*? Most would hold this to be logically impossible; it breaks what philosophers call the law of non-contradiction. The apparent paradox of the framing device follows just this form. The framing verses are characterized by both constancy and change: constancy in that they have the same lyrics and musical accompaniment as well as almost the same vocal delivery; change in that they are heard by the listener in profoundly different ways. They are both the same and yet not the same; they are both different and yet not different.

Van Zandt's "Tecumseh Valley" presents the framing device's apparent paradox by offering the first verse, which can be heard by the listener in certain ways and then repeating that verse in such a way that it is heard quite differently. With the first verse, perhaps the song is an expression of love, and this is our first image of a stunning individual. Alternatively, the listener might be influenced by the minor chords and hear this first verse as the mistaken portrayal of someone who will turn out to be quite vicious and the song as a whole gearing up to be a tale of malicious heartbreak. But it is only by means of our journey through the song's narrative that we come to adequately hear the elegiac quality of the framing verses, that we hear the last verse as lamenting the loss of someone who is, in the eyes of the narrator, truly special. In the case of "Tecumseh Valley," it is the story that, at least in part, transmutes the opening image into an epitaph.

However, the framing device does not merely work by using a narrative to fill out an austere opening image. Listen to "Tecumseh Valley" a hundred times. Commit to memory the story of the young woman who, out of desperation, turns to prostitution and is found alone and dead by her own hand under the stairs of the local saloon. Memorize the words and melody. Still, the first and last verses are heard differently. That the framing verses strike one as different is not just due to knowledge acquired during the course of the song; the difference is not merely an *epistemic* difference.

Further, the framing device can be successfully employed in songs that lack a narrative. Consider Van Zandt's "Snow Don't Fall," a short but arresting song that Van Zandt considered one of his best.[7] The opening verse offers a series of rather enigmatic images: "Well, snow don't fall on summer's time, wind don't blow below the sea / My love lies 'neath frozen skies and waits in sweet repose for me."[8]

Before this verse returns at the end of the song, another verse and a bridge are sung. The middle verse offers several images in quick succession, almost all having to do with a particular woman—her eyes, lips, legs, hair, and thoughts. The brief bridge, that he doesn't need to see his love "To know she casts her glance at me," connects the "love" of the first verse with the "her" of the middle verse.[9] With the final verse, a repetition of the words of the first, we might feel as if we have more images held in our minds—that the background against which we hear the final verse is augmented. But no narrative has been offered, no story given. In fact, the verse and the song as a whole remain as enigmatic as ever. We don't need to make sense of it, and yet we *still* hear it differently. And again, this persists across repeated listenings. We can hold the images of the middle verse in mind, we can remember the connection offered in the bridge, yet the last verse *still strikes us differently* than the first.

If it is not merely an epistemic issue—not just because new knowledge has been acquired over the course of listening to the song—and if it is not only because of the expanded connotations of the images with which we become familiar after repeated listenings, then how are we to make sense of the fact that we hear these verses so differently? To better grasp what is at stake in this apparent paradox, to ensure that it is firmly in hand, and for assistance in resolving or dissolving it, Wittgenstein's work on aspect perception and his holism with regard to linguistic meaning are helpful.

Wittgenstein on Seeing Aspects and Semantic Contextualism

Ludwig Wittgenstein was an Austrian-born philosopher who spent much of his life working on questions in the philosophies of language, logic, and mind at the University of Cambridge. It is hard to overstate his impact on 20th- and 21st-century philosophy as well as the social sciences and even the arts—impressive indeed, considering he only published one book of philosophy during his life: the *Tractatus Logico-Philosophicus*. But if during his lifetime his publications were scant, he was expansive in his unpublished philosophical writing on a wide range of topics. He is perhaps best known for his investigation into how meaning is unavoidably and profoundly context-dependent—an investigation that can help us more responsibly engage with the apparent paradox of the framing device in country music.

To be told that meaning in language is contextual can seem a trifle. Of course, one might think, words do not always mean the same in all contexts. Just consider "duck." The soldier is not talking to his comrade about waterfowl, when he urges him to take cover from enemy fire; nor is the child at the edge of the park's pond issuing orders when she spots the approaching birds. But to take contextualism to be merely the claim that words have various meanings in various contexts is to misunderstand the depth and complexity of Wittgenstein's point. Alternatively, one might take Wittgenstein as endorsing some sort of shallow relativism, where words just mean whatever we happen to currently agree that they mean— perhaps depending on the vogue social practices or political trends of the day. This, too, would be to misunderstand Wittgenstein.

Rather than offering a new philosophical theory of meaning, Wittgenstein is primarily concerned with disabusing us of the mistaken views or "pictures" with which we approach questions of meaning.[10] Such pictures insist that there is some determiner of meaning—such as a definition, rule, thought, image, mental experience, or even a divine entity—that *fixes* the meaning of our words and signs generally. For example, someone might think that "brick" means what it does because at some specific time in the past a person pointed to a rectangular piece of hardened clay and offered an utterance that we represent with the sign "brick." Here, the meaning-determiner would be a convention begun by an initial baptism-like act, and all "correct" usages of the term depend upon that initial act. Or perhaps one might claim that "pain" means what it does because it *points to* a mental experience: a pain experience; and if no such mental experience is being referred to when I grumble, "I am in such pain," then the word "pain" is not being legitimately used.

What these pictures get wrong is that they attempt to make the interpretation of any given word, sign, or act irrelevant by fixing its meaning with a meaning-determiner, where correct usage or understanding depends solely on accordance with the meaning-determiner. However, any candidate meaning-determiner is always subject to further interpretation; thus, it is open to *deviant* interpretation.[11] Any candidate meaning-determiner is always subject to misinterpretation in the future. For example, when that builder first pointed at the piece of hardened clay and uttered "brick," how are we to be sure that he was talking about the object as a whole and not its color, shape, or texture? The pointing gesture itself, by which "brick" and the hardened clay were supposedly linked, is a matter of interpretation (why do my eyes trace the line extending from the index finger and not the thumb or the curved ring finger?). We can only convince ourselves that meaning is fixed if we remove the use of a word, sign, or act from the circumstances in which it is employed. As Wittgenstein scholar David Stern succinctly puts it: "A change in the context of application can yield a change in meaning, and therefore meaning cannot be identified with anything independent of context."[12]

The thing is, we *do* mostly understand when someone teaches us a new word by pointing at an object, and we *do* mostly understand when someone sincerely complains to us that they are in pain. We are so adept at doing so because of the rich context within which these activities take place—what G.E.M. Anscombe in her translation of Wittgenstein's *Philosophical Investigations* renders as "stage-setting"—and which we take for granted when we interact with others, participate in language, or interpret a sign.[13] These activities are not taking place in a vacuum but in very specific contexts as well as amidst a broad and rich tapestry of shared practices, our shared "form of life."[14] It is by the specific context that we are cued to understand words, signs, or acts in the appropriate ways. Yet, this "weave of our lives" comes to escape our notice, we forget the important role of context, and we insist that there must be context-independent meaning-determiners, all because this background is so fundamental to any and all experience.[15] It becomes hidden by its sheer proximity to us.

Though we lack sublime meaning-determiners that fix the meaning of our words, we are not stuck with shallow relativism. This stage-setting in which linguistic usage takes place runs very deep. Rather than whimsy or social trends, our communication makes sense because of the role it plays in our form of life. And just as certain aspects of how we live our lives are (to us) seemingly unquestionable and unchangeable, so too are certain aspects of our use of language.

Wittgenstein broadens this contextualism beyond the overtly linguistic when he investigates what he refers to as seeing aspects.[16] Seeing aspects, or aspect perception more generally, refers to a perceptual phenomenon wherein we perceive a sensory object as changing in one respect while remaining the same in another.

Consider the image of Jastrow's famous duck-rabbit. The image strikes some at first as a duck, but they can come to see it instead as a rabbit. However, such a perceptual change is not reflected in the image itself changing at all. The lines on the page remain the same, yet we see it differently. Before it was a duck; now it is undeniably a rabbit. Or consider the faces of two of my acquaintances who are siblings. After months of knowing both of them, I am struck by a similarity in their faces that I had not noticed before. Their faces have not changed, yet I now see them differently. In each of these cases, the object of perception remains the same, yet a new "aspect" of that object is "lighting up."[17]

Wittgenstein presents the lighting up of aspects in a very similar way to how I have been presenting the apparent paradox of the framing device. In fact, we can reformulate the framing paradox as follows. When I listen to the repeated verse at the end of "Tecumseh Valley," a new aspect has lit up for me; though the sensory object appears to remain the same, I hear it under a new aspect.[18]

Wittgenstein recognized that we might be tempted in various ways to misunderstand the paradox of seeing aspects. Now that we have reformulated the framing paradox along the lines of seeing aspects, we can apply his words of caution to our own apparent paradox. First, the difference cannot be due to some distant attendant quality—for example, "When I heard the first verse, I was snapping my fingers, but during the last verse I was tapping my toes." This may be the case, but it is irrelevant to the claim that the perceptual object *itself* both does and does not seem to change. Second, the difference cannot be due to a different physiological process *in me,* for example: "The manner in which my cochlea converted the sound of the first verse into a nervous signal and transmitted it along the

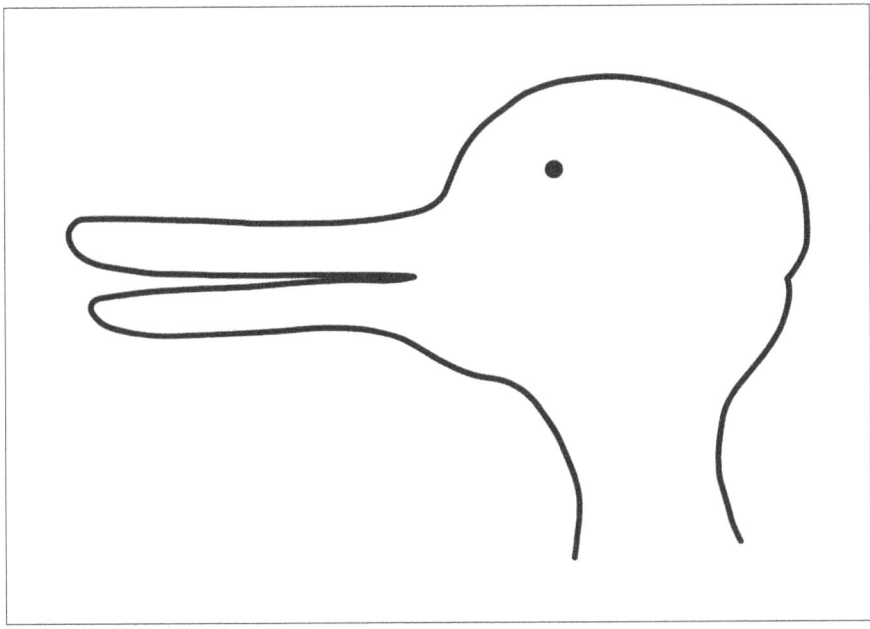

Figure 1: Jastrow's Duck-Rabbit (image recreated by author).

vestibulocochlear nerve was different than during the last verse." This, too, Wittgenstein holds, is irrelevant to the paradox.

Wittgenstein also anticipates an objection to this apparent paradox: "No, no, no," the objection goes. "We don't *hear* the verses differently; we hear them exactly the same. Rather, we *interpret* them differently." Wittgenstein responds that this objection depends upon a mistaken view of how we experience anything because it presupposes a clear distinction between pure perception, on the one hand, and interpretation, which acts upon that perception, on the other. Surely, interpretation takes place when listening to and parsing the lyrics of a song; however, according to Wittgenstein, there is no unprocessed given that we receive in pure form *and then* to which we apply our concepts. Experience is not so easily divided into two distinct steps: the first of receiving a perceptual object, and the second applying a concept to that object.

How are we to attempt to resolve this apparent paradox? A first response is that sometimes there is something identifiable that *does* change: the listener. In certain cases, the listener has come to know something about the content presented in the first verse or acquired further and enriching connotations to the first verse's images. But such an attempted resolution does not do justice to the depth of the paradox as discussed above; it only explains the difference *sometimes*.

A famous passage from Wittgenstein's *Philosophical Investigations* goes as follows: "What is your aim in philosophy?—To show the fly the way out of the fly-bottle."[19] This passage characterizes the sort of philosophy that Wittgenstein sees himself as practicing: an activity that disabuses us of the pictures that hold us captive to certain ways of thinking. This disabusing is done by removing the temptation of these pictures, which in turn is done by identifying the mistaken presuppositions that underlie them. We should consider, then, if the framing device only appears paradoxical because we approach it under the sway of an inappropriate picture of how language functions. Perhaps once outside of the fly-bottle—outside of a particularly tempting picture of how language works—the apparent paradox dissolves.

It turns out that the framing paradox does depend upon a certain picture of language: that language operates in the same way in different contexts. Though in certain circumstances we are quick to acknowledge the importance of context for language use (remember the soldier and child at the park from above), we are nevertheless tempted to take repeated signs (such as words or sentences) to be a repetition of meaning (i.e., repeated semantic content) *because* that is how language works in most cases. Sometimes repeated signs just *do* involve repeated semantic content—such as a repeated announcement in an airport terminal—but that is only appropriate in the usual cases—the paradigmatic cases. There are other (perhaps less common but still important) cases in which repetition of signs should not be taken to be repetition of semantic content. Poetry and song can be such exceptional cases, where a different picture of language and meaning is appropriate. In "Tecumseh Valley," the first verse is repeated only at the level of signs. With regard to semantic content, there is no mere repetition. The last verse is *heard* by the listener differently because it *means* something richer, more complex, and different.

The paradox dissolves when we realize the significant difference between the first and last verses of "Tecumseh Valley." Sure, the signs are repeated, but the signs that constitute the verses are not the only means we have to explain their difference. How I might describe the first verse to a close friend who had never heard "Tecumseh Valley" would be different than my description of the last verse. The non-descriptive, expressive reactions that I have while listening to the two verses also would be different because they occasion different emotional responses for me. The signs that make up these verses are just one aspect among others, such as forms of expression when describing, non-descriptive expressive reactions, and emotional or affective responses.[20]

Dissolving the paradox of the framing device by rejecting that the verses are the same encourages us to make use of a holistic approach when engaging with poetry and song. We should not simply equate verses because of the repetition of signs. The verses mean what they do because of their context, and the context for each verse is importantly different.[21] The paradox is dissolved when we attend to the wider context and forgo the picture of how language works in just the paradigmatic cases. This is an important boon of poetry and song: they loosen the hold that certain pictures of language have over us, opening us up to the multifarious ways that collections of signs can mean.

In *Philosophical Investigations*, the reader is reminded that the paradoxes at issue in the text do not (for the most part) arise in everyday life—that they arise from a particular philosophical perspective that seeks to isolate words, signs, sentences (even verses!) from their context and the circumstances in which they are ordinarily used. Relatedly, the person listening to country music is not likely to hear "Tecumseh Valley" as a paradoxical provocation. However, the philosophically interested listener will find in the framing device a moving example of the context-based way that meaning is conveyed. The apparent paradox of the framing device and its dissolution shows that in art and song, we are called to entertain new or more complicated pictures—for example, one in which sameness is not merely a function of repeated signs and musical accompaniment.

Country Music and the Elevation of the Ordinary

Framing devices are not solely found in country music—consider "In Search of Little Sadie" from Bob Dylan's *Self Portrait*—however, the device has found success in country songwriting because of a particular preoccupation of the genre: the elevation of the ordinary.[22] This occurs when an everyday object or experience is introduced then transmuted over the course of the song into a representative of or gesture to something much more far-reaching and weighty. "Black Diamond Strings" by Guy Clark, which also makes use of the framing device, begins with a description of a brand of tough, cheap guitar strings that are only played by someone who can't get anything better.[23] But it turns into a portrait of a driven, yet struggling musician, with the tough, cheap strings reflecting his gritty character. Terry Stafford's "Amarillo by Morning" (famously recorded by George Strait in 1982) presents the narrator driving overnight from San Antonio to Amarillo yet uses this seemingly prosaic experience as a meditation on the struggles and solitude of a contemporary rodeo cowboy.[24]

The framing device aids in the elevation of the ordinary because we are at first offered an everyday, even unassuming image in the first verse, then in the last verse, we are shown how that image has come to mean so much more. Further, not only is the everyday elevated, but with the framing device it is self-consciously elevated; the structure reminds the listener—by repeating the signs of the first verse—that a transmutation has taken place. With the elevation of the ordinary, we are again reminded of the importance of context, as over the course of the song the prosaic object or event is de-contextualized and re-contextualized, rising from its humble origins to concern something much more wide-reaching. The framing device provides a song structure perfectly suited for such a task.

The framing device in country music might strike the philosophically inclined as having the form of a paradox, yet it appears paradoxical only when we are held captive by a particular picture of how language works. When the grip of such pictures is loosened and the repetition of signs is shown to be only one way of relating the two framing verses, the verses are shown to be significantly and importantly different. It is in the process of engaging with poetry and song that we can come to find that our ordinary pictures of language are not universally applicable. Art, especially poetry and song, provides the salutary benefit of loosening the grip that such pictures of language have on us, not by showing them to be faulty, but by disabusing us of the conviction that such pictures must *always* apply. Country music is especially inclined to use this device because of its attendant preoccupation with elevating the ordinary. This makes country music an especially illuminating example of the oft-forgotten, context-dependent manner in which meaning is conveyed.

Notes

1. Van Zandt, Townes. 1977. "Tecumseh Valley." *Live at the Old Quarter, Houston, Texas.* Tomato/Fat Possum.

2. *Ibid.*

3. Clark, Guy. 1995. "Dublin Blues." *Dublin Blues.* Wilkinson, Miles (prod.) Asylum Records; Elektra Records.

4. Shaver, Billy Joe. 2004. "Fame." *Billy and the Kid.* Colton, Tony (prod.) Compadre Records.

5. Williams, Hank. 1949. "I'm So Lonesome I Could Cry." B-side to "My Bucket's Got a Hole in It." Williams, Clarence (prod.) MGM Records.

6. Van Zandt, Townes. 1972. "Snow Don't Fall." *The Late Great Townes Van Zandt.* Clement, Jack; Eggers, Kevin (prods.) Poppy; Clark, Guy. 1975. "L.A. Freeway." *Old No. 1.* Wilburn, Neil (prod.) RCA Records. Shaver, Billy Joe; Hall, Hillman. 1973. "Omaha." *Honky Tonk Heroes.* Waylon Jennings (rec. artist; prod.) RCA Victor. Guthrie, Woody. 1989. "Lonesome Valley." *Library of Congress Recordings.* Rounder. Foley, Blaze. 2010. "Rainbows and Ridges." *Sittin' by the Road.* Remmert, Fred (prod.) Lost Art. Williams, Lucinda. 1980. "Louisiana Man." *Happy Woman Blues.* White, Mickey (prod.) Smithsonian Folkways.

7. Zollo, Paul. 2003. "Townes Van Zandt." *Songwriters on Songwriting.* Cambridge: Da Capo Press, 443–452.

8. Van Zandt, Townes. 1972. "Snow Don't Fall." *The Late Great Townes Van Zandt.* Poppy.

9. *Ibid.*

10. Wittgenstein, Ludwig & Anscombe, G.E.M. & Hacker, P.M.S. & Schulte, J. 2009. *Philosophical Investigations*, Chichester: Wiley. [*PI*] See also Stern, David. 1997. "Heidegger and Wittgenstein on the Subject of Kantian Philosophy." *Figuring the Self: Subject, Individual and Other in German Idealism.* Klemm, D., and Zöller, G. (eds.) Albany: SUNY Press, 245–259.

11. Stern, David. 2004. *Wittgenstein's* Philosophical Investigations: *An Introduction.* Cambridge: Cambridge University Press, 20.

12. *Ibid.*

13. Wittgenstein, *PI*, §257.

14. *Ibid.*, *PI*, §23.

15. *Ibid.*, *PI*, II, 240, §362; cf. "tapestry of life" in *PI*, II, 183, §2.

16. *Ibid.*, *PI*, II, 204, §118.

17. *Ibid.*

18. One might object by pointing out that the sensory object does not stay the same. As a new instance of singing and musical accompaniment, it is decidedly *not the same* object. However, I suggest that a new aspect could light up even if the recording of the first verse is simply copy and pasted by a recording engineer at the end of the song. It could be the same sensory object (just repeated), and yet a new aspect can still light up.

19. *Ibid.*, *PI*, §309.

20. For further discussion see Ahmed, Arif. 2017. "Wittgenstein on Seeing Aspects." *A Companion to Wittgenstein.* Glock, H.-J., and Hyman, J. (eds.) Hoboken: John Wiley & Sons, 528–529.

21. That repeated choruses do different work at their various locations in a song is acknowledged by certain songwriters. For a discussion see Pattison, Pat. 2009. *Writing Better Lyrics: The Essential Guide to Powerful Songwriting.* Cincinnati: Writer's Digest Books.

22. Dylan, Bob. 1970. "In Search of Little Sadie." *Self Portrait.* Johnston, Bob (prod.) Sony Music Entertainment.

23. Clark, Guy. 1995. "Black Diamond Strings." *Dublin Blues.* Asylum Records; Elektra Records.

24. Stafford, Terry; Fraser, Paul. 1982. "Amarillo by Morning." *Strait from the Heart.* Strait, George (rec. artist). Mevis, Blake (prod.) MCA Records.

Does Country Music Suck?

S. Evan Kreider

It's surprisingly common to hear people say, "I like all kinds of music … except country." In less polite conversations, they might even go so far as to say, "Country music sucks!" Indeed, country is one of the genres which members of the music-consuming public are most likely to say "sucks" rather than simply saying "I don't care for it" or "It's just not my thing" (as they might say of other genres). However, a bit of clarification is needed to make sense of this claim. What exactly is it for music to "suck"? And once this concept is properly clarified, can we indeed say that country music sucks? With the help of philosophical aesthetics, we will consider some possibilities of what the claim "Country music sucks!" might entail. However, we will also see that the claim is false, as it rests on certain misconceptions about country music. Additionally, it will be made clear that standards which might be used to attempt to justify such a claim are inconsistently applied, since the charges leveled against country music could just as easily be aimed at genres of music that the critic in question presumably does not think "suck."

Formal Failure?

Broadly construed, aesthetic formalism is the idea that we can identify and evaluate works of art based on their various formal features. For example, a painting is made up of lines, shapes, colors, etc., while a song is composed of melody, harmony, rhythm, and so on. Formalism has roots at least as far back as Aristotle, who analyzed tragedies in terms of plot, character, thought (dialogue), and other elements. Early modern philosophers such as Francis Hutcheson further developed the foundations of aesthetic formalism by drawing attention to more generalizable features of beauty (whether natural or artistic), such as the order and complexity of the objects that prompt aesthetic pleasure in the viewer or listener. Fully developed theories of modern formalism are arguably a product of 20th-century philosophers such as Clive Bell who advanced a notion of "significant form" in his 1913 work, *Art.*[1]

According to Bell, what makes works of art different from other objects is that they have "significant form." Bell was specifically speaking of painting and related visual art forms, their formal qualities such as line, shape, and color, and the particular way that those individual formal qualities are arranged. Not merely a random collection of elements, they are related and combined into a coherent whole that prompts an aesthetic feeling in the viewer. This feeling is distinct from other emotional responses that we experience in non-aesthetic contexts. Of course, non-aesthetic objects also have form, but not the significant form that can move us to experience this special aesthetic feeling. According to Bell, nothing else is required other than the perceptual experience of significant form. Knowledge of the artist's intention, background information or historical context, familiarity with objects represented in the art, etc., are unnecessary for aesthetic experience.

Some critics implicitly draw from formalist accounts of aesthetics when criticizing country music. They point to the standard formal elements of music and then claim that those elements are ineffectively or improperly used in country music, which then fails to evoke the same aesthetic feeling they experience when listening to their preferred genres of music such as rock or classical. For example, they might claim that the typical chord changes in country music are too simplistic and repetitive. The rhythm of country music is similarly criticized for lacking "swing" and being too "square" or (problematically, as we'll discuss later) "white." Other, more subtle formal elements, such as the stylistic ornamentation used in country singing and playing (for example, the distinctive sliding up to notes of the steel guitar) are characterized as corny or trite. However, these criticisms seem unfair considering they are either inaccurate (i.e., false or exaggerated) or inconsistent (i.e., not applied equally to other genres).

The claim that country music's chord changes are simplistic, repetitive, or even cliché has some initial plausibility. Many country songs do in fact have simple, well-worn chord changes, using as few as three or four chords such as Dolly Parton's "Jolene"[2] and Hank Williams' "Your Cheatin' Heart."[3] However, this criticism is unfair in two ways. First, it cherry-picks examples of songs with simple chord changes without acknowledging country songs with more sophisticated forms. For example, Willie Nelson's "Always on My Mind"[4] has a jazzier influence that uses at least twice as many chords as the preceding examples, with the added jazz flavor of slash chords (chords with a different bass note than the usual root of the chord) and walkups (as heard in the bass and the piano in the chorus section, where the notes appear to "walk up" the scale from the first chord to the target chord). For another example, consider Johnny Cash's "I Walk the Line,"[5] which modulates to a whole new key with each verse! Another reason why the criticism is unfair is that other genres, presumably approved by the critic, are just as simple. Many, many rock tunes are "three chords and a dream." Songs such as "Wild Thing"[6] by the Troggs and "Louie Louie"[7] by The Kingsmen are composed of a mere three chords, but that didn't make them any less popular.

The next criticism is that country music is rhythmically "square" or "white." Many genres of popular music are written in the 4/4 time signature; that is, every measure has four beats (each of which is called a quarter-note—thus 4/4). In genres such as rock, blues, and jazz, the emphasis is usually on the backbeats (i.e., the second and fourth beats of each measure). Listeners of such genres generally clap on the two and four and dance in a manner that emphasizes those beats.

It's claimed that country music sounds "square" because it emphasizes the first and third beats instead. Again, there is an initial plausibility to this, considering the number of country songs in which the bass plays on the first and third beats; for example, listen to the bass parts on "I Walk the Line" and "Folsom Prison Blues"[8] (both by Johnny Cash), which do indeed occur on the "square" beats. However, this is once again unfair on two counts. First, country music does in fact provide some emphasis on the two and four, although it's not quite as heavy-handed as in other genres: though the bass emphasizes the one and three in the aforementioned tunes, careful attention to the drums (especially the snare drum) reveals stronger attention to the two and four. Second, there's nothing inherently "cooler" or "more hip" about emphasizing the two and four rather than the one and three. Either approach allows for serious musicianship and music appreciation, and to criticize one approach by the standards of another seems to be a simple misapplication of values, which to some degree are going to be relative to genre.

Finally, there is the criticism that certain country ornamentations are "corny" or trite. This includes various little slides and bends up to notes, used in a very obvious way by steel guitar players, but also imitated by vocalists and instruments other than steel guitar. Critics often mock these ornamentations by imitating them vocally in an exaggerated manner: "Bew bew bew BWOOOWWWWWWW!!!" Similarly, they mock vocals by pronouncing them in a way reminiscent of "white trash" stereotypes (an incredibly problematic criticism, to which we will return in a later section). Once again, this criticism is misplaced. Many styles of music, from classical to blues to rock, use similar ornamentation. The particular use of it may vary slightly from genre to genre, but the basic technique is still the same: in classical music, it is referred to as a grace note, while in rock and blues, it is referred to as a bend. The exact placement of the bend may differ; for example, grace notes in classical and bends in blues and rock often occur just before the note and at a slightly lower volume, while "slip notes" (as they are called in country piano, popularized by Floyd Cramer) in country often occur directly on the beat and at a louder volume. However, they are essentially the same technique with a slightly different emphasis, and once again, the criticism appears to be based on the misapplication of standards from other genres to country, which, to some degree, is a matter of musical relativism.

Lyrical Lapses?

Song lyrics occupy an interesting space between music and literature. They have formal features such as rhythm and rhyme that could be analyzed in purely musical terms, but they also contain content, literal or otherwise. Some philosophers such as Aristotle have argued that such content should serve to improve the audience morally or intellectually. Though Aristotle specifically discusses tragic plays in his work, *Poetics*, there is a long tradition of extrapolating a more general theory of aesthetic didacticism and applying it not only to plays but also to novels, poems, and other forms of literary art, which could include song lyrics as well. According to Aristotle, the purpose of tragedy is to evoke the emotions of fear and pity and to effect a catharsis of them.

One traditional interpretation of catharsis was to see it as a "purging" of the relevant emotions, allowing for a kind of psychological therapy, as it were. This view coheres nicely with some psychological views (especially those of Freud and related thinkers) that our emotions, especially negative ones such as fear and pity, require the occasional release, hopefully in a healthy and non-destructive way such as watching a horror movie to help work out one's fears and anxieties. However, a number of recent scholars have argued that catharsis entails a kind of "perfection" of the relevant emotions. This view coheres nicely with Aristotle's writings on moral virtue, which involve (in part) a perfecting of emotional responses by training them to fall within a mean between extremes. For example, the virtue of courage involves a mean of fear (i.e., appropriate amounts of fear, in the appropriate situations, at the appropriate time, toward the appropriate objects, etc.) rather than the extremes of too much fear (i.e., the vice of cowardice) or too little fear (i.e., the vice of recklessness). Simply put, this interpretation suggests that Aristotle sees literature as something that should help us to develop virtue and to become better people.

With this in mind, the lyrics of country music have also been the target of criticism, specifically the content of those lyrics rather than their formal characteristics, and their criticisms echo the aesthetic didacticism of Aristotle. Some claim that country lyrics are trite and lack substance, choosing instead to sing about yet another romantic heartbreak or wax poetic about a horse or pickup truck, neither of which has a great deal of moral merit. Others level a more serious claim, that the lyrics are not simply morally banal, but morally objectionable, advancing themes that are anti-feminist, heteronormative, and even explicitly violent. Once again, the problems with these criticisms are two-fold. In some cases, they are simply untrue. In other cases, they may be true, but they are equally true of other genres of music.

To be fair to the critic, there are plenty of such songs. Waylon Jennings' "Cedartown, Georgia"[9] certainly fits the bill. The narrator sings of how he married a gal from Cedartown, moved her down to New Orleans, and spent his days working hard to support her. However, he soon finds her cheating on him with other men, at which point he buys himself a .22 and concludes by telling us that there are "gonna be a lotta kin folks squalling and a-grieving / 'Cause that Cedartown gal ain't breathing." Similarly, Willie Nelson's "Red Headed Stranger"[10] tells the tale of the titular stranger who casually kills a woman who attempts to steal his horse and gets away with it "of course." Johnny Cash's "Cocaine Blues"[11] recounts the drug-addled murder of an unfaithful woman, seemingly without remorse, still referring to her toward the end of the song as "that bad bitch." These three songs are a mere sample of the numerous country songs with similar themes.

Of course, such themes are hardly unique to country music. "A Good Idea"[12] by Bob Mould's band Sugar describes a young man who drowns his girlfriend for seemingly no reason and without warning. Guns N' Roses "Used to Love Her"[13] proclaims just that, along with the fact that he "had to kill her" (and sung in a rather gleeful manner). In "Blood on the Floor,"[14] Fleetwood Mac's Jeremey Spencer sings the point of view of a man who killed his "darling" for cheating on him and whose only regret is having been caught because of the evidence named in the title. These rock examples have their roots in classic blues music, such as Robert Johnson's "32–20," the rifle used in the song to cut his baby "half in two" if she should "get unruly and thinks she don't wanna do." Again, these are just a small sample of such songs from genres such as rock and blues, but they illustrate that it's unfair to criticize country music specifically for the misogyny and violence that can be found in the lyrics of certain country songs.

Furthermore, many country songs avoid such topics, explicitly speak against them, or advocate much more positive and inclusive themes. Martina McBride's signature song "Independence Day"[15] calls attention to the tragedy of domestic abuse. Dolly Parton's "Just Because I'm a Woman"[16] calls out the double standard of men expecting women to remain "angels" before marriage, while they feel free to "take a good girl and ruin her reputation." Miranda Lambert's "Y'all Means All"[17] is an ode to the LGBTQIA+ community. In many instances, contemporary country music has moved away from the more traditional and occasionally problematic viewpoints and values of older country styles.

Class Condescension?

Given the inaccuracies and inconsistencies—one might be tempted to say "hypocrisies"—of the criticisms of country music, we might begin to wonder if the objections of most critics are less rooted in musical analysis and more in something else entirely. Given country music's popularity or lack thereof among various demographics, it's only natural to suspect that the real source of criticism lies in something more socio-political. Philosophers such as Karl Marx have suggested that our very way of looking at the world, from our basic economic conditions through cultural phenomena such as ethics, religion, and the arts, is very much colored by our socio-economic class.

According to Marx, human beings are first and foremost material creatures, driven by material needs. As a result, economics—systems for the production and exchange of material goods—are at the root of human societies. The economic base is the foundation on which the social superstructure—that is, all non-economic aspects of society (such as religion, politics, and art)—is built. Indeed, the social superstructure is essentially a reflection of and determined by the economic base. This includes music, the form and content of which mirrors the economic realities of the societies in which it is present.

Perhaps because of the importance of economics to society, humans see the world through their economic contexts. Each society's dominant ideology is that of the most powerful class, but each class also has its particular class consciousness that colors the ways in which they see and interact with the world. This would include music and musical tastes as well. It's not hard to make the case that under capitalism, the most successful forms of music would be those that are generated by and reflective of capitalist means and modes of musical production (the American Top 40 once brought to us by Casey Kasem, for example). However, it also explains why some forms of music appeal to some groups of people more than others, and thus why there are various charts for not only pop but also country, soul, dance, and other genres of music, each of which sells to some social groups more than others.

Unfortunately, one can't help but think that some criticisms of country music come from a place of ideology rather than aesthetics. As mentioned above, critics often mock the voices of country singers in a way that implies that their singing sounds "low-class." Jokes about country lyrics and their supposed focus on drinking and pickup trucks also seem to include at least a tinge of classism. Since country music is more popular in certain geographic areas such as the American South, critics of country are more likely to hail from other parts of the country that may harbor negative stereotypes of Southerners and their musical tastes. Once again, their criticisms fail because they are inconsistently applied or straightforwardly false.

The inconsistency comes once again from comparisons to genres of which the country music critic presumably approves. If country music is "low class" then so is rock and roll. Rock music has long championed itself as music for the "common people," historically replacing supposedly more sophisticated genres such as jazz in popularity. Rock is also known for explicitly singing the praises of the "working man" as evidenced by songs such as Rush's "Working Man"[18] and Styx's "Blue Collar Man."[19] If these songs deserve respect, then so too should Dolly Parton's "9 to 5"[20] or Loretta Lynn's "Coal Miner's Daughter."[21]

Moreover, it's simply not true that all country music reflects "low class" people or contexts. In fact, many popular country songs communicate themes that transcend any particular socio-economic station. Hank Williams' classic "I'm So Lonesome I Could Cry"[22] sings of the universal experience of loneliness, with imagery of the night sky that anyone anywhere in the world could gaze upon while wishing for company. Tim McGraw's "Live Like You Were Dying"[23] tells of an unsettling medical diagnosis, then used as inspiration to live life to the fullest and become a better person. And Dolly Parton's "I Will Always Love You"[24] is, of course, a bitter-sweet song about the all-too-familiar theme of the end of a meaningful relationship. Nothing about any of these songs suggests anything limited to any one socio-economic group, much less one of "low class."

Country Conclusions

In the final analysis, criticisms of country music are not well-grounded, seeing as they are either false or inconsistently applied. Furthermore, the motivation behind these criticisms may be ideological rather than aesthetic. The genre of country music deserves just as much respect as any other genre. Indeed, country music doesn't suck at all.

NOTES

1. Bell, Clive. 1913. *Art*. Kessinger Publishing.
2. Parton, Dolly. 1973. "Jolene." *Jolene*. Ferguson, Bob (prod.) RCA Victor.
3. Williams, Hank. 1952. "Your Cheatin' Heart." Rose, Fred (prod.) MGM Records.
4. Carson, Wayne; James, Mark; Christopher, Johnny. 1982. "Always on My Mind." *Always on My Mind*. Nelson, Willie (rec. artist). Moman, Chips (prod.) Columbia Records.
5. Cash, Johnny. 1956. "I Walk the Line." *Johnny Cash with His Hot and Blue Guitar!* Phillips, Sam (prod.) Sun Records.
6. Taylor, Chip. 1966. "Wild Thing." The Troggs (rec. artist). Page, Larry (prod.) Fontana Records.
7. Berry, Richard. 1963. "Louie Louie." *The Kingsmen in Person*. The Kingsmen (rec. artists). Flip Records.
8. Cash, Johnny. 1955. "Folsom Prison Blues." *Johnny Cash with His Hot and Blue Guitar!* Phillips, Sam (prod.) Sun Records.
9. Vickery, Mack; Smith, Sammi; Cobble, Charlie. 1971. "Cedartown, Georgia." *Cedartown, Georgia*. Davis, Danny; Atkins, Chet; Light, Ronny (prods.) RCA Nashville.
10. Stutz, Carl; Lindeman; Edith. 1975. "Red Headed Stranger." *Red Headed Stranger*. Nelson, Willie (rec. artist; prod.) Columbia Records.
11. Arnall, T.J. 1968. "Cocaine Blues." *Johnny Cash at Folsom Prison*. Cash, Johnny (rec. artist). Johnston, Bob (prod.) Columbia Records.
12. Mould, Bob. 1992. "A Good Idea." *Copper Blue*. Sugar (rec. artist). Mould, Bob; Giordano, Lou (prods.) Rykodisc/Creation Records.
13. Guns N' Roses. 1988. "Used to Love Her." *G N' R Lies*. Clink, Mike (prod.) Geffen Records.
14. Spencer, Jeremy. "Blood on the Floor." *Kiln House*. Fleetwood Mac (rec. artist; prods.) Reprise Records.
15. Peters, Gretchen. 1993. "Independence Day." *The Way That I Am*. McBride, Martina (rec. artist). RCA Nashville.
16. Parton, Dolly. 1968. "Just Because I'm a Woman." *Just Because I'm a Woman*. Ferguson, Bob (prod.) RCA Victor.
17. Lambert, Miranda. 2021. "Y'all Means All." *Queer Eye*. Dick, Luke (prods.) Netflix.
18. Lifeson, Alex; Lee, Geddy. 1973. "Working Man." *Rush*. Rush (prods.) Moon Records, Anthem Records, Mercury Records.
19. Shaw, Tommy. 1978. "Blue Collar Man (Long Nights)." *Pieces of Eight*. Styx (rec. artist; prods.) A&M Records.
20. Parton, Dolly. 1975. "9 to 5." *9 to 5 and Odd Jobs*. Perry, Gregg (prod.) RCA Nashville.
21. Lynn, Loretta. 1970. "Coal Miner's Daughter." *Coal Miner's Daughter*. Bradley, Owen (prod.) Decca Records.
22. Williams, Hank. 1949. "I'm So Lonesome I Could Cry." B-side to "My Bucket's Got a Hole in It." MGM Records.
23. Nichols, Tim; Wiseman, Craig. "Live Like You Were Dying." *Live Like You Were Dying*. McGraw, Tim (rec. artist). Gallimore, Byron; McGraw, Tim; Darran, Smith (prods.) Curb Records.
24. Parton, Dolly. 1974. "I Will Always Love You." *Jolene*. Ferguson, Bob (prod.) RCA Records.

III

The Good (Country) Life

The Dilemma of Freedom and Belonging

Gordon P. Barnes

If you listen closely to any number of the classics of country music, you'll discover a recurring theme, a tale of two people: the one who *stayed* and the one who *left*. In "Blue Kentucky Girl," Loretta Lynn tells the tale from the point of view of the one who stayed as she sings about a country boy who left her to see the world but implores him, "Some morning when you wake up all alone / Just come on home to your blue Kentucky girl."[1] The protagonist longs for her "country boy" to come home to her; it's all she wants. However, in many of these stories, the one who stayed wonders if they made a mistake, if they are missing out on a better life. In her classic hit, "Is There Life Out There?" Reba McEntire imagines a woman who married when she was only twenty and now wonders if she isn't missing out on something more, a life beyond her home or even her family: "She's done what she should / should she do what she dares?"[2] Put differently, the young woman doesn't want to leave, but she also can't help but wonder what the world might hold for her outside of her current familial context. Again, this is a story of the one who stayed but now wonders if she should have left.

However, in some of these stories, the one who stayed isn't the only one who eventually has doubts. In some instances, the one who left also comes to regret their choice. This is Willie Nelson's lament in his classic hit "Heartaches of a Fool." The song recounts the story (from the first-person perspective) of a boy who saw the vast possibilities the world could provide him and dreamed that he would one day earn his fame and fortune. However, achieving his goals eventually led him to leave behind his sweetheart who would've loved him forever because he shortsightedly thought he could go at it alone: "And look at me / I'm the king of a cold lonely castle / The queen of my heart is gone."[3]

Lynn's "Blue Kentucky Girl" and Nelson's "Heartaches of a Fool" seem to be telling the same story from two different points of view, the view of the one who stayed, and the view of the one who left. What's striking, and perhaps a bit puzzling, is that *both* of these protagonists are unhappy in the end.

The story of the one who left is often embodied by what we might call the *Honky Tonk Man*: the familiar character of the man who chooses the adventurous life on the road and everything that comes with it. This character appears from the earliest days of country music. In "Honky Tonk Blues," Hank Williams tells the story of a young man who leaves his home to experience life in the city. But by the end of the story, he's had enough of urban living: "I'm going to tuck my worries underneath my arm / And scat right back to my pappy's farm / And leave these honky tonk blues."[4] This is a recurring theme in Williams' music. He tells the very same story in "Lost Highway," recounting traveling as a young, twenty-two-year-old man when he was "neither good nor bad, just a kid like you / And now I'm lost, too late to pray / Lord, I've paid the cost on the lost highway."[5] The story of the Honky Tonk Man doesn't end with Hank Williams. Dwight Yoakam tells a similar tale in the fittingly titled "Honky-Tonk Man," singing that he can't seem to quit the life of the Honky Tonk Man because of his penchant for girls and music, despite where such a lifestyle may inevitably lead him. "But when my money's all gone / I'm on the telephone singing / Hey hey mama, can your daddy come home?"[6]

So it seems, the Honky Tonk Man appears almost inevitably beset by regret. However, in the end, the ones who stay seem as if they can be just as contrite as the ones who leave. Each longs for the life of the other. The one who stayed wonders what it would have been like to leave; the one who left now wants to go home. Why is that? In this essay, I'll argue that these stories reveal a fundamental dilemma of human existence: *the dilemma of freedom and belonging.* As human beings, we all want freedom, and we also want to *belong.* Both of these things matter to us a great deal. However, as we will see, freedom and belonging are in tension with each other. In one sense, it is impossible to have both. Thus, we face a fundamental dilemma between freedom and belonging. So I will argue.

The Nature of Freedom and Belonging

We all want to be free. This desire is well expressed by The Chicks in their classic hit, "Wide Open Spaces," as the song alludes to the universal familiarity of the desire to step out into the world: "Who's never left home, who's never struck out? / To find a dream and a life of their own / A place in the clouds, a foundation of stone."[7] The desire for freedom is a recurring theme in many of The Chicks' greatest hits, such as songs like "Ready to Run" and "Set Me Free" (examples to which we will return by the end of this essay). Again, everyone wants to be free.

But if the desire to be free is so innate, why do those who leave come to regret their decision? After all, they got what they wanted; they're free! Why are they now unhappy? It seems as if country artists are providing us with an answer. Those who leave are free, but they are also *alone*. They don't really be*long* anywhere or with anyone. The value of belonging is one of the recurring themes in the music of Alabama. In "High Cotton," they describe the comfort that comes from belonging to a loving family; the singer describes how, as he has gotten older, he sees the light and warmth of his parents, and he can now appreciate everything they did for him: "They kept us warm and kept us fed / Taught us how to look ahead." However, looking back, he now understands; he can see that they were walking "in high cotton."[8] In another Alabama hit, "Love in the First Degree," the lyrics describe how falling in love can lead a person to choose belonging over freedom. The singer admits that he once thought that love was like a prison that he should reject. However, after love finally comes his way, he is willing to take a gamble, and even if love really is like a prison, he pleads to his lover that she's left him defenseless, but he's "only got one plea / Lock me away inside of your love / And throw away the key."[9] As we can see, the protagonist in this song sees his choice as one between love and freedom, and he chooses love. He seems to think that love and freedom are, to some extent, incompatible. Is he right about that?

There are ways of using your freedom that will make it more difficult to belong. If a person chooses a career that requires them to move frequently or spend most of their time working, then it will be more difficult for them to form strong relationships. Outside of work, such a person's relationships are likely to be transitory. That's the point of Dolly Parton and Kenny Rogers' classic hit "You Can't Make Old Friends," that when "someone new walks in / I will smile and shake their hands / But you can't make old friends."[10] Some ways of living and some career choices will make it difficult to form the kinds of relationships that constitute *belonging*. That much is obvious enough, but freedom and belonging are incompatible in a much more significant way.

The authors of these songs have grasped a fundamental dilemma of human existence: the dilemma of freedom and belonging. The dilemma is again that we all want to be free, and we all want to belong, but freedom and belonging are in tension with one another. Why? To understand the dilemma, we need to delve deeper into the nature of freedom and the nature of belonging. Let us begin with freedom.

Human beings are rational animals, in the sense that we act *for reasons*. Our ability to act for reasons empowers us, but there is a way in which it also limits us. To see this, consider the following example from the philosopher Peter van Inwagen.[11] Suppose that I come to a red light at a busy intersection. A steady stream of cars is crossing the intersection in both directions in front of me. I am not in a hurry to get where I am going. If I were to hit the gas and fly through the red light, I would risk being hurt or killed in an accident, not to mention being arrested for reckless driving. Thus, I have a compelling reason to stop at the red light and remain there until the light turns green. By contrast, I have *no reason* to hit the gas and fly through the intersection. In this situation, could I hit the gas and fly through the intersection? No, I really couldn't, at least not if I am being rational. As a rational being, I am compelled to stop because I have every reason to stop and no reason to fly through the intersection. In this way, my rationality limits my freedom, or so it seems. This may be surprising, but it's true. The point is that our freedom is limited by our reasons. As a rational being, you cannot act contrary to compelling reasons. If you have compelling reasons to do something and you recognize that you have such reasons, then you will do it. So, while human beings may be free in some important sense, our freedom is not without limits.

Now, let us consider belonging. When I use the term "belonging," I am referring to being a part of relationships such as marriage, family, friendship, and those found in any close community. One of the most important facts about belonging, in this sense, is that if you truly belong to or are a part of one of these relationships, then the wants and needs of the other people in the relationship always give you a very strong reason to act on their behalf. Consider marriage. If I am truly committed to my spouse in the way that constitutes a loving marriage, then if my wife needs something, I have a very strong reason to provide it for her. It is important to be very clear about this: if I am in a committed, loving marriage, then the fact that my wife needs something is, by itself, a very strong reason for me to provide it for her. If my wife needs help getting out of bed in the morning, then I have a very strong reason to help her. The same principle applies to being a parent, a friend, or even a good neighbor. If my son needs something, then that is a very strong reason for me to provide it for him, if I can. Likewise, if my friend needs something, then that is a strong reason for me to provide it, again, if I can. If I am really committed to these relationships—to my spouse, my children, and my friends—then the needs of these people give me reasons to act, whether I like it or not.

Moreover, in many situations, the fact that one of these people needs something will be a *compelling* reason for me to provide it. That is because, in many situations, the fact that one of these people needs something will be a stronger reason than any other reason I have. Suppose that my son falls and breaks his arm. I am the only person with him, and he needs to go to the hospital right away. This gives me a compelling reason to stop whatever I am doing and take him to the hospital. As a rational person who loves my son, I could not do anything else. And this would also be true if it were my spouse, or my good friend, or even my neighbor. It is a consequence of really belonging to these relationships that the needs of these people can give me compelling reasons to act. In some cases, even the mere *wants* of these people will give me compelling reasons to act on their behalf. This is an important part of what it means to belong to a marriage, a family, or a community. If you belong to one of these groups, then the needs and wants of the members of the group give you strong reasons to act, and sometimes those reasons are compelling—you really *have to* act on them.

This is especially clear in the case of parenthood. To be a parent—to really be committed to parenthood—entails that your children's needs are compelling reasons to act on their behalf. No one describes this better than Faith Hill. In "You Can't Lose Me." A little girl who is small for her age takes a long time to finish a field day race, but when she does, her mother is at the finish line waiting for her with nothing but words of encouragement and the reminder that "you're gonna lose the race from time to time / But you're always gonna find / You can't lose me."[12] This is part of what it means to be a parent and to really belong to a family. The needs of your children are compelling reasons to act on their behalf.

The Tension Between Freedom and Belonging

We are now in a position to understand why freedom and belonging are in tension with one another. If you really belong—in a marriage, a family, or even a friendship—then the needs and wants of the other people in those relationships will sometimes give you compelling reasons to act on their behalf. When this happens, you will not be free to act in any other way. Thus, being in a marriage, a family, or a friendship will often put you in situations in which you have a compelling reason to act for other people. In these situations, that is how you *must* act; in a very literal sense, you cannot do anything else. In this way, truly belonging is incompatible with complete freedom. When you choose to belong in any of these ways, you are choosing to limit your freedom.

The incompatibility of freedom and belonging is described beautifully in a more recent (but still classic) country hit. In "The Mother," Brandi Carlile perfectly captures the sacrifice of freedom that comes with motherhood as the mother in the song describes how, now that she's a mother, she is no longer alone (even inside her own mind) and that she's forever connected to her child in a way that inevitably leads to sacrifice. As such, she comforts her child by reminding her that she'll hold her while she's sleeping even though the mother wishes she could go because "all [her] rowdy friends [are] around, accomplishing their dreams / But I am the mother of Evangeline."[13] Carlile describes motherhood as being "tethered to another," and that is exactly right.

This, then, is the dilemma: we can be completely free, or we can have genuine belonging, but we cannot have both. To really belong—to a marriage, a family, or a friendship—is to have your freedom limited by the needs and wants of other people. Nevertheless, as these songs attest, many people choose belonging. Why? One answer is that we are simply built for it. Human beings are social animals, through and through. We need to belong to be happy. Those who choose complete freedom over belonging, like the Honky Tonk Man, eventually suffer the "Heartaches of a Fool." That is why so many people choose to belong.

However, not every group of people limits the freedom of their members to the very same degree. Some spouses, some families, and some "friends" manipulate and abuse their significant others in ways that diminish or even destroy the value of belonging with them. At the level of community, Hank Williams attests to the ways in which a community can impinge on the freedom of its members. Williams addresses this in "Mind Your Own Business" in which a group of busybodies seems to be poking their nose into Williams' relationship, to which he responds "Why don't you mind your own business? / 'Cause if you mind your own business, you sure won't be minding mine."[14] When communities interfere with the freedom of their members in ways that are unnecessary or harmful, it diminishes the value of belonging to that community.

Some have experienced more mistreatment by their community than others. Women, in particular, have often been the victims of manipulation and abuse by their spouses, families, and communities. Thus, it is no wonder that women often face a very difficult choice between freedom and belonging. No one has sung about this more, or better, than The Chicks, as they seem to take up the voice for women who have been mistreated by their own communities: "Why, oh, why do you keep me tethered? / You've taken enough from me / Why not just set me free?"[15] Here, again, we find the word "tethered," but in this instance, it's used not with affection but resentment. In a relationship that restricts a person's freedom too much, belonging becomes suffocating and loses much of its value.

At their worst, spouses, families, and friends can be extremely abusive. In those cases, belonging loses its value, and it makes more sense to choose freedom or at least freedom from that *particular* relationship. This is often why some people choose freedom over belonging. Their families and communities have become manipulative, oppressive, or even abusive. When that happens, the value of freedom for those who have been mistreated becomes greater than the value of belonging or at least belonging to that *particular* community. Of course, in some situations, it can be extremely difficult for a person to free themselves from an abusive relationship. If a person is under the constant threat of violence, with no easy path of escape, they will find some way to defend themselves. That is the moral of The Chicks' classic hit, "Goodbye Earl." In the song, when Wanda gets a restraining order against her abusive husband, Earl, he attacks her anyway and puts her in intensive care. Wanda's friend, Mary Anne, rushes to help her, and "She held Wanda's hand as they worked out a plan / And it didn't take 'em long to decide / That Earl had to die."[16] That is what happens when communities allow some members to abuse others. In an abusive community, belonging ceases to be a good thing.

To some extent, we have to choose between freedom and belonging. We cannot have complete, unlimited freedom while also really belonging to a group of other people. In order to belong, we must accept limitations on our freedom. It is easy to lose sight of this fact. We would all love to have unlimited freedom, but if we want to enjoy the benefits of belonging, then we need to face the fact that this is only possible through restrictions on our freedom. However, with that said, we all need at least a little bit of *both* freedom *and* belonging. We need at least some true freedom as well as genuine belonging. If we are to achieve both, then we must build and sustain relationships—marriages, families, and communities—that are worth belonging to, which means that those relationships must give us at least a little bit of freedom too.[17]

NOTES

1. Mullins, Johnny. 1965. "Blue Kentucky Girl." *Blue Kentucky Girl*. Lynn, Loretta (rec. artist). Bradley, Owen (prod.) Columbia Records.

2. Longacre, Susan; Giles, Rick. 1992. "Is There Life Out There." *For My Broken Heart*. McEntire, Reba (rec. artist). Brown, Tony (prod.) MCA Nashville.

3. Nelson, Willie; Breeland, Walt; Buskirk, Paul. 1981. "Heartaches of a Fool." *Greatest Hits (& Some That Will Be)*. Grusin, Dave; Jones, Booker T.; Mardin, Arif; Pollack, Sydney; Rosen, Larry; Russell, Leon (prods.) Columbia Records.

4. Williams, Hank. 1952. "Honky Tonk Blues." *Moanin' the Blues*. Rose, Fred (prod.) MGM Records.

5. Payne, Leon. 1949. "Lost Highway." Williams, Hank (rec. artist). Rose, Fred (prod.) MGM Records.

6. Horton, Johnny. 1986. "Honky-Tonk Man." *Guitars, Cadillacs, Etc., Etc.* Yoakam, Dwight (rec. artist). Anderson, Pete (prod.) Reprise Records.

7. Gibson, Susan. 1998. "Wide Open Spaces." *Wide Open Spaces*. Dixie Chicks (rec. artists). Chancey, Blake; Worley, Paul (prods.) Monument Records.

8. Murrah, Roger. 1989. "High Cotton." *Southern Star*. Alabama (rec. artists). Lee, Larry Michael; Leo, Josh (prods.) RCA Nashville.

9. Hurt, Jim; DuBois, Tim. 1981. "Love in the First Degree." *Feels So Right*. Alabama (rec. artist). Shedd, Harold (prod.) RCA Nashville.

10. King, Ryan Hanna; Schlitz, Don. Smith, Caitlyn. 2013. "You Can't Make Old Friends." *You Can't Make Old Friends*. Huff, Dann (prod.) Warner Music Nashville.

11. Van Inwagen, Peter. 1989. "When Is the Will Free?" *Philosophical Perspectives*, Vol. 3. Ridgeview Publishing Co., 399–422.

12. Bruce, Trey; McHugh, Thom. 1996. "You Can't Lose Me." *It Matters to Me*. Hill, Faith (rec. artist). Hendricks, Scott (prod.) Warner Bros. Nashville.

13. Carlile, Brandi; Hanseroth, Phil; Hanseroth, Tim. 2018. "The Mother." *By the Way, I Forgive You*. Cobb, Dave; Jennings, Shooter (prods.) Lower Country Song; Elektra Records.

14. Williams, Hank. 1949. "Mind Your Own Business." Rose, Fred (prod.) MGM Records.

15. Maguire, Martie; Maines, Natalie; Strayer, Emily; Antonoff, Jack; Abraham, Ben. 2020. "Set Me Free." *Gaslighter*. The Chicks (rec. artists). Antonoff, Jack; Geiger, Teddy (prods.) Columbia Records.

16. Linde, Dennis. 2000. "Goodbye Earl." *Fly*. Dixie Chicks (rec. artists). Chancey, Blake; Worley, Paul (prods.) Monument Records.

17. This essay is dedicated to my favorite fans of country music: Marine Barnes, Robert Barnes, Heidi Liebert, Amy Liebert, Amy Liebert, and Brenda, Joe, and Emily Thompson.

Storytelling and the Good Life

Jenna Yuzwa

Country music is often characterized by its simplicity and the stories that unfold through its lyrics. While storytelling may have a variety of functions, the kind of storytelling that takes place within country music seems to serve a particular purpose; it can move its listeners to be (or at least want to be) a certain type of person. What kind of person might country music move its listeners to be? And how might such music move them through the stories it tells?

Country music may move its listeners to be *virtuous* people, thereby promoting their own flourishing. To practice the virtues as a constitutive part of one's own flourishing is an idea that can be traced back to ancient philosophers, most notably Aristotle. In what follows, we'll consider how some of the songs within country music move listeners to exercise virtues such as courage, pride, and kindness. And it is the simplicity of country music that may move its listeners to be virtuous. The simple aspects of the genre (e.g., the accessibility and relatability of these songs) encourage listeners to practice virtue, and as such, to ultimately live the good life.

Virtue in Country Music

Again, taking a closer look at the work of Aristotle can help us understand how the simplicity of storytelling in country music can move listeners toward the good life. Some of the most fundamental issues Aristotle sought to address were how humans ought to live, what the best life for a human being is, and what kind of person a human should strive to be. According to Aristotle, the best and happiest life is one that involves actively exercising virtues such as courage, truthfulness, and friendliness, among others. With all of this in mind, let's first consider a country song that exemplifies the virtue of courage and moves its listeners to be courageous.

"Independence Day," by Martina McBride, is perhaps one of the most powerful country songs of the 1990s. Narrated from the point of view of a young girl whose father abuses her mother, she recounts the story of how, at the age of just eight years old, she flees her chaotic home in order to attend the fair on Independence Day. When she returns, she finds the family home set ablaze and implies that her mother started the fire, presumably to escape the violence of her partner, seeing no other available recourse. As listeners, we aren't told whether the mother made it out alive; we only know that the little girl is taken to a county-run home. It's left to the listener to determine the morality of what has conspired, and while the narrator doesn't take a stance on this, she perhaps alludes to what she is thinking: "Now I ain't sayin' it's right or it's wrong / But maybe it's the only way...."[1]

In this song, the woman abused at the hands of her husband evidently felt she had no other option to escape the violence than to set her home on fire with her husband inside. She resorts to what seems to be her only hope to bring an end to her partner's abuse. Crucially, though, the song recounts the devastating consequences that can result from domestic violence; the daughter is now left without her mother (because the mother either perished in the fire or the child was removed from her care by the authorities). Escaping a situation of domestic violence is incredibly difficult and those experiencing the abuse are often in the most danger when they attempt to flee. Though this can be difficult to fully grasp while in the midst of the chaos of domestic violence, it is almost always the case that the longer a victim stays, the more perilous their situation becomes.

Both the mother and daughter at the heart of McBride's anthem exemplify the virtue of courage, but the story moves listeners to exercise courage as well. There is courage in doing what one must in order to put an end to violence and abuse. And there is courage in sharing a story about a topic that was and still can be a source of shame or a taboo. Ultimately, however, the takeaway of "Independence Day" is that listeners who may be experiencing domestic violence themselves may be given the courage to leave before it gets to a point where the sort of tragedy that occurs in the song occurs in their own lives.

Indeed, McBride has received many fan letters about the song. One of these letters was from a woman who had been experiencing domestic violence, but upon hearing the song, came to the realization that her situation wasn't her fault and that she needed to leave.[2] However, the song may also encourage the listener who hasn't experienced domestic violence to take a stand on an often uncomfortable and difficult issue and to advocate for victims. The song's author, Gretchen Peters, noted that when "Independence Day" hit the airwaves, conversation around domestic violence increased in a way that hadn't really been seen before.[3] This phenomenon seems to demonstrate the exercise of another sort of courage that comes in the form of dialogue and the enacting of social change.

"Independence Day" is just one example of a country song exemplifying or encouraging virtue. But before we proceed with additional examples, it would be worth taking a closer look at the concept itself; what exactly is a virtue (on Aristotle's view)? Getting clear on this notion is important since it is central to (Aristotle's arguments about) the good life. "Virtue" or "excellence" is the typical translation of the ancient Greek word, *aretē*. It is a firm, consistent, and reliable character trait, such as courage, truthfulness, or friendliness. One who has the virtue of courage will not simply behave courageously on some occasions and not others; they will practice it regardless of the circumstances. Virtues are chosen for their own sake and are constitutive of the good life, not a means to an end. They are also determined by the right reason. Thus, one who, for example, provides what looks to be on the surface, a rather generous donation to a charitable organization, but only does so for the tax benefits, is not virtuous since they do not act for the right reason.

Additionally, the virtuous agent not only *behaves* virtuously; they also *feel* a certain way about behaving virtuously. That is, such a person takes pleasure in and is not pained by carrying out virtuous actions. If the person acts kindly but is inwardly begrudging of their kind act, they are not truly virtuous. Finally, virtue must be actively practiced. It is inadequate to carry out some virtuous action at some points but not others or to merely talk about being virtuous. Virtue must be exercised in a manner that is ongoing and consistent.[4]

How does one determine what the virtuous action is in a given situation? For Aristotle, virtue is a mean between the two extremes of vice. The two extremes of vice consist of excess at one end and deficiency at the other. For example, for the virtue of courage, the vice of excess would be overconfidence or being rash, while the vice of deficiency would be cowardice. One who practices virtue aims for the mean and to avoid the vices of excess and deficiency. But one does not aim for the mean only with respect to the action they choose; they also aim for the mean in regard to how they feel about said action. Again, being virtuous involves having the appropriate feelings about the act in question. Thus, the actor must determine what the mean is with respect to their feelings about the action.[5]

To think practically about how one might locate virtue as a mean between the vices of excess and deficiency, let's now consider another country song that exemplifies and encourages virtue. Consider the virtue of pride as the mean between the two extremes of excess (what Aristotle would call "empty vanity") and deficiency (or "undue humility"). In

"Coal Miner's Daughter," Loretta Lynn sings about growing up rich in love but poor in material possessions. Though life for the family was never easy as the family often lacked basic necessities, Lynn nevertheless retains a sense of pride with respect to how she was raised and in being a coal miner's daughter.[6]

Though some may perceive the destitution of the Lynn family as shameful, for Lynn, the hard work and the ability to make the best out of what they had, despite their poverty, is a source of pride. Yet this pride is measured; it's not excessive. Lynn isn't arrogant about her father's work or their family's lifestyle; she is instead appropriately proud of who they are. As a result, "Coal Miner's Daughter" exemplifies the virtue of pride and avoids the vices of deficiency or undue humility, and of excess, or empty vanity.

Having analyzed the notion of virtue (and how virtue may be exemplified in country songs), we can now turn our attention to another important concept for Aristotle: *eudaimonia*. This ancient Greek term is often translated as "happiness" or "flourishing." However, for Aristotle, happiness is not merely a fleeting good feeling or a cheerful disposition, and a happy life is not one spent accumulating wealth and riches, nor is it a life centered around the pursuit of physical pleasures. Instead, happiness is a type of activity.[7]

To our modern ears, this can sound a bit odd, but recall that eudaimonia may also be understood as flourishing or well-being. On Aristotle's view, to flourish as a human being is to actively practice the virtues, and virtues are constitutive of the good life. What we've suggested so far is that the stories told through country music may move listeners to practice the virtues. Because of this, it can be argued that country music promotes flourishing or eudaimonia. To make sense of this claim, we'll take a close look at some additional stories found within country music.

Shaping Moral Character Through Stories

Country music is not the only genre that has the capacity for storytelling, but telling stories is particularly important to country. Songwriters vividly capture the experience of the characters at the heart of their songs, recounting narratives that the listener can effortlessly connect to and identify with. Consider a tragic love story told through a song like "Whiskey Lullaby" by Brad Paisley and Alison Krauss. The broken-hearted former couple at the center of this piece each attempts to drown their sorrows by drinking, but each eventually decides to take their own life.[8] Consider also the more light-hearted example of Jo Dee Messina's "You're Not in Kansas Anymore." In this song, one of the characters has grown up on a farm in Kansas but dreamt of going to Los Angeles. When he expresses this dream to someone, they warn him that he "can't be too careful that's for sure" but they nevertheless promise to be there for him no matter what: "So write my number on your wall / And call me anytime at all." And, ultimately, they're happy for him even though (or because) he's not in Kansas anymore.[9]

Having canvassed some of the kinds of stories country music tells, we're now in a position to consider storytelling more generally and what it might be capable of within the medium of music. What exactly is special about storytelling in the first place? Psychologist Jerome Bruner has argued that storytelling is a means by which we think about the world and engage in problem-solving. In this way, it is an exercise of the mind.[10] But stories may not merely be a means of keeping the mind active; they may offer healing power and serve a therapeutic purpose. As Michael Wilson has pointed out, it was during the late 20th century that the belief that stories possessed healing qualities arose. It was thought that folktales passed on through the oral tradition contained a particular kind of wisdom that was somehow disposed of by scientists and scholars following The Enlightenment but that such wisdom could be recovered by the storyteller.[11]

However, at its core, Wilson suggests that "as a human activity storytelling is not only our primary mode of communication, it is also a fundamental marker of what it means to be human."[12] That is, our ability and tendency as human beings to share and interpret communication in narrative form have grown and developed as our species has developed in other areas. Storytelling also provides us with a means of dealing with personal experience. More specifically, it is not merely about communicating one's experience but also a way of processing said experience.[13]

I don't reject these ideas about what storytelling can do. Indeed, it is a means by which we may keep our minds active, but stories may also have certain types of healing properties, and the act of sharing stories crucially distinguishes us from other sentient beings, helping us to work through our personal experiences. Yet, this doesn't seem to be the whole picture either; I would contend that stories have functions beyond these. That is, they can help us cultivate our moral character. Recall that earlier, I argued that country songs may move us to practice the virtues and thereby promote our flourishing as human beings, and it is the stories within country music that may move us in this way, that may foster our moral character. But even more narrowly, what I now want to suggest is that the stories told through country music enable us to do this precisely because they are told through simple art since simple art is both accessible and relatable.

Simplicity, Agency, and the Good Life

What does it mean for country music to be considered art that's "simple"? Philosopher John Dyck notes that country music is simple in that it is direct and straightforward. It is both lyrically and sonically simple. For example, many country songs are built upon a set of three basic chords. Think of Dolly Parton's "Jolene,"[14] Johnny Cash's "Ring of Fire,"[15] or John Denver's "Take Me Home, Country Roads."[16] Or consider the lyrical simplicity behind songs like "One Way Ticket (Because I Can)" by LeAnn Rimes.[17] This celebratory, hopeful anthem tells a story about a newly single woman on the brink of embracing her newfound freedom following heartbreak and her confidence in her capability to fall in love again. Besides buying a one-way ticket to make the most of her independence, Rimes sings, "I'm gonna go out dancing in the pouring rain / And talk to someone I don't know (because I can) / I won't let fear clip my wings and tell me how high I can fly."[18] She convinces herself and the listener that whatever fear and doubt she might have had following her heartbreak—perhaps feeling like she could not be in love again—will no longer hold her back. In short, country music is, as Dyck notes, accessible, uncomplicated, and easy to both play and consume.[19]

What, if anything, might be valuable about simple art? We may begin to address this question by contrasting simple art with subtle art. One argument, presented by philosopher Alex King, is that the latter type of art is valuable because it enables one to actively engage with the art in question and, in turn, to exercise agency.[20] The inverse of this, as Dyck notes, is that simple art does not seem to allow for active engagement; it does not demand that we give it attention or focus. As a result, simple art does not provide us with an opportunity to exercise agency. Yet, Dyck maintains that simple art affords us an opportunity to exercise our agency in a different way; namely, it allows us to exercise our agency of use. When we experience simple songs, such as many of those in country music, we can decide to use them in a greater variety of ways in our day-to-day lives. In other words, simple songs make broader applications possible, and we frequently tend to adopt such music for personal uses, playing it as we see fit. In this way, we exercise agency over the sorts of contexts and situations in which we use the music. The sort of variety in the ways we use these songs would not be possible were they not simple. To be sure, Dyck thinks that the more subtle the art, the greater the restrictions on its use and, in turn, on one kind of agency.[21]

However, simple music (such as country) allows listeners to exercise their agency in a different kind of way; it is one that has not yet been accounted for, though I will argue for it here. As we saw previously, country music's simplicity makes it both accessible and relatable to listeners. It is precisely this accessibility and relatability that move listeners to practice a given virtue. Listeners do not need to engage in a set of intellectual gymnastics to grasp the message or meaning of a country song. There is little to no ambiguity as to what a song might be saying and no need to engage in abstractions or to ponder in puzzlement.

Instead, what is often found in country songs is direct and straightforward. Put differently, country songs do not require specialized knowledge or complex language to grasp, and listeners can frequently identify with the experiences of the characters in the songs. As a result, listeners are more easily moved to practice the virtues. And, when listeners are moved to practice the virtues captured by a country song, they are, in turn, capable of exercising agency over their own well-being. They are in a position to promote their own flourishing. To further support this idea, consider again McBride's "Independence Day" and Lynn's "Coal Miner's Daughter." Consider also an additional example, "Humble and Kind" by Tim McGraw.

In McBride's "Independence Day," the simplicity of the story—the straightforward, very real, very possible aftermath of trying to leave a domestic violence situation—plays out in a manner accessible to the listener. This is important because it powerfully carries the message to those who may be in a similar situation to get out as soon as possible. One need not question what is happening in the story or what the meaning of the song might be. A listener who is in the same situation as the mother in "Independence Day" may very well see herself in this character, which makes the story particularly relatable. With this accessibility and relatability in mind, the hope is that one would be moved to courageously remove themselves from the abusive situation. In this way, one's flourishing or eudaimonia is promoted. An individual who is able to leave a relationship involving domestic violence ultimately has the opportunity to regain their autonomy, to restore their emotional and physical safety, and to therefore exercise agency over their own well-being. In situations of domestic violence, those subjected to such trauma do not need subtle art that is cognitively demanding; they need music that inspires them to do what must be done in order to escape. "Independence Day" does just this.

A similarly accessible story (with a protagonist with whom listeners can identify) is found in "Coal Miner's Daughter." Upon its release, plenty of listeners would have either worked in the coal mines themselves or had family who did. That said, the song has an appeal much broader than and stretches well beyond the coal mining community because of its message about hard work in the face of adversity. It's about finding ways to not simply make do in the face of struggles (such as poverty) but to be joyful in them as well.

Such a message stands the test of time and is relatable to listeners who find themselves facing similar challenges, and through the song, Lynn encourages said listeners to take pride in themselves. Rather than viewing themselves in a degrading light or in a way that victimizes themselves as a result of their circumstances, Lynn moves listeners to not only appreciate the non-material riches they may have (e.g., familial support and love) but also to cultivate a healthy level of self-worth with respect to the work ethic that develops out of the sorts of struggles Lynn's family and others have faced. As much as listeners could see themselves in the woman or even the daughter at the heart of McBride's "Independence Day," they could similarly identify with Lynn's narrative in "Coal Miner's Daughter." The message of being proud of your roots is presented in a direct and straight-forward manner that moves listeners to practice such pride and in turn, promotes their eudaimonia, thereby affording said listeners a unique kind of agency.

The final example worth considering here is Tim McGraw's "Humble and Kind." This piece exemplifies the virtue of humility, but since we've already considered the related virtue of pride, it would be worth focusing here on what the song says about the virtue of kindness. The sort of story-telling that occurs in the song differs from the previous two in that it may be described as more of a dialogue involving a speaker attempting to teach the listener about the types of things they should do in order to main-tain a certain kind of character (namely, one that is humble and kind). By contrast, "Coal Miner's Daughter" and "Independence Day" exemplify the virtues of courage and pride and do so by recounting an experience or event that unfolded which gives the listener an opportunity to reflect on the virtue in question. In "Humble and Kind," the listener instead becomes the character being directly spoken to by the singer. The singer provides advice about the sort of actions one should do to be kind: "Visit grandpa every chance that you can / Hold the door, say 'Please,' say 'Thank you' / Help the next one in line."[22]

The simplicity of this song, not unlike the previous two, embodies both accessibility and relatability. The listener can easily grasp the sorts of actions they should take in order to be a kind person. It also isn't difficult to imagine the singer at the center of this song taking on a personal role in relation to the listener since the very things we hear from the singer are likely to be the sorts of things we've heard from a loved one such as a par-ent, grandparent, or any meaningful figure who contributed to our char-acter development. In this way, then, the listener is moved to practice the virtue of kindness which in turn is constitutive of their own flourishing; listeners can exercise agency over their happiness. They can choose the good life.

All things considered, the simplicity of the stories in country music need not be considered a weakness or a deficiency of the genre. Instead, we have reason to celebrate country music's simplicity for its capacity to promote our individual flourishing as human beings. The very simplicity that involves accessibility and relatability is the kind of simplicity that, when used to present stories involving virtue, moves its listeners to practice those virtues themselves. As the virtues are constitutive of human flourishing, those who can be moved to be virtuous will in turn be on their way to eudaimonia. In this way, country music has the capacity to enable individuals to exercise a unique kind of agency over their own well-being.

NOTES

1. Peters, Gretchen. 1994. "Independence Day." *The Way That I Am*. McBride, Martina (rec. artist). Worley, Paul; Seay, Ed; McBride, Martina (prod.) RCA Nashville.

2. Country Music Hall of Fame and Museum. 2022. "Martina McBride's 'Independence Day' | The Story and People Behind a Song with a Lasting Impact." *YouTube*.

3. *Ibid.*

4. Aristotle. 2009. *Nicomachean Ethics*. Ross, David (trans.), Brown, Lesley (ed.) Oxford University Press.

5. *Ibid.*

6. Lynn, Loretta. 1970. "Coal Miner's Daughter." *Coal Miner's Daughter*. Lynn, Loretta (rec. artist). Bradley, Owen (prod.) Decca.

7. Aristotle.

8. Randall, Jon; Anderson, Bill. 2004. "Whiskey Lullaby." *Mud on the Tires*. Paisley, Brad (rec. artist). Rogers, Frank (prod.) Arista Nashville.

9. Nichols, Tim; Turner, Zack. 1996. "You're Not in Kansas Anymore." *Jo Dee Messina*. Messina, Jo Dee (rec. artist). Gallimore, Byron; McGraw, Tim (prod.) Curb.

10. Bruner, J. 1990. *Acts of Meaning*. Harvard University Press.

11. Wilson, Michael. 2022. *Storytelling (Arts for Health)*. Emerald Publishing Ltd.

12. *Ibid.*

13. *Ibid.*

14. Parton, Dolly. 1973. "Jolene." *Jolene*. Ferguson, Bob (prod.) RCA Victor.

15. Cash, Johnny. 1963. "Ring of Fire." *Ring of Fire: The Best of Johnny Cash*. Cash, Johnny (rec. artist). Law, Don (prod.) Columbia Nashville.

16. Denver, John. 1971. "Take Me Home, Country Roads." *Poems, Prayers & Promises*. Denver, John (rec. artist). Okun, Milt and Ruskin, Susan (prods.) RCA.

17. Rimes, Leann. 1996. "One Way Ticket (Because I Can)." *Blue*. Rimes, LeAnn (rec. artist). Howard, Chuck and Rimes, Wilbur C. (prods.) Curb.

18. *Ibid.*

19. Dyck, John. 2021. "The Aesthetics of Country Music." *Philosophy Compass*, 1–14.

20. King, Alex. 2017. "The Virtue of Subtlety and the Vice of a Heavy Hand." *British Journal of Aesthetics*, 119–137.

21. Dyck.

22. McKenna, Lori. 2016. "Humble and Kind." *Damn Country Music*. McGraw, Tim (rec. artist). Gallimore, Byron; McGraw, Tim (prod.) Big Machine.

Law and Virtue
in Outlaw Country

ERIC C. BROOK

One of the longstanding points of interest throughout the history of ethics, both East and West, has to do with the relationship between law and virtue. Within these discussions, broad and pressing philosophical questions about identity, authenticity, freedom, and justice have come to the fore. Answers to such questions in the form of ethical instruction and advice are often passed down through art and music. The musical artists most associated with Outlaw Country, those who came to be known as The Highwaymen (Johnny Cash, Waylon Jennings, Willie Nelson, and Kris Kristofferson), deal with such questions in compelling ways by putting the relationship of law and virtue on display for the general public, not only through their songs but also in their lives and actions.[1] The musical genre of Outlaw Country refers to two things: the cluster of musical artists who were identified as "outlaws" in their own context by the middle of the 1970s and the lyrical content of that genre, which deals directly with the figure of the outlaw. The historical and biographical data that informs the full picture of what is meant by Outlaw Country is extensive.[2] So, this essay is centered around what may be gleaned mostly from the lyrical content of Outlaw Country, though some historical details are included when they are relevant.

Our primary focus will be on the way in which Outlaw Country shows that an outlaw may be virtuous though lawless. As such, Outlaw Country makes a philosophical point that is upheld by the *aretaic* or virtue traditions of ethics in both Eastern[3] and Western philosophy. Outlaw Country is a cultural expression that arises within the Western context, so the philosophical point of reference will be the Western Classical tradition.[4] Within this framework, Outlaw Country helpfully demonstrates a problematic relationship between law and virtue. It is not a guarantee that a person's life will be virtuous simply by following the law.[5] Furthermore, it is entirely possible that a person, such as an outlaw, can transgress a law for virtuous reasons.

Not all, or even most, of the lyrics of Outlaw Country refer directly to outlaws or anything related, like cowboys. But, when they do, just like other outlaw genres, Outlaw Country represents both vicious and virtuous outlaws. Representatives of the Law, such as sheriffs and judges, may themselves be vicious outlaws. The ethical status or identity of either is never defined in relation to the Law, and whenever the artists of Outlaw Country describe the behavior of vicious outlaws, they do not endorse it, especially when those outlaws are agents of the Law.

Across the various outlaw genres, "the Law" to which the outlaw is opposed, usually refers to the overlapping institutional framework of legislative, judicial, and executive power structures. This kind of Law refers to positive law, as opposed to something more directly rooted in ethical theory, such as natural law.[6] However, in the Classical world that informs all subsequent ideas about law in the West, unwritten social codes and obligations are also referred to as "law," and they carry the force of positive law. The Greek word for law, *nomos*, often denotes what is customary, and is frequently translated simply as "custom" or "convention." The outlaw of Outlaw Country may refer to an agent who is opposed to either or both definitions of the law. As we will see with the singers and songwriters of Outlaw Country, they usually only embody this unconventional understanding of the outlaw. Nevertheless, when they live this kind of outlaw life, they draw inspiration and direction from cowboys who have historically been more directly lawless. Our attention in this essay will be given to the way Outlaw Country deals with virtuous outlaws.

Narrative Identity and Ethics

Narrative ethics, which emphasizes storytelling as the proper context for understanding ethical norms,[7] directly connects to the approach to virtue in Outlaw Country. The outlaw is a narrative figure whose character is accessed through story. Approaching ethical questions from the perspective of narrative allows for the opportunity to think about normative behavior outside of something more than abstract moral principles or guidelines. Legal principles follow this more abstract approach, thus placing the Law at a practical disadvantage for understanding, evaluating, and implementing ethics. Casuistry then becomes the main challenge for the execution of justice in the context of the Law. In narrative ethics, we move from the narrative context to the ethical content, seeking to maximize what is best for all agents or persons in that situation. Perhaps more than most genres, country music relies upon storytelling, and the trope of the outlaw in Outlaw Country provides a recurring narrative scope for ethical reflection, both on the part of the performer and the audience.

The narrative identity of the outlaw in contemporary parlance mostly refers to the 19th-century figure associated with things like ranching, horses, guns, saloons, and cowboys, usually in the American Old West. The immediate context of Outlaw Country refers to the musical collective of performers and songwriters who successfully forged their musical careers contrary to the dictates of the conventions of the established institutions in Nashville and, in the process, transformed the genre of country music itself. These musical artists were designated "outlaws" due to their embrace of counter-cultural norms that were sweeping across the world beginning in the 1960s, evident in their dress and attitude, and what we might call style. These same artists embraced and identified with the narrative context of the outlaw and utilized that metaphor for their own poetic and commercial interests, while at the same time internalizing and expressing the ethical ethos of the outlaw.

Following the framework of the narrative representation of outlaws across other genres, Outlaw Country maintains a narrative context for ethical content. For example, Outlaw Country songs often include the common trope about lawless characters who find themselves wanted for crimes due to decisions that were made in tragic situations. Such tragic circumstances are, by definition, fraught with ethical ambiguity, so when singers or songwriters represent agents as victims of circumstance, they are showing ethical sensitivity in a way that the Law cannot. Thus, there may be no legal ambiguity for certain actions, but the narrative context may ethically exonerate the outlaw in the eyes of other ethical agents, such as in gunfights due to cheating in gambling. Thus, narrative ethics provides the means and context for understanding the ultimate point that an agent may be virtuous though lawless.

Virtues of Authenticity

Though the designation of musical artists as "outlaws" was originally very much a promotional ploy on the part of the Nashville recording industry, the moniker is not entirely vacuous. The artists themselves identified with the outlaw narrative in terms of their own lives, but not unequivocally so. Though these country artists were not always the most virtuous of people in all respects, in their music they embraced the ideals of the virtuous outlaw, specifically regarding motivations (e.g., being "good-hearted"). As such, Outlaw Country reinforces the classical aretaic emphasis upon ethical genuineness and authenticity.[8] Indeed, a significant part of the appeal that Outlaw Country has had for audiences, even to this day, is precisely the perception of authenticity that it presents.

Though associated with the clothing of the outlaw, when Johnny Cash wore all black, no one took him to be doing so just as a promotional schtick. He was truly the "Man in Black"[9] who embodied this persona because he advocated for those who are unjustly oppressed and victimized in society, often through the force of law. As Willie Nelson sang after Cash's death, "He wrote his songs from deep within / And he hit the stage with a crooked grin / He and I were both Highwaymen."[10] Here, Nelson associates Cash's authenticity with his outlaw status as a highwayman. Merle Haggard follows this up in the same song, recounting the fact that Cash had never spent any real time in prison, but when he performed "Folsom Prison Blues," it was plainly obvious that he'd paid his debt to society. And Haggard contextualizes Cash's outlaw persona in terms of genuineness, reminding us that (even though he wore black), Cash had real affection for folks, and they returned that affection.[11]

With Cash and the other Highwaymen like Waylon Jennings and Willie Nelson, what audiences saw is what they got. Nelson sang, "You callin' us heathens with zero respect for the law / But we're only songwriters just writing our songs and that's all." Such words would seem to diminish their "outlaw" status, but Nelson reassures us that the Highwaymen only write what they've lived (and they live what they write).[12] Nelson actually wrote these lyrics in protest to his treatment by the Nashville establishment, those he calls "Mr. Music Executive" and "Mr. Purified Country."[13]

The intentional sense of authenticity on the part of the Highwaymen has to do with the way they looked up to the exemplars who came before them and shaped their own narrative identity. Before Outlaw Country ever appeared, country and western music had already long identified with the narrative identity of the cowboy. Not every, or even most, cowboys are outlaws, but nearly all outlaws out west were cowboys first. As a result, when looking at the representation of the outlaw in Outlaw Country, it is not always clear where the line may be drawn between the cowboy and the outlaw. At that border between cowboy and outlaw lies an overlapping nostalgic horizon in Outlaw Country.

Nelson's songs reflect this ambiguous space between cowboy and outlaw. In "So You Think You're a Cowboy," he wrote: "So you think you're a cowboy but you're only a kid / With a mind to do everything wrong."[14] Given the potential lawless context of the cowboy, alone out on the range, it is easy to fall into lawlessness, even unintentionally. Nelson shows the trajectory from cowboy in "Somewhere in Texas, Part 1" to outlaw in

"Somewhere in Texas, Part 2." In Part 1, Nelson sings of a young cowboy who dreams of living in an earlier time because "'he knew that he could have been / The best cowboy the world had ever known."[15] In Part 2, after a night of dancing to the music of Bob Wills, this same young cowboy, "going home in his pickup," is unaware that a man "on the same side of town" has robbed a store using a truck matching the description of the truck the young cowboy is driving. During the robbery, the store owner was shot and killed, but before he died, he mistakenly identified the innocent cowboy, and as a result, the Law "tried him and sent him away."[16] Once this young cowboy is on the other side of the Law through false conviction and imprisonment, he will forever be marked as an outlaw.

Across the various outlaw genres, including Outlaw Country, if an innocent cowboy has the misfortune of being mislabeled as an outlaw, it almost guarantees that he will actually become an outlaw. The sympathy that people have held throughout time for the outlaw often derives from the sense that these people have been falsely branded. As such, the life of the outlaw is the cowboy's tragedy. In the spoken word introduction to Cash's "Slow Rider,"[17] Cash personified the outlaw John Wesley Hardin, who speaks in his own voice, telling us that there are a lot of stories floating around about him; in fact, "they say I've killed forty men." And he recounts the narrative of how he killed a man when he was fifteen years old "to save my life but then I had to do it again / Then every bum in the country that was fast with the gun started lookin' for me." Cash later sang about Hardin on his album *Johnny Cash Sings the Ballads of the True West*, again employing a spoken-word narration for the song "Hardin Wouldn't Run."[18] For Hardin, the outlaw life was simply the inevitable result of false accusations and self-preservation.

Freedom and Justice

Historically, the virtue that stands out most when considering the rule of law is justice. The law is putatively set forth to uphold justice, but it is entirely possible to live maximally as a just person without the consultation of law. Laws may also be unjust, and justice demands the virtuous agent to transgress unjust laws. Hence, an outlaw may be virtuous contrary to law in two ways: whenever the law is practically irrelevant to the achievement of virtuous character and whenever an agent transgresses unjust laws.

Although Outlaw Country may also exemplify vicious disregard for the law, there are enough examples of virtuous transgression to show that Outlaw Country proves to be a significant positive resource for ethical reflection on the relationship between law and virtue. The main concern of justice for the Highwaymen has to do with freedom, specifically the injustice of being unjustly deprived of freedom through false conviction and imprisonment (often leading to death), the slavery of a chain gang, or the confinement of an Indian Reservation. In all these examples, the Law is vicious and operates as an agency of injustice. Furthermore, as we saw above, people may find themselves victims of unjust laws, which effectively transform them into outlaws. Obviously, these virtuous and victimized outlaws are opposed to these vicious laws, and the outlaws of Outlaw Country (at times, being themselves victims of these laws) stand up as virtuous agents of justice by bringing attention to the injustice of the Law.

Johnny Cash sang extensively against all three of the above forms of injustice, such as his famous concert at Folsom Prison in 1968. The concert album's 1999 re-release includes the song "Joe Bean," in which Cash tells the macabre story of Joe Bean who is on death row for killing a man in Arkansas (a state to which Bean has not been).[19] With exaggerated irony, Cash sings: "He killed twenty men by the time he was ten / He was an unruly kid / Yes, they're hanging Joe Bean for the one shooting"[20] (a shooting which Bean did not do). And Cash points out to the prisoners that they (along with himself) could all have been in Bean's position. This indicates that Bean was arrested because he was a "usual suspect," like Kristofferson's character in "Best of All Possible Worlds" who asks his arresting officer why he has never seen "a man locked in that jail of yours / Who wasn't just as lowdown poor as me?"[21] More poignant for the time in which this song was written and for the ethical point it makes, Kristofferson later said that his music publisher would not let him release the song as he originally wrote it: "black or poor as me."[22] Again, like Nelson's young cowboy somewhere in Texas, the Law may unjustly condemn and imprison (and even kill) the innocent.

In Cash's "Chain Gang,"[23] another young man (not unlike Nelson's innocent cowboy inclined toward freedom) is unjustly arrested when a "man walked up and said, 'Come with me / You're broke, and son, that's vagrancy.'" The young man is condemned to the forced labor of a chain gang and a resulting crushing sense of hopelessness. The chain gang represents something more than the false imprisonment of the innocent. It involves a dehumanizing existence, where prisoners "work like a dog on a chain gang,"[24] whether or not they're guilty of any crimes. Again, when Cash wore all black, he said, "I wear it for the prisoner who has long paid for his crime."[25] It is precisely this severity of punishment that he had in mind when Cash sang "I Got Stripes"[26] at Folsom Prison. Cash brought attention to the plight of the imprisoned there, at one point chuckling in the middle of the song "The Wall" and commenting, "Ain't it the truth? They're mean bastards, ain't they?"[27]

During his recorded concert at San Quentin State Prison the following year, Cash recounted the various other concerts he had done in prisons. In "Starkville City Jail,"[28] Cash sang about his own experience of being unjustly arrested and falsely imprisoned. He told the inmates at San Quentin that he was thrown in jail in Starkville, Mississippi, for picking flowers. Cash knew that this singular experience with the Law hardly qualified him to identify with his audience, recounting the story almost in jest. But in his good-hearted way, Cash told the prisoners that he'd been thinking of them, and "I tried to put myself in your place, and I believe this is how I would feel."[29] He then performed the song "San Quentin," and in this respect, Cash employed the empathetic resources of narrative to formulate an ethical stance of justice against the Law.

Cash did roughly the same thing in his advocacy of justice for Native Americans, though it did not require absolute empathy. For some time, Cash mistakenly believed he was descended from indigenous Americans, and it was during this time that he dedicated a whole album to his own people: *Bitter Tears: Ballads of the American Indian*. Cash is dressed like a stereotypical Indian on the cover of the album. In "As Long as the Grass Shall Grow,"[30] Cash sings a narrative of the unjust treatment of the "Senecas" who are identified as "an Indian tribe of the Iroquois nation." Their story is the standard history of the way Native Americans have been oppressed by the unjust laws of the United States. Cash sings of the lawful treaty, made in good faith by the Indians, that was violated by "Uncle Sam," who built a dam and flooded the sacred graves of Native American ancestors, and "on the Seneca reservation, there is much sadness now."

In Aristotelian language, whenever laws are self-serving and bereft of a sufficient account for virtue, particularly the virtue of justice, these laws have a false teleology, which compromises the ethical weight that should be accorded to such laws. Kristofferson made this same point in "The Law Is for Protection of the People," when he narrates about young men who are mistreated in various ways by law enforcement, "'cause the law is for protection of the people / Rules are rules and any fool can see." More transcendently, Kristofferson averred, "don't wonder who them lawmen was protectin'" when they nailed Jesus to the cross.[31] In short, unjust laws are no laws at all by any meaningful definition. Throughout history, legal systems often become complicit in structured systems of evil and vice, such as the Nuremberg Laws of Nazi Germany. For Outlaw Country, whenever laws infringe upon freedom, those laws are unjust.

As we have seen in the narrative accounts of outlaws, innocent cowboys, "the true sons of freedom,"[32] are often in the wrong place at the wrong time and find themselves at odds with laws that are not designed to facilitate their freedom, making such laws unjust. These cowboys could be anyone. For Nelson, "cowboys are average American people / Texicans, Mexicans, black men, and Jews."[33] These cowboys, now as outlaws, then assert their prerogative for freedom and justice against unjust laws. The artists of Outlaw Country follow these same outlaw sensibilities in their music when they speak out against institutional evils. For them, the hypocrisy of the Law was often at the forefront. Outlaw Country takes freedom as an optimal state that makes the successful acquisition of virtue possible.

This state of freedom is both the precondition and goal of a virtuous life, being respectively (in Aristotelian terms) the formal and final causes of virtue. In the words of Waylon Jennings, "I like living easy, I like being free / Living free and easy brings out the best in me."[34] The music of Outlaw Country shows how the Law may easily impede this virtuous goal by getting into people's business, with no real regard for the general well-being of people, despite claims of being for the protection of the people. The Law is either irrelevant at best, or an impediment at worst, to an agent's ethical character. The main impediments of the Law for a virtuous life are those instances in which laws infringe upon one's exercise of freedom.

Outlaw Country typically demonstrates a live-and-let-live approach to life that may interfere with strict adherence to fastidious norms of the Law. This kind of empathetic approach to justice, which Cash utilized for his prisoners, fits with the outlaw notion of freedom: "The eagle flies wild and free / I watch him rise on the breeze / I don't bother him, he don't bother me."[35] The animals live just and free lives with no regard for the rule of law. In this respect, justice is natural and does not require the conventions of the Law. Humans find freedom and justice in the same way. In "I've Got a Life of My Own," whatever concerns others might have for him, Kris Kristofferson insists that they don't try to make him part of a plan. He should either be accepted for who he is, or they should let him be. Freedom is something that not everyone understands, but "I got a life of my own / I said I ought to know where to sow my own seeds / And when I oughta leave it alone."[36] Virtuous humans are more likely to know what is best for themselves, even if what they want runs contrary to the Law.

Jennings articulated the overall approach of Outlaw Country to the rule of law in "Don't You Think This Outlaw Bit's Done Got Out of Hand." Despite their lawless image, the artists of Outlaw Country, for the most part, did not live like thugs or gangsters. They were not known for brawling and violence. In fact, Cash and Nelson were famous for their kindness and gentleness. But none of the Highwaymen had any regard when it came to drugs. They had respect for the law to an extent, but they recorded at least one song "about the night [law enforcement] spent protecting you from me / Someone called us outlaws in some old magazine / New York sent a posse down like I ain't never seen."[37] Jennings then recounts in the song an incident where federal agents tracked a shipment of drugs to the studio where he was recording. Before the cocaine got to Jennings, it was intercepted and flushed by someone in his entourage. Nevertheless, Jennings was booked for possession and surmises, somewhat tongue-in-cheek, that his outlaw image must have contributed to his arrest. Even though the purchase and consumption of cocaine was illegal, the charges were dropped against Jennings because of a bad warrant, which once again illustrates one of the main points of Outlaw Country: the Law itself may also be lawless.

Outlaws are virtuous in the same way that anyone else might be virtuous, such as when they live authentic lives that are well-intentioned toward justice and freedom. Unfortunately, the Law may not have these same virtuous goals, which creates a vicious and tragic situation for people who are simply trying to live their own lives without interfering with the lives of others. The artists of Outlaw Country faced similar circumstances as their outlaw narrative counterparts, and so they identified with them in their lives and music. They challenged the rules and conventions of established institutions and rightfully earned their designation as outlaws. In the process, Outlaw Country has provided a clear didactic means by which to work through the philosophical problem of what exactly the relationship is between law and virtue. In so doing, the Highwaymen of Outlaw Country show themselves to be virtuous outlaws, and they show the rest of us what that means.

Notes

1. Each of the members of The Highwaymen are recognized as representatives of Outlaw Country due to their ability to decide what they wanted to do with their musical expression, which means that even though the lyrics of Outlaw Country are not always, or usually, written by The Highwaymen themselves, they chose the songs they wanted to perform. They had power over their own self-expression, and the lyrical content of their music is essential to that representation. I will, therefore, treat their lyrics as reflecting their own sensibilities and choice, even when they did not directly pen the actual words sung. However, it should be made clear that all The Highwaymen are among the most celebrated lyricists and songwriters in the history of music.

2. To get more of that kind of information regarding Outlaw Country, see Streissguth, Michael. 2013. *Outlaw: Waylon, Willie, Kris, and the Renegades of Nashville.* It Books. Cash, Johnny. 2003. *Cash: The Autobiography.* HarperOne. Jennings, Waylon. 1998. *Waylon: An Autobiography.* Warner Books. Nelson, Willie, and Ritz, David. 2016. *It's a Long Story: My Life.* Back Bay Books. Miller, Stephen. *Kristofferson: The Wild American.* 2010. Omnibus Press. Deusner, Stephen M. 2018. "What Exactly Makes a Country Outlaw?" *The Pitch*; Hight, Jewly. 2018. "Country Music's Outlaw Legacy, Behind Glass." *The Record*; Stewart, Nathan McLaren. 2021. "What Is Outlaw Country? A Guide to Its History and Artists." *Holler.*

3. Cf. Sin, William. 2017. "*The Water Margin*, Moral Criticism, and Cultural Confrontation." *Dao: A Journal of Comparative Philosophy.* Vol. 16, 95–111. The novel *The Water Margin* (*Shuihu Zhuan* 水滸傳) is also often translated as *The Outlaws of the Marsh.*

4. See Hursthouse, Rosalind, and Pettigrove, Glen. 2023. "Virtue Ethics." *The Stanford Encyclopedia of Philosophy.* Zalta, Edward N., and Nodelman, Uri (eds.) MacIntyre, Alasdair. 2007. *After Virtue: A Study in Moral Theory.* University of Notre Dame Press.

5. Aristotle, *Nicomachean Ethics,* 1144a.

6. *Ibid.,* 1134b.

7. Newton, Adam Zachary. 1997. *Narrative Ethics.* Harvard University Press; Phelan, James. 2014. "Narrative Ethics." *Handbook of Narratology.* Hühn, Peter, Meister, Jan Christoph, Pier, John, and Schmid, Wolf (eds.); De Gruyter. Ricoeur, Paul. 1991. "Narrative Identity." *Philosophy Today.* Vol. 35:1, 73–81.

8. Nehamas, Alexander. 1999. *Virtues of Authenticity: Essays on Plato and Socrates.* Princeton University Press.

9. Cash, Johnny. 1971. "Man in Black," *Man in Black.* Cash, Johnny (prod.) Columbia Records.

10. Haggard, Merle. 2015. "Missing Ol' Johnny Cash." *Django and Jimmie.* Nelson, Willie, and Haggard, Merle (rec. artist). Cannon, Buddy (prod.) Legacy Recordings.

11. *Ibid.*

12. Nelson, Willie. 1984. "Write Your Own Songs." *Music from Songwriter.* Jones, Booker T. (prod.) Columbia Records.

13. *Ibid.*

14. Nelson, Willie. 1979. "So You Think You're a Cowboy." *The Electric Horseman: Music from the Original Motion Picture Soundtrack.* Grusin, Dave, Rosen, Larry, Nelson, Willie, and Pollack, Sydney (prod.) Columbia Records.

15. Nelson, Willie. 1983. "Somewhere in Texas (Part I)." *Tougher Than Leather.* Nelson, Willie, and Spears, Bee (prod.) Columbia Records.

16. *Ibid.*

17. Cash, Johnny. 1960. "Slow Rider." *Ride This Train.* Law, Don, and Quaglieri, Al (prod.) Columbia Records.

18. Cash, Johnny. 1965. "Hardin Wouldn't Run." *Johnny Cash Sings the Ballads of the True West.* Law, Don, and Jones, Frank (prod.) Columbia Records.

19. Freeman, Bud, and Pober, Leon. 1999 (1968). "Joe Bean." *Johnny Cash at Folsom Prison.* Cash, Johnny (rec. artist). Johnston, Bob (prod.) Columbia Records.

20. *Ibid.*

21. Kristofferson, Kris. 1970. "Best of All Possible Worlds." *Kristofferson.* Foster, Fred (prod.) Monument Recording.

22. Streissguth, Michael. 2013. *Outlaw: Waylon, Willie, Kris, and the Renegades of Nashville.* It Books, 48.

23. Howard, Harlan. 1963. "Chain Gang." *Blood, Sweat and Tears.* Cash, Johnny (rec. artist). Law, Don, and Jones, Frank (prod.) Columbia Records.

24. *Ibid.*

25. Cash, Johnny. 1971. "Man in Black." *Man in Black.* Cash, Johnny (prod.) Columbia Records.

26. Cash, Johnny, and William, Charlie. "I Got Stripes." 1999 (1968). *Johnny Cash at Folsom Prison.* Cash, Johnny (rec. artist). Johnston, Bob (prod.) Columbia Records.

27. Howard Harlan. "The Wall." *Ibid.*

28. Cash, Johnny. "Starkville City Jail." 1969. *Johnny Cash at San Quentin.* Johnston, Bob (prod.) Columbia Records.

29. Cash, Johnny. "San Quentin." *At San Quentin.* Johnston, Bob (prod.) Columbia Records.

30. La Farge, Peter. 1964. "As Long As the Grass Shall Grow." *Bitter Tears: Ballads of the American Indian.* Cash, Johnny (rec. artist). (prod. Law, Don and Jones, Frank) Columbia Records.

31. Kristofferson, Kris. 1970. "The Law Is for Protection of the People." *Kristofferson.* Foster, Fred (prod.) Monument Recording.

32. Shaver, Billy Joe. 2020." We Are the Cowboys." *First Rose of Spring.* Nelson, Willie (rec. artist). Cannon, Buddy (prod.) Legacy.

33. *Ibid.*

34. Jennings, Waylon. 1982. "Shine." *Black on Black*. Moman, Chips (prod.) RCA Victor.

35. White, Tony Joe, and Rector, Ricky Ray. "Up in Arkansas." 1994. *Waymore's Blues (Part II)*. Jennings, Waylon (rec. artist). Was, Don (prod.) RCA Nashville.

36. Kristofferson, Kris. 1976. "I've Got a Life of My Own." *Surreal Thing*. Anderle, David (prod.) Monument.

37. Jennings, Waylon. 1978. "Don't You Think This Outlaw Bit's Done Got Out of Hand." *I've Always Been Crazy*. Jennings, Waylon, and Albright, Richie (prod.) RCA Victor.

IV

Country Music Politics

The "Country" in Country

WALTER BARTA

Country music has a special tie to its country of origin. More specifically, American country music has a special tie to the American national identity. As such, country artists express and embody an interesting philosophical stance toward patriotism: the affection one has for one's country.[1] As country singer Lee Greenwood puts it in "God Bless the USA," the patriotic American country song par excellence, when we listen to some good American country music, we can't help but feel "proud to be an American."[2] Looking philosophically at some of the most famous country songs, we can see that country music has a lot to say about what patriotism is, how patriotism is possible, and how patriotism should be practiced.

Patriotic Sacrifice

Where exactly does patriotism find its origin? The word "patriot" derives from the Latin "*patria*," which roughly translates to "country" (or, more specifically, "fatherland"), and thinking about the nature of patriotism can be found as far back as the philosophers of ancient Greece and Rome. In the Greek context, in Plato's dialogue *Crito*, the philosopher Socrates, imprisoned for crimes against Athens, is offered the chance to escape from prison and flee abroad.[3] But, perhaps counterintuitively, Socrates stays behind to stand before the Athenian court and meet his fate. Socrates' reasoning is an appeal to a kind of patriotism: he argues that he is indebted to the city of his birth.[4] In the Roman context, after conspirators assassinated Julius Caesar, in the chaos that followed in which the Roman Republic was dissolved and the Roman Empire established, one of the senators of Rome (sympathetic to the conspiracy) was the philosopher Marcus Tullius Cicero. During the turmoil, Cicero wrote his magnum opus, *On Duties*, a philosophical work in which he enumerated the various moral duties that a person has, including the duty to one's country.[5] Not long after finishing this work, Cicero would be put to death by Caesar's loyalist Mark Antony for opposing imperial ambitions and remaining true to the Republic.

As Socrates and Cicero embody it, patriotism may actually be the ultimate duty, even requiring the sacrifice of the patriot's own life. In country music, self-sacrifice for one's country can be observed as one of the most commonly recurring motifs, as country songs frequently pay homage to "the men who died."[6] Although Socrates and Cicero were executed for their philosophical principles (though both philosophers served as soldiers as well), the patriot in question usually dies as a soldier, as depicted in The Chicks "Travelin' Soldier"[7] or Toby Keith's "American Soldier."[8] In "Ragged Old Flag" by Johnny Cash, patriotism is expressed through the extended metaphor of the "ragged old flag," which represents the ravages of war through which the country has nonetheless persevered.[9]

But the deaths of soldiers are often depicted as a "cost" that is paired with a benefit. The responsibility for risking one's life is paired with the liberty and equality made possible by the continued protection of the country. In as much, patriotism is one half of a social contract, in which the country and the compatriots form a reciprocal relationship, willing to sacrifice themselves for the benefits that the country has provided and will continue to provide. Country music often makes this social contract explicit. In "America" by Waylon Jennings, the reciprocal relationship between country and compatriot is referred to as "promise and follow through."[10] In "Where Were You (When the World Stopped Turning)" by Alan Jackson, this responsibility is referenced like a form of survivor's guilt, an indebtedness to the previous generations that made the country possible.[11] In "Some Gave All" by Billy Ray Cyrus, the relationship is framed as a mutual gift exchange in which "all gave some, but some gave all," such that a country is only preserved because of and constituted by that relationship.[12] Trace Adkins' "Arlington" makes the connection between the patriot, death, and country even more explicit, alluding to Arlington, the site of the National Military Cemetery, a specific location that is made meaningful by the soldiers who sacrificed to serve their country.[13] In such songs, the relationship between the dead and the living is one of mutual gratitude; the living are thankful for the sacrifice of the dead, and the dead are thankful that their sacrifice meant something. As Adkins puts it, they are "thankful for those thankful for the things we've done."[14]

However, although patriotism is a persistent feature of human society, and is partially defended by philosophers like Socrates and Cicero, patriotism often exists in tension with other philosophical ideals. Although the country artist says, "There ain't no doubt I love this land,"[15] the philosopher says, "doubt everything." "Everything" includes local, provincial loyalties, like those born out of the perceived importance of our place of birth and that therefore give rise to our patriotism. So, philosophy forces us to further interrogate our relationship with country music and its relationship with its country of origin.

The Heart of Patriotism

The first substantive question the philosopher might ask the country artist might be, can we even be patriots at all? This philosophical question arises from a counterintuitive observation: there is a sense in which, it could be argued, that countries are not even *real*. Of course, there is also another sense in which countries are very much real! Amerigo Vespucci did land on a real beach. John Hancock scribbled on some real paper. Abraham Lincoln lived in a real log cabin. These men really lived. Presumably, philosophers aren't doubting these material facts (with perhaps the exception of a handful of absolute skeptics).

But in a different sense, countries are *imaginary*. When looking at a map and tracing the borders of a country, one might realize that the borders could theoretically be drawn in any combination of ways (what we sometimes derisively call "gerrymandering"). The only reason borders are the way they are is due to a sequence of historical contingencies that could have gone quite differently. Indeed, when they go into space and look down at Earth, astronauts are often awed by the observation that there typically are no visible national borders, an observation celebrated as the "overview effect."[16] In her song "From a Distance," country singer Nanci Griffith sings about this effect as well: that national identities tend to disappear when considered from a god's-eye view.[17]

However, there is another sense in which countries are even more real than the topography on which they are overlaid. In our daily lives, we may not have to face the realities of traversing rivers, forests, and purple mountains majesty, but we do have to deal with the realities of property lines, zoning laws, and border crossing stations. Countries are real to us because we have socially constructed them and subsequently must deal with and operate within those social constructions. In other words, countries are as real as we make them.

These social constructions of national identity are what historian and political theorist Benedict Anderson calls "Imagined Communities."[18] We have never met and never will meet every person in our country, and yet, we may still feel that there is some sense in which we share an identity with them. You may live in California, and I may live in Texas, but a shared imagined community brings us together. Thus, we are capable of forming bonds with people we have never met, creating what country singer Jake Owen calls a "small town world," everyone in that "world" being on intimate terms because of a shared imagined identity.[19] In other words, a *nation* is a product of collective *imagination*.

For example, we can see the formation of national boundaries made apparent in a different Nanci Griffith song from the same album. Unlike "From a Distance," which dissolves national boundaries, "Lone Star State of Mind" sets up national identities: "But here I sit alone in Denver / Sippin' California wine / I'm in a lone star state of mind."[20] The song brings together various American locations, central with "Denver," west with "California," and south with "lone star state." This is a motif among many country songs. For example, in "American Kids," Kenny Chesney recounts a slice of life of people from "New York to L.A."[21] And in Greenwood's classic, he lists several American locations, including Minnesota, Tennessee, Texas, Detroit, Houston, New York, and Los Angeles.[22] Like maps, these songs are plotting out the boundaries of the nation and, in as much, constructing the national identity.

But a nation is not just its borders, it is also the community of people occupying those borders, and many other songs make a point to create this kind of communal identity. In her song "American Heart," Faith Hill, borrowing her title from Greenwood, says of Americans, "We're all the same."[23] And in her song, "All American," Mickey Guyton imagines a community in which personal differences are dissolved into a collective "we": "here we are, all American."[24] In both songs, the use of the rhetorical "we" demarcates the national identity of "American" and imbues listeners with a communitarian ethos. In "Everyday America," by Sugarland, the "we" is replaced by "everybody" who is "dreaming big" and "just getting by."[25] And these activities are relatable enough to most of us to inspire a common bond. Thus, even if we have never actually bought lemonade from a child on a corner (like Rodney Atkins apparently has, according to his song "It's America"), we can imagine those hypothetical children somewhere as part of our extended community; and this might actually cause us to take action in that extended community: "people came from miles around just to help the neighbors out."[26]

But how do imagined communities form? We do not form a nation by systematically meeting every other member of the nation. Rather, these communities form through shared cultural transmissions. Benedict Anderson thinks that the invention of the printing press was the inciting event in the founding of many national identities.[27] The ability to mass produce print was instrumental in the concretization of a national language and a national literature, which made it possible for millions of people who had never met to have a common cultural experience. But cultural transmission also includes music, especially self-consciously patriotic country music. In modern times, it is not just the printing press but radio, television, and digital media that have come to dominate human attention. Since the spread of these media, country music has occupied its niche as the poster child for the spreading of national identity in the form of music.

The psycho-socio process works something like this. The song evokes a certain set of intense feelings and references a specific national identity. Then, the listener's mind associates these feelings with the nation. Thus, the love of the country is inspired by country music. Patriotism is born in this connection. This process is made explicit through national anthems, which operate as theme songs for countries, with the direct intent of inspiring loyalty. Songs like "God Save the King" in the United Kingdom and "The Star-Spangled Banner" in the United States are prime examples of this tradition. The process operates implicitly in other songs. American country songs often self-consciously attempt to define what an "American" is by using descriptions and anecdotes that seem quintessential to the national identity, defining America, what the nation "is" in the collective imagination. We can look to songs like "It's America" by Rodney Atkins,[28] "American Country Love Song" by Jake Owen,[29] "American Spirit" by Thomas Rhett,[30] or "Chicken Fried" by Zac Brown Band.[31] All of these country songs use this common structure: the list. They define the American Experience by listing: it's this, it's that, it's this, it's that.... The American experience is (at least according to Zac Brown) a Friday night that includes cold beer and fried chicken and "a pair of jeans that fit just right / And the radio up."[32] Fill in the blanks with your own quintessential American experience.

These songs also often self-consciously acknowledge the role of music in identity formation. Atkins includes music ("It's a Springsteen song") in the definition of America.[33] Jake Owen mentions the "Radio DJ."[34] And Zac Brown Band encourages listeners to turn "the radio up," which acknowledges that the hypothetical listener may be listening on a radio to their song.[35] Thomas Rhett asks, "if you hear it, that American spirit" and "listen to the lyrics," which is an acknowledgment that the American Spirit, what it means to be American, is spread by the transmitted message itself, what the singer is singing about and the audience is hearing, constituting the national identity.[36] Even Taylor Swift's debut single "Tim McGraw" is an acknowledgment of how previous country music, like that by Tim McGraw, has affected and continues to affect her identity formation, such that listeners' experiences are defined in terms of a song and anytime they "think Tim McGraw."[37] Every song is sung someplace, and the place influences the song, but the song also influences the place. This is how culture self-replicates through references and media awareness and creates the identities of its listeners.

In Defense of Patriotism

In addition to questioning the metaphysical status or identity of any particular nation, an additional patriotism-related issue the philosopher might ask the country artist might be, should we even be patriots at all? The contemporary moral philosopher Alasdair MacIntyre has given a particularly clear and cogent defense of patriotism as a virtue.[38] To MacIntyre, all moral ideals are inextricably tied to the social identities of the people who adopt them. Thus, national identity being one such identity, national patriotism must be part of one's personal identity and one's moral ideals. As MacIntyre himself puts it, "the questions of *where* and *from whom* I learn my morality turn out to be crucial for both the content and the nature of moral commitment."[39] Or reworded by Dolly Parton in "Color Me America," "I am red, white and blue" and "I want justice for us all."[40]

However, patriotism is not without its critics. Writer and critic Samuel Johnson worried about the abuse of patriotic appeal as a political tool, and famously called patriotism "the last refuge of scoundrels."[41] Other critics point out that the problem is that patriotism is either grounded in a belief that a country is the *best country* or in an identification with *our country*, but both of these positions turn out to be somewhat difficult to defend.

We may be patriots because we believe that our country is the *best country*. Many country songs express this attitude of exceptionalism. In American country music, American exceptionalism is often celebrated as a justification for American patriotism. For example, in "Where the Stars and Stripes and the Eagle Fly," Aaron Tippin calls America an "extraordinary place."[42] And, while he acknowledges that there are other places, he emphasizes that America is the best, "it ain't the only place on earth, but the only place that I prefer."[43] As Rodney Atkins puts it elsewhere, there is "no place else I'd rather build my life" than the USA.[44] Similarly, in "Only in America" by Brooks & Dunn, aside from the obvious exceptionalism reflected in the word "only" in the title, America is referred to in the superlative as "the promised land," invoking religious prophecy, which is so great because it is a place "where we dream as big as we want to."[45] In "American Flag on the Moon" by Brad Paisley, American exceptionalism is glamorized again, with the example of the American space program: the USA was the first country to land humans on the moon, which actually is exceptional.[46] But exceptionalism has problems, as many philosophers have argued, even as early as the 4th century by Augustine of Hippo.

Augustine was bearing witness to the fall of Rome to the Goths, and as a Christian, he was wont to defend Rome as the home of the Catholic Church. But at the same time, Augustine believed that any given terrestrial community, what he called an Earthly City, is not the same as the ideal Christian community, what he called the Heavenly City (or *City of God*).[47] The former city most loves *itself*; the latter city most loves *the greatest good*. Thus, at least for Augustine, there is tension between patriotism and higher values. Furthermore, as other philosophers have pointed out, only one country can actually be the "best country," so almost all patriots must be mistaken about their country's exceptionalism, and so patriotism is perhaps not the most informed loyalty.[48]

That said, perhaps the stalwart patriot could still bite the bullet: yes, there is only one best country, and it just so happens to be us! The patriot might even support this claim by citing some features of their country that truly are exceptional. So, an American country singer might, with some reasonable basis, provide exceptional features of America. Personal biases aside, America certainly has a few things in its favor. Since Thomas Jefferson wrote the *Declaration of Independence*, America has held claim to being the first country that was deliberately founded (not organically grown) and established according to a set of philosophical principles, making America fairly exceptional compared to most countries.

However, this can be followed up by the critique that, even if we happen to be born in the best country, it is not obvious why we should be loyal to the country itself and not the ideals that the country exemplifies. So, even if America is the best because of its moral principles, should we celebrate "America" itself, or should we celebrate the moral principles? This dilemma is evidenced in country music, since singers are always singing about liberty and equality, not necessarily the importance of patriotism itself. For example, in "American Saturday Night," Brad Paisley points out that "everywhere has something they're known for, but it usually washes up on our shores," which is to say that America is the best because it combines the best things about other countries (from "Italy" to "China").[49] However, we might rightfully ask Paisley, is it *America's* diversity we are celebrating or diversity *generally*? The former is patriotism; the latter is perhaps just liberalism, which would be tantamount to switching loyalties if our country ever gave up its moral principles.

Alternatively, we may be patriotic because our country is *our country*. Many country songs express this attitude of tribalism. One's personal identity as a citizen of one's country is often the most important part of patriotism. For example, in "I'm American" by Billy Ray Cyrus, there is a strong emphasis on the personal pronoun "I" and identifying oneself as American, not due to any claims to exceptionalism, but due to the personal fact of one's birth and upbringing.[50] As Cyrus says, "this country made me who I am," and thus, for better or worse, one's identity is tied to one's country.[51] As Thomas Rhett similarly puts it, "that's just how it is around here, and we love it."[52] In "Home" by Dierks Bentley, the emphasis is likewise on the fact that a country, like America, is someone's home, with all the emotional baggage loaded in that term.[53] For Bentley, it is not because of exceptionalism but in spite of non-exceptionalism that we feel patriotism: "this is still the place that we all call home."[54]

But, like exceptionalism, tribalism has problems. If everyone is loyal only to one's own country, then there must be as many loyalties as countries, everyone with their own conflicting loyalties. (Not to mention, if our loyalty is based on the happenstance of our birthplace, then if we had been born somewhere else, our loyalty would have been completely different.) The tribalism implied means that patriotism is not impartial or universalizable, which seems distinctively contrary to moral principles, given that almost all systems of morality stress the importance of impartial and universalizable codes of conduct. Worse still, this tribalism tends (perhaps inevitably) toward war because everyone has a duty to defend their country against everyone else.

This is what the author Leo Tolstoy, famous for his novel *War and Peace*, points out in his essay "Patriotism, or Peace?" in which he frames the issue as a dilemma because he does not think that patriotism *and* peace are compatible.[55] To Tolstoy, patriotism is a paradox: I go to war for my country, you go to war for your country, both of us are virtuous, but we are opposed to one another. The conflict is so tragic because both sides are ultimately acting from the same patriotic impulses to *our country*, but it is nonetheless irreconcilable because neither side shares an *our country* in common. Some of the more militaristic motifs in country music seem to manifest Tolstoy's concern. For example, after the tragedy of 9/11, a proliferation of American country songs advocated for retaliatory war, like "Courtesy of the Red, White and Blue" by Toby Keith, which seems to valorize the war in Afghanistan as a self-righteously avenging military campaign.[56] This is a far sight from Nanci Griffith's hope for world "harmony."[57] Unfortunately, even with their hearts in the right place, what patriots like Keith may fail to consider is that the call-to-arms that their music encourages for their compatriots may be the same kind of call-to-arms that also inspires their enemies.

Being more charitable to self-defensive impulses, though, we might suggest that there is a version of patriotism that is more morally justifiable. Political thinker George Orwell, famous for his novel *Nineteen Eighty-Four*, advocated for a version of patriotism that is purely defensive, distinct from and opposed to offensive versions of it, like nationalism or imperialism.[58] We can see defensive patriotism born out in country music as well. Mostly, patriotic country music celebrates the self-sacrifice of defending one's country, not in service of jingoism and expansionism. For example, this is made clear in Chely Wright's song "The Bumper of My S.U.V."[59] Like Orwell, Wright disambiguates defense from offense, stipulating that, just because I have a bumper sticker honoring the troops, "doesn't mean I want war."[60] There is an important moral difference between tribalistic warmongering and patriotic self-defense.

All these criticisms considered, we can still accept the most intuitive part of MacIntyre's defense of patriotism: even though ideas are abstract, they are always instantiated in time and place and embodied in people, so ideology and country are not fully distinct; we must appreciate our origins with our beliefs. If so, we might not even be able to clearly distinguish *our country* from the *best country* anyway, since the identity of the nation and the ideals of the citizens are intertwined. For Americans, the flag is a symbol of freedom, and our national identity as Americans is constitutive of our moral identity as lovers of freedom. So, in order to defend our moral ideals, we have to defend the specific country and people upholding those ideals. Perhaps, then, patriotism cannot be strictly separated from morality, for better or worse. So, while we can strongly discourage tribalism and exceptionalism, we can hardly help feeling a little bit patriotic while listening to our favorite country songs.

Notes

1. Primoratz, Igor. 2020. "Patriotism." *The Stanford Encyclopedia of Philosophy* (Winter Edition), Zalta, Edward N. (ed.)

2. Greenwood, Lee. 1983. "God Bless the USA." *You've Got a Good Love Comin'*. Crutchfield, Jerry (prod.) MCA Nashville.

3. Plato. 1954. *The Last Days of Socrates, translation of Euthyphro, Apology, Crito, Phaedo*. Hugh Tredennick.

4. *Ibid.*, 51c–51d

5. Atkins, E.M.; Griffin, M.T. 1991. *Cicero: On Duties. (Cambridge Texts in the History of Political Thought)*. Cambridge University Press, 57–58.

6. Greenwood.

7. The Chicks. 2002. "Travelin' Soldier." Home. Maines, Lloyd (prod.) Columbia Nashville.

8. Keith, Toby. 2003. "American Soldier." *Shock'n Y'all*. Stroud, James (prod.) DreamWorks Records.

9. Cash, Johnny. 1974. "Ragged Old Flag." *Ragged Old Flag*. Bragg, Charlie (prod.) Columbia.

10. Jennings, Waylon. 1984. "America." *Waylon's Greatest Hits, Vol. 2*. Bridges, Jerry; Scruggs, Gary (prods.) RCA Nashville.

11. Jackson, Alan. 2001. "Where Were You (When the World Stopped Turning)." *Drive*. Stegall, Keith (prod.) Arista Nashville.

12. Cyrus, Billy Ray. 1992. "Some Gave All." *Some Gave All*. Scaife, Joe; Cotton, Jim (prods.) Mercury.

13. Adkins, Trace. 2005. "Arlington." *Songs about Me*. Hendricks, Scott (prod.) Capitol Nashville.

14. *Ibid.*

15. Greenwood.

16. *White, Frank. 1987. The Overview Effect: Space Exploration and Human Evolution.* Houghton Mifflin Harcourt.

17. Griffith, Nanci. 1987. "From a Distance." *Lone Star State of Mind*. Gold, Julie (Writer); Brown, Tony (prod.) MCA.

18. *Anderson, Benedict. 1983. Imagined Communities: Reflections on the origins and spread of nationalism. Verso Books.*

19. Owen, Jake. 2016. "American Country Love Song." *American Love*. Copperman, Ross; McAnally, Shane (prods.) RCA Nashville.

20. Griffith, Nanci. 1987. "Lone Star State of Mind." *Lone Star State of Mind*. Gold, Julie (Writer), Brown, Tony (prod.) MCA.

21. Chesney, Kenny. 2014. "American Kids." *The Big Revival*. Cannon, Buddy (prod.) Blue Chair.

22. Greenwood.

23. Hill, Faith. 2012. "American Heart." Gallimore, Byron (prod.) Warner Bros. Nashville.

24. Guyton, Mickey. 2021. "All American." *Remember Her Name*. Chapman, Nathan (prod.) Capitol Nashville.

25. Sugarland. 2007. "Everyday America." *Enjoy the Ride*. Gallimore, Byron; Bush, Kristina; Nettles, Jennifer (prods.) Mercury Nashville.

26. Atkins, Rodney. 2008. "It's America." *It's America*. Hewitt, Ted (prod.) Curb.

27. Anderson, 44–46.

28. Atkins.

29. Owen.

30. Rhett, Thomas. 2015. "American Spirit." *Tangled Up (Deluxe)*. Frasure, Jess (prod.) Valory.

31. Zac Brown Band. 2008. "Chicken Fried." *The Foundation*. Stegall, Keith (prod.) Live Nation.

32. *Ibid.*

33. Atkins.

34. Owen.

35. Zac Brown Band.

36. Swift, Taylor. 2006. "Tim McGraw." *Taylor Swift*. Chapman, Nathan (prod.) Big Machine.

37. *Ibid.*

38. MacIntyre, Alasdair. 1984. *Is Patriotism a Virtue?* (The Lindley Lecture). University of Kansas.

39. MacIntyre. Sect. III.

40. Parton, Dolly. 2003. "Color Me America." *For God and Country*. Wells, Kent; Smith, Tony (prods.) Welk Music Group.

41. Boswell, James. 1986. *The Life of Samuel Johnson*. Hibbert, Christopher (ed.) Penguin Classics, 182.

42. Tippin, Aaron. 2001. "Where the Stars & Stripes & The Eagle Fly." *Stars & Stripes*. Bradley, Mike; Watson, Biff (prods.) Lyric Street.

43. *Ibid.*

44. Atkins.

45. Brooks & Dunn. 2001. "Only in America." *Steers & Stripes*. Wright, Mark (prod.) Arista Nashville.

46. Paisley, Brad. 2014. "American Flag on the Moon." *Moonshine in the Trunk*. Wooten, Luke (prod.) Arista Nashville.

47. Augustine of Hippo, 2004. *City of God*. Penguin Classics.

48. Keller, Simon. 2007. *The Limits of Loyalty.* Cambridge University Press.

49. Paisley, Brad. 2009. "American Saturday Night." *American Saturday Night.* Rogers, Frank (prod.) Arista Nashville.

50. Cyrus, Billy Ray. 2011. "I'm American." *I'm American.* Buddy Cannon (prod.) Buena Vista.

51. *Ibid.*

52. Rhett.

53. Bentley, Dierks. 2011. "Home." *Home.* Beavers, Brett; Wooten, Luke (prod.) Capitol Nashville.

54. *Ibid.*

55. Tolstoy, Leo. 1987. "On Patriotism" and "Patriotism, or Peace?" *Writings on Civil Disobedience and Nonviolence.* New Society, 51–123, 137–47.

56. Keith, Toby. 2002. "Courtesy of the Red, White and Blue." *Unleashed.* Stroud, James (prod.) DreamWorks Nashville.

57. Griffith, "From a Distance."

58. *Orwell, George. 1994. "Notes on Nationalism." Essays. Penguin.*

59. Wright, Chely. 2004. "The Bumper of My S.U.V." *The Metropolitan Hotel.* Dualtone.

60. *Ibid.*

Bards and (Prison) Bars

JAKOB R. GIBSON *and* TOBIAS T. GIBSON

Conceptions of country music in the present day take many forms, and many stereotypes surrounding the genre emphasize a number of popular themes such as trucks, beer and whiskey, and women which can be found throughout many of its highest charting songs. One theme that is regrettably overlooked but is equally, if not more influential on the development of the genre, is that of prison and social inequality. Foundational artists such as Merle Haggard, Johnny Cash, and Tom T. Hall, among others, have all penned music detailing run-ins with the law, interactions with the criminal system, and prison life and death. There are many themes evident throughout these songs: social inequities that lead to prison sentencing, enduring punishment, an unjust legal system, and the ripple effect of the punishment doled out to prisoners.

The links between mainstream country music and the criminal justice system emerged fully in the 1960s and '70s when artists such as Cash and Haggard actively contributed to the cultural maelstrom that swept through the United States and manifested into anti–Vietnam protesting, rising drug use, and a historic spike in crime throughout the nation.[1] Cash, in particular, wrote about the prison experience in a manner that ran counter to the conservative rhetoric espoused by leading politicians of the late '60s such as Richard Nixon, George Wallace, and Ronald Reagan, all of whom spoke on some level about the need for "law and order" as a means of curtailing the rash of crime and peaceful protesting of the period. Cash's lyrics implored listeners to sympathize with the men behind bars; they also painted a vivid picture of the harsh realities of what it's like to live in prison. The live recordings of his albums "At Folsom Prison" and "At San Quentin" add an extra layer to his message as the reactions from those inmates—with which the listener is meant to identify—can be heard alongside the music itself.[2]

The crime spike of the 1960s and '70s was one of the dominant storylines in American criminal justice during the 20th century, with another being the resulting emphasis on criminal punishment and alterations to the prison system in the following decades. This second point is emphasized by the astronomical rise in America's incarceration rate since the early '70s; at the beginning of the decade a mere 98 out of every 100,000 Americans were imprisoned whereas by 1980, that figure had jumped to 140 per 100,000.[3] Both numbers pale in comparison to the most recent figure, published in November 2023, which indicates that 355 out of every 100,000 Americans are imprisoned.[4]

Sociologist Loïc Wacquant coined the term "hyperincarceration" to describe this phenomenon and argues that the present-day American model of criminal justice targets citizens "first by class, second by race, and third by place."[5] Each of these factors can be explained by the swift turn toward a more punitive model of criminal justice that was first endorsed by the federal government during the Lyndon B. Johnson administration, which created new programs focused on law and order that set the stage for a cultural shift toward harsher, more determinate sentencing as well as bipartisan agreement on prison expansion.[6] Much of the rhetoric surrounding this shift has advanced a retributivist approach to justice, emphasizing the need to punish the crimes of the past while failing to address the root causes of crime and work toward a future where it may be lessened. This has fostered a system where solutions are a secondary concern and recidivism is critically high, with one analysis conducted by the U.S. Department of Justice across 24 states indicating that within one year of release, 43 percent of formerly incarcerated people were rearrested, and within 10 years of their release, 82 percent of individuals released from those state prisons were rearrested at least once.[7]

Foundational Philosophies of Criminal Law and Justice

Well before the advent of criminal law and justice, as we understand them today, the German philosopher Immanuel Kant laid out his political philosophy. Kant was a staunch proponent of a retributivist model of criminal punishment, arguing that the only justification for punishment was the guilt of the criminal at hand, with alternatives such as rehabilitation being insufficient.[8] Kant also possessed such an approval of the ultimate criminal punishment—the death penalty—that it has been reliably characterized as insistence.[9] In keeping with his adherence to the "eye for an eye" rationale, he believed that, as there was no true equivalent to death, the only suitable punishment for murder could be death.

Bridging the gap between Kantian theory and the modern American system is the French historian and philosopher Michel Foucault. In his 1975 work, *Discipline and Punish*, Foucault outlined his view of the progression of criminal law and justice up to that point, where the systems he observed had largely moved away from torturing and killing criminals in favor of a program of rehabilitation, a model he thought "to punish less, perhaps; but certainly to punish better."[10]

In the present day, criminal justice and the American system that peddles it are dependent on a continuing societal need for criminal reform and deterrence. One function of criminal justice within the United States is that of justified punishment. Some scholars, such as Michael S. Moore, have articulated that, perhaps, justified punishment is the sole purpose of criminal law.[11] This model is referred to as the punitive view and ostensibly combines criminal procedure and evidentiary rules with the tenets of criminal law to justify the punishments the system doles out. This model goes against the curial view, which contends that the criminal court, its trials, and its myriad of procedures are the main components of criminal law, rather than the punishments that such courts dole out.[12] Punishment is still a key element in the curial view, of course, but it is not the central tenet. A third and final model, the communitarian view, offers a theory that criminal law is intended to respond to wrongdoing on behalf of every member of the affected community. This model couples well with the curial view to illustrate a version of criminal law as a vehicle for giving much-needed answers to afflicted communities.[13]

All three of these models feature in at least one of the songs covered throughout the remainder of this essay, with the punitive view being elucidated most frequently. We see the punitive model at play in every song discussed, while the curial and communitarian models are present in Merle Haggard's "Mama Tried" and Tom T. Hall's "A Week in a Country Jail," and in Steve Earle's "Ellis Unit One" and Marty Robbins' "The Chair," respectively. Within these, and similar songs, run many threads related to theories of punishment, retributive justice, and legal punishment, which this essay aims to explore, both from the perspective of the imprisoned and the imprisoner. Collectively, these songs offer a critique of the criminal justice system and implicate the idea that society is served by punishing with a prison sentence. The modern American prison system is not only alien to the country artists listed above and their contemporaries, but it runs counter to the philosophies of life they wrote about as well.

"A lonesome whistle blowin'"

In Merle Haggard's "Mama Tried,"[14] we learn of a rebellious young man, growing up in a "family meek and mild," without his father who had died. His first memory was knowing that he wanted to leave home, on the train with the lonesome whistle. Like many American males growing up without a father, his mom tried to beat the odds that had been cast in her and her son's way. Yet, as Haggard confesses, despite his mother's best attempts at giving him a moral education, it never quite stuck. Even with some help from the larger community, her son was unable to control his worst impulses.

But we also learn that there was not much support for the single, widowed mother and her child. Without help, the mother worked endlessly and tried to give her son a good life, and though she tried to bring her son up well, he refused. To be sure, the subject of the song does inform the listener that his plight is his own doing. But Haggard's lamentations on disappointing his mother while incarcerated in California's San Quentin prison in the late 1950s indirectly tell a tale where he is not solely at fault for his lot in life.[15]

A study published by the American Medical Association in 2007 indicated that "significant associations" could be drawn between an individual being raised under the guidance of a single parent and being arrested or convicted, with particular emphasis on violent crimes or crimes resulting in property damage.[16] This study, which was conducted on the basis of existing literature not taking a broad enough approach to the coverage of single-parent households, bore damning results, including documenting heightened rates of anxiety, diminished educational success, and worsened economic opportunities, all of which can contribute to the increased criminal activity that the study assessed among its subjects.

The Judge, the Jailer, and His Wife

Tom T. Hall, in "A Week in a Country Jail," tells a story about being arrested in a small town for speeding—while "sittin' at a red light." Although he is reassured that he'll face the judge the following morning, it takes a week for the judge to arrive to court, and the exploits of the protagonist, his cellmates, and their jailers are outlined in the meantime. This tale, woven by Hall, a man aptly nicknamed "the Storyteller," imparts themes of state domination, punishment, and atonement. Hall's semi-autobiographical look into the hierarchy of a country jail paints a picture of country justice and mild corruption on the part of Hall's jailer. Along the way, the Sheriff edifies our protagonist about the state of law in town (this is definitely not Indianapolis). He and a fellow prisoner were able to get some beer, but they "had to pay him double 'cause he was the man in charge / And the jailer's job was not the best in town."[17]

Here we see evidence of state domination, where group agents—i.e. the sheriff, the jailer, and the officers that arrested Hall—are clearly exerting their collective agency on him, as evidenced by the "shared beliefs or joint intentions among the members of the group" that typically characterizes group agency domination in the view of thinkers such as Quentin Skinner and Phillip Pettit.[18] Such thinkers within the neorepublican tradition often associate domination with acts that people in power have the capacity to do by virtue of their status, rather than limiting their scope to acts which are carried out, and in "A Week in a Country Jail," Hall, albeit humorously, does feel that power. By the time he's released, again a week after being told he would be and after being seemingly arrested on a trumped-up charge, the judge takes every last nickel he has and tells him, "let this teach you not to race."[19]

The Lessons of "The Chair"

One of the most contentious issues in the American penal system is the death penalty. Marty Robbins' haunting lyrics in "The Chair" are about a death row prisoner summoned to his end. The prisoner's fear is palpable—he's been unable to sleep, he is unable to contain his fear, and he begins to weep. So overcome is he with fear that he is pushed and carried to the chair—"blind with fright." As he is strapped in, the chaplain encourages him to believe that "faith in God will cause Him to forgive."[20] The prisoner is not consoled, because although he has his faith, "but still I want to live."[21]

Beyond the ethical debate about the death penalty, it is also clear in the music of the country bard that the guards on death row also feel the pain, grief, and finality of death row. Steve Earle's "Ellis Unit One" is told from the perspective of the prison guard, and the listener learns much about the prison system and its impact on local economies and the individuals who are employed there. The subject of the song returns home after a stint in the Army, gets married, and is hired on at the prison as he suspected he would because that's what his father and uncles had done.

He learned about the old days of the electric chair, before lethal injection, when crowds would gather outside when an inmate was put to death. Yet, although lethal injection is civilized, the death clearly impacted the prisoners, their families, and the victims' families: "I've helped to drag 'em when they could not stand / I've heard their mamas cryin' when they heard that big door slam / I've seen the victim's family holdin' hands."[22]

Most disturbingly, the prison guard—who, regardless of one's politics or view on the death penalty, is certainly innocent of a crime that would lead to legally punishing him—takes his work home with him. His reality as a death row prison guard begins to haunt his dreams, with the potential of him being subjected to the very capital punishment that he leads prisoners to. In one harrowing example, Earle recounts a dream the guard had, where he himself had awoken to find himself stuck and strapped down, with something cold and black filling his lungs, lamenting to himself that he was beyond even the help of Jesus, implying that there was no place for God in Ellis Unit One. This presents a glaring ethical consideration about not only how we treat prisoners, but also about the societal impact of the prison system.

Country Philosophies and Real-World Implications

While this essay discusses classic country songs and couches that discussion in philosophical works, there are lessons within these lyrics and the often high-minded, often abstract thinking of philosophers. Since the 1970s, when the Supreme Court ruled that the death penalty was unconstitutional (*Furman v. Georgia, 1972*)—and then overturned that decision a short time later (*Gregg v. Georgia, 1976*), capital punishment has consistently been a contentious political, legal, and ethical battle within the U.S. Marty Robbins and Steve Earle, in songs written roughly twenty-five years apart, offer a peek into *why* the ongoing discussion surrounding the death penalty is important.

Similarly, Tom T. Hall's "Country Jail" offers an amusing, but poignant, look into a failed, corrupt local legal system. Regardless of whether one, knowingly or not, adheres to a retributive, justified form of justice or a punitive one, it is easy to recognize the injustice of being jailed (for "racing") while stopped at a stop light. About a decade ago, after the city of Ferguson, Missouri, saw weeks of protest, some of it violent—and internationally televised—the Department of Justice issued a report on the city's police department and courts. Some of the findings, in brief, include the claim that "Ferguson's law enforcement practices are shaped by the City's focus on *revenue* rather than by public safety needs ... contributing to a pattern of unconstitutional policing," including directives like "the City Finance Director wrote to Chief Jackson that 'unless ticket writing ramps up significantly before the end of the year, it will be hard to significantly raise collections next year.'"[23] Compare this to the opening of "Country Jail," in which Hall recounts the story of sitting at a red light where he's accused by two men of speeding through their town.[24]

Moreover, according to the report, "[t]he municipal court does not act as a neutral arbiter of the law or a check on unlawful police conduct."[25]

Again, in comparison, after being held for a week, the protagonist of "Country Jail" had his day in court, where the judge (after taking all of his money) tells him, "let this teach you not to race."[26] In short, the classic lyrics of these country crooners, beyond making a good song, were illustrative of real situations, and played a role in the real ethical debates that roiled the nation in the 1970s—and remain relevant today.

NOTES

1. Worrall, John L. 2019. "The Politics of Policing." *Oxford Handbook of the History of Crime and Criminal Justice*, ed. Paul Knepper and Anja Johansen, 58. Oxford University Press; see also Geary, Daniel. 2013. "'The Way I Would Feel About San Quentin': Johnny Cash & The Politics of Country Music." *Daedalus*. vol. 142, no. 4, 64–72.

2. Geary, "San Quentin," 64, 67.

3. Meranze, Michael. 2016. "Histories of the Modern Prison: Renewal, Regression, and Expansion." *Oxford Handbook of the History of Crime and Criminal Justice*, ed. Paul Knepper and Anja Johansen, 689. Oxford University Press; see also Kalish, Carol B. 1981. "Prisoners in 1980," research from the website of the Bureau of Justice Statistics. Bureau of Justice Statistics.

4. Carson, E. Ann, and Kluckow, Rich. 2023. "Prisoners in 2022—Statistical Tables," research from the website of the Bureau of Justice Statistics. Bureau of Justice Statistics.

5. Wacquant, Loïc. 2010. "Class, Race & Hyperincarceration in Revanchist America." *Daedalus*. vol. 139, no. 3, 74.

6. Meranze, 689.

7. Lahdon, Tenzing. 2023. "From the Desk of BJA—November 2023: Justice Matters." Published by the Bureau of Justice Assistance.

8. Rauscher, Frederick. 2022. "Kant's Social and Political Philosophy." *Stanford Encyclopedia of Philosophy*. Stanford University.

9. *Ibid.*

10. Gutting, Gary, and Oksala, Johanna. 2022. "Michel Foucault." *Stanford Encyclopedia of Philosophy*. Stanford University.

11. Moore, Michael S. 1997. *Placing Blame: A Theory of Criminal Law*. Oxford University Press, 28–29; see also Edwards, James. 2018. "Theories of Criminal Law." *Stanford Encyclopedia of Philosophy*. Stanford University.

12. Edwards.

13. *Ibid.*

14. Haggard, Merle. 1968. "Mama Tried." *Killers Three*. Nelson, Ken (prod.) Capitol Records.

15. Collins, Ace. 1996. *The Stories Behind Country Music's All-Time Greatest 100 Songs*. Boulevard Books, 98–100.

16. Fergusson, David M., et al. "Exposure to Single Parenthood in Childhood and Later Mental Health, Educational, Economic, and Criminal Behavior Outcomes." *Archives of General Psychiatry*. JAMA Network.

17. Hall, Tom T. 1969. "A Week in a Country Jail." *Homecoming*. Kennedy, Jerry (prod.) Mercury Records.

18. List, Christian; Pettit, Phillip. 2011. *Group Agents: The Possibility, Design, and Status of Corporate Agents*. Oxford University Press, 19-41; McCammon, Richard C. 2025. "Domination." *Stanford Encyclopedia of Philosophy*. Stanford University.

19. Robbins, Marty. 1971. "The Chair." *The Greatest Hits of Marty Robbins*. Robbins, Marty (prod.) Columbia Records.

20. *Ibid.*

21. *Ibid.*

22. Earle, Steve. 1996. "Ellis Unit One." *Dead Man Walking.* Robbins, Tim and Robbins, David (prods.) Columbia Records.

23. DOJ Civil Rights Division. 2015. "Investigation of the Ferguson Police Department." *Department of Justice* website, 2. United States Department of Justice.

24. Hall.

25. DOJ Civil Rights Division, 3.

26. Hall.

Country Music Is Conservative

ANTHONY PETROS SPANAKOS
and IAN J. DRAKE

On March 10, 2003, in a concert in London, England, Dixie Chicks' lead singer, Natalie Maines, announced on stage, "Just so you know, we're on the good side with y'all. We do not want this war, this violence, and we're ashamed that the president of the United States is from Texas."[1] At first, it was a non-event. The U.S. ambassador to the UK attended the concert and met with the group afterward (with no reported mention of Maines' onstage remarks) and, for about four days thereafter, media in the U.S. made no mention of the remarks until the Drudge Report and Freerepublic.com started to publicize and criticize Maines' remarks.[2]

In the following months, Dixie Chicks records were publicly destroyed by steamrollers,[3] Lipton, a corporate producer of instant iced tea, canceled its advertising contract with the group for fear of boycott, and their music was effectively removed from country music radio airplay. Within a few days of the initial backlash, Maines conceded her onstage remarks were "disrespectful." Yet, in 2006, she withdrew her concession and claimed President Bush deserved no respect. Twenty years later, in 2023, Maines, still the lead singer of the since-renamed The Chicks, proudly proclaimed the kerfuffle was a "defining moment" that "set us free."[4]

The Dixie Chicks controversy is interesting not because the group took a stand against a Republican president, but because they took *any* partisan stand. Most country artists have not openly embraced conservative or liberal/progressive political causes or partisan affiliations, adhering to the "Michael Jordan rule." In 1990, North Carolina native Jordan refused to endorse Democratic candidate for Senate Harvey Gantt, reportedly claiming, "Republicans buy sneakers, too."[5] Taylor Swift saw the backlash against the Dixie Chicks, too, and later said, "you're always one comment away from being done."[6]

Although there is little scholarship on the political affiliations or opinions of the country music industry's audience,[7] most scholars and popular writers describe the genre and audience of country music as conservative.[8] The scant evidence on the topic suggests the audience trends to the political right. For example, in 2004, country music fans were twice as prevalent among Bush supporters (30 percent) as Kerry supporters (15 percent), and R&B and hip-hop fans were 19 percent of Kerry supporters, but only 4 percent of Bush supporters.[9]

More recently, in 2017, one blogger, Carson Taylor, combined data from YouTube, Google Trends, and Spotify to tentatively conclude that the audience for country music is from less densely populated states, which tend to vote more conservatively.[10]

The Traditional Roots of Country Music

The geographic origins of country music are in the South. Originally called "folk" and later "hillbilly," country music, as with most American forms of music, was a hybrid genre derived from the merging of styles and instruments from different ethnic groups that migrated to the Spanish, French, and English colonial possessions in North America in the 16th and 17th centuries. The English, Highland Scots, Scotch-Irish, Catholic Irish, Welsh, Germans, Spanish, French, Mexicans, Native Americans, and Africans all contributed to the origins not only of country music, but also of blues, jazz, and rock and roll.[11] Most historians agree that the songs and instruments of these groups were a reflection of their ethnic origins in Europe and Africa, combined with their experiences in rural, frontier-oriented settlements in America.

One version of the story of settlement in North America is that of a rural-urban divide: coastal urban commercial development and rural inland lag. This urban-rural (or "town and country") division persisted well into the 20th century and was reflected in the music that originated in rural areas.[12] As a pair of noted historians of country music have noted, describing the folk music of the early national period and that of the 19th century, "[r]ural southerners responded affectionately to songs that reaffirmed the values of home, family, mother, and God, and they took to their hearts songs about dying orphans, neglected mothers, blind children, maidens who died of broken hearts, and eastbound trains that carried penniless children to see their poor blind convict fathers."[13] In short, the rural origins of folk music were correlated to a concern with place and produced a nostalgic defense of the virtues of inland rural areas against vice-ridden, libertine cities.

The widespread use and commercial potential of radio in the 1920s brought folk music commercial success and exposure throughout the United States. Although the first commercial recording was probably in New York City in 1922,[14] "hillbilly music" was thought of as a southern phenomenon. Fiddlers and singers would perform live on the radio and scouts from music publishers (often located in the northeast, especially New York City) would travel to the South to find talent to market to a regional, and, later, a national audience.[15] The talent scouts also sought out talent in opera, blues, and jazz, searching for songwriters and singers who could write and perform "old-time tunes." The search made folk (and jazz and blues) music available to the nation. But the needs of the music market also contributed to the shaping of that music by industry insiders.

This has led some critics and scholars to think of country music as having a "fabricated authenticity,"[16] something not unique to this genre, as producers often tailor their art to satisfy the taste of consumers. This question is especially important for country music because it seeks to communicate an earnest traditionalism born of time, place, and experience, all of which can sometimes lead to a particular moral and political outlook.

Country Music and Conservativism

Asking "Is country music conservative?" typically just means something like "Do fans and artists vote Republican?" and, indeed, country music fans are more inclined than those of other genres to do so. But that does not mean that country music is necessarily conservative in a partisan way. Yet, country music *is* definitely conservative in a philosophical way. It sees beauty in tradition and life and seeks to "conserve it," a definitional point for Roger Scruton.[17] It relies not on ideology but on a disposition or, as conservative thinker Michael Oakeshott wrote, a response to disorder and a perception of a world in flux.[18] And it venerates the places and experiences of dwelling, themes raised by Byung-Chul Han.[19]

The remainder of this essay will examine a range of country music songs in order to explore these themes: desire to conserve the good/beautiful things of life; the disposition toward a changing world; and the understanding of place and dwelling. Ultimately, the conservatism of country music is less about party as it maps better onto the more recent social cleavage of "somewheres vs. anywheres" (i.e., people who identify with a very specific place as opposed to people who are more cosmopolitan).[20] But it also raises difficult, uncomfortable, and very political questions about what should be conserved.

People usually begin thinking of politics with ideas of left (progressive) and right (conservative) even though conservative and progressive programs vary according to country and historical period. Nineteenth-century Protestant missionaries and Japanese imperialists were progressive forces in the final days of the Joseon Dynasty in Korea while the Russian and Chinese Court's influences were more conservative. From the late 19th century to the present, American conservatives have favored, then rejected, and favored again trade restrictions and protection of national industry. The Chinese communist party during the Cultural Revolution attempted to extirpate Confucian influence in society, and in the beginning of the 20th century, it financed Confucius Institutes around the world.

It is also relevant that the term "conservative" is often used outside of politics. Architectural designs may seek to conserve habits of everyday life, and an aging jogger may seek to conserve energy during the course of a run. Accountants make conservative forecasts about expected revenues—something appreciated even by progressive investors—and tech executives, many being socially and politically progressive, are remarkably conservative in the amount of screen time they allow their children and often oppose employee unionization efforts.

For our purposes, it is worth separating a partisan position (which we will call Conservative) from a philosophical one (conservative). There is much diversity among Conservatives in any country or across the world (the Republican Party in the U.S., the Labour Party in Great Britain, Fidesz in Hungary, the Bharatiya Janata Party in India, and the Liberal Democratic Party in Japan). In this essay, *Conservative* will refer to ideas and policies advocated by members of the Republican Party and associated think tanks and groups.

A conservative philosophical position does not map perfectly onto that of conservatives. A conservative believes that there are things of great, often permanent, value and beauty in society. Many of these are the result of human effort. They are vulnerable to decay over time due to lack of attention or to deliberate efforts of others. The conservative's world is inherited and passed on to others in the form of a tradition, a world. Surely not all of this is worthy of praise and preservation, but much is, and the conservative has the responsibility and obligation to conserve that which is of value and pass it to future generations. The conservative aims to "conserve" that which is beautiful, good, and true in the physical, social, and political world.

The English philosopher Roger Scruton's entry into conservatism was through aesthetics because beauty tells us we are "at home in this world."[21] It is in appreciation of beauty that Scruton defined a conservative as "someone who wishes to conserve something."[22] But what *should* be conserved? Here, conservative is not an ideology but a disposition.[23]

An ideology knows in advance what is good, bad, and ugly at all times and places. It is universally applicable precisely because it is abstract. But conservatives reject abstractions. They do not simply reside in a place. The home, town, country, and even civilization are places of dwelling,[24] the sort of experience replete in country music lyrics. This may sound parochial, if the term is used as a pejorative, and the conservative knows little of "universal" goals (justice, development, and so on) but is very vested in local concerns. The conservative is neither concerned with abstractions nor with ideology but with prudential living in a world which is subject to changes, small and great, benevolent and baneful.

Chronicles of Time and Place

Country music is not limited to the United States (e.g., country music star Shania Twain hails from Windsor, Ontario, Canada), and many countries have some form of music associated with narrating experiences of the encounter of folk and rural traditions with modernization and urbanization projects (e.g., *Sertaneja* music in Brazil). In the case of the U.S., the dichotomy between rural-urban continues as do narratives of simple, traditional, and hard-scrap living, famously summarized in a self-deprecating song performed by David Allan Coe. "It was not the perfect country & western song; because he hadn't said anything at all about mama; or trains, or trucks, or prison, or getting' drunk."[25]

In a more serious vein, the idea of living slowly in response to, and perhaps suffering from, a world in rapid change continues to resonate. In one of the more perspicacious readings of the 2016 Brexit vote in Britain and the election of Donald Trump in the U.S., British journalist David Goodhart separated people not by political party but by whether they could live "anywhere" or whether they were "somewheres"—people with deep roots to a place, its culture and traditions.[26] The anywhere is the person who claims to be a "global citizen," can move and live anywhere with little friction and loss of moral compass and social orientation. The somewhere is like our conservatives for whom beauty, tradition, and connection to the past and coming generations is experienced in particular places that are not easily traded. As such, they must be actively conserved, even or especially when so much in the world aims at its dissolution. Although country music includes many different performers and themes, the voice of Goodhart's somewhere whose disposition is to conserve the beauty and preserve authentic dwelling in a particular place is a shared motif.

Place was central to Merle Haggard and Roy Burris' "Okie from Muskogee," not only a hit record but a flag placed in a culture war. An "okie," a pejorative familiar to readers of *The Grapes of Wrath*, was some-one from what might now be called "flyover country," a foreigner and second-class citizen in a city in his or her own country. The song rejects the LSD-favored lifestyle of burning draft cards by people with long, unkempt hair. Rather, the "we" in the song want to live as they should and to be free, and they live in "a place where even squares can have a ball / We still wave Old Glory down at the courthouse / And white lightning's still the biggest thrill of all."[27]

The hippies clearly represented a challenge to the social and aesthetic norms of the Okies. The song notes differences in hair, dress, and choice of drug (LSD v. white lightning, whiskey). But these and, presumably, much else contribute to something far greater which allows the singer to believe that his group is living right and free. It is this that the singer wishes to protect from outside forces. Moreover, the town is still a place where "the college dean" is respected, football is still big, and Old Glory (the U.S. flag) is being waved. All of these are aspects of a life lived in a particular place and country, of which the singer is proud. He is a member of the life in that place and wishes to conserve its beauty.

The late Toby Keith's "Courtesy of the Red, White and Blue (the Angry American)"[28] is an heir to "Okie from Muskogee" in its brash flag-waving lyrics. The narrator's father was severely injured while serv-ing in the army but nevertheless flew the American flag in the family's yard until the day he died because he wanted his children to grow up and be happy in the land of the free. The father's sacrifice is not decried; Keith acknowledges the sacrifice was made so that Americans can live in peace and have the luxury of sleeping comfortably at night. The country pro-vides peace through its soldiers, and recognition of this can be seen in how we live and act. The father's dedication to the flag and efforts to teach such to his children, everyone saluting the flag so we can sleep in peace, repre-sent a relation to a cherished tradition and a way of dwelling. Keith's song was very much seen as a response to many artists (such as Maines) and public intellectuals' criticism of the Bush administration and the war in Iraq. While not a pro–Republican song *per se* (and therefore not necessar-ily Conservative), the song depicted an attitude of a people who knew who they were, knew they were attacked, and were ready to light up the world of their adversaries. They had families, a home, and a country to protect.

Some 20 years later, even patriotic conservatives soured on the war efforts in Iraq and Afghanistan, increasingly aware of the social breakdown in rural (and urban) America, particularly in the form of opioid-related deaths, other forms of drug addiction, wage stagnation, and a rise in loneliness and depression. YouTube star Oliver Anthony touched a nerve in such a context with a number of songs. The one to gain the most traction, "Rich Men North of Richmond," was very critical of politicians and the top 10 percent of income earners living around the nation's capital (and in other urban areas) who were deliberately harming people living in smaller cities and the country. He laments that politicians aren't looking out for (hard-working Americans such as) miners, but instead are looking out for minors (on an island; a sly reference to the Jeffrey Epstein scandal). He also grieves the young men committing suicide at an alarming rate because the country is continually kicking them down.[29]

The song is a protest song, one that calls attention to the intentional destruction of American life by elites and politicians. It highlights how some groups take advantage of the system while politicians do not care for others in their care, such as miners. Miners are particularly important in recent politics as their profession is considered "dirty" and "anti-environmental" (and therefore morally repugnant). Many miners and other various manual laborers believe that the attitude of the Obama and Biden administrations toward them is evident in an Obama then Biden quip that miners need to learn how to code. The quip may reflect technical expertise in labor economics but it fails to see the lived experience: "I've been sellin' my soul, workin' all day / Overtime hours for bull—pay / So I can sit out here and waste my life away."

Anthony's "Virginia" is a rumination on living in a place which is an ineradicable part of that person's identity. For the singer, one does not choose a place to live, one cannot remove himself from that place, even if this place is of little value to the people who count. The song begins with Anthony recounting his time on his back porch picking at his banjo, accompanied by little more than his dreams. Growing up down old backroads, he sings that when he grows old he'll tell the young what those who came before told him: "Lord, they don't sing songs about Virginia / But Virginia, she's always singin' to me." This Virginia is contrasted with the U.S. more generally in "Rich Men North of Richmond," in which he laments what the world has become for him and people of his ilk.[30]

Both Anthony songs show that the urge to conserve is connected to the challenge of change and decay. When one dwells in a place that is a home and hearth and not simply a place to be "from," one sees the beauty in what is inherited and feels a need to preserve it for others (the young Anthony hopes to educate and the family members Keith wants to protect). Although it was President Obama who pitched coding as the answer for jobs in depressed communities which were built by manual labor, the attitude is not limited to the Democratic Party or progressives. Certainly, many Conservatives would agree, though perhaps not publicly. But a conservative will be suspicious of technically designed answers to places the expert does not know. The expert knows an academic subject in a way that is different from the way the conservative knows where he or she lives and what he or she has inherited. The conservative is favorably disposed to a way of living which is under attack and knows that deliberate effort is needed to preserve beauty, goodness, and truth in this world and to transmit those things to succeeding generations. It is in this way that country music is conservative.

NOTES

1. Malone, Bill C., and Tracey E. Laird. 2018. *Country Music USA*. University of Texas Press, 552.

2. St. John, Warren. 2023. "The Backlash Grows Against Celebrity Activists," *New York Times*.

3. Moss, Marissa R. 2022. *Her Country: How the Women of Country Music Became the Success They Were Never Supposed to Be*. Henry Holt, 48.

4. In 2006, she withdrew her concession and claimed President Bush deserved no respect. The group released a new album in 2006 featuring the song "Not Ready to Make Nice" which peaked at #23 on the *Billboard Hot* 100 but then it did not make another studio album until 2020, under the new name "The Chicks." In 2023, Maines proudly proclaimed the kerfuffle was a "defining moment" that "set us free." The band now lists the causes (Planned Parenthood, Headcount, the Human Rights Campaign, etc.) it supports on their website and elsewhere, information which is probably valuable to its committed but much smaller fanbase. See Keller, Erin. 2023. "The Chicks have no regrets being canceled for Bush remark: 'Set us free,'" *N.Y. Post*.

5. Lutz, Tom. 2020. "Michael Jordan insists 'Republicans buy sneakers too' quote was a joke," *The Guardian*.

6. The head of a global brand empire, Swift has deliberately chosen to take on political commentary in recent years, as have BTS and many others responding to the demands of vocal groups in their millennial and generation Z fan base. See Willman, Chris. 2020. "Taylor Swift: No Longer 'Polite at All Costs,'" *Variety*.

7. Taylor, Carson. 2017. "Mapping Country Music's Politics," *Medium*.

8. Malone, Tracey, 553.

9. Jones, Jeffrey M., and Joseph Carroll. 2024. "Music, Cars, and the 2004 Election," *GALLUP*.

10. Taylor, Carson. 2017. "Mapping Country Music's Politics," *Medium*.

11. Malone; Tracey, 1–5.

12. Fay, Molly. 2014. "City Country: The Paradox of Country Music in Urban America." *New Errands: The Undergraduate Journal of American Studies*; Cooper, Tonya. 2012. "'Sometimes I Live in the Country, Sometimes I Live in Town': Discourses of Authenticity, Cultural Capital, and the Rural/Urban Dichotomy in Alternative Country Music." PhD diss., Open Access Te Herenga Waka-Victoria University of Wellington.

13. Malone, Tracey, 19.

14. *Ibid.*, 42.

15. Cusic, Don. 2008. *Discovering Country Music*. Bloomsbury, 17–18.

16. Peterson, Richard A. 1997. *Creating Country Music: Fabricating Authenticity*. University of Chicago Press, 2.

17. Scruton, R. 2018. *Conservatism. An Invitation to the Great Tradition*. All Points Books.

18. Oakeshott, Michael. 2015. *Experience and Its Modes*. Cambridge University Press.

19. Han, Byung-Chul. 2020. *The Disappearance of Rituals: A Topology of the Present*. John Wiley & Sons.

20. Goodhart, David. 2020. *The Road to Somewhere*. Millemari.

21. Hörcher, Ferenc. 2023. *Art and Politics in Roger Scruton's Conservative Philosophy*. Palgrave MacMillan, 152.

22. Scruton.

23. Oakeshott.

24. Han.

25. Goodman, Steve; Prine, John. 1975. "You Never Even Called Me by My Name." *Once Upon a Rhyme*. Coe, David Allan (rec. artist). Bledsoe, Ron (prod.) Sony Music Entertainment.

26. Goodhart.

27. Burris, Roy Edwards; Haggard, Merle. 1969. "Okie from Muskogee." *Okie from Muskogee*. Owen, Fuzzy (prod.) Capitol Records Nashville.

28. Keith, Toby. 2002. "Courtesy of the Red, White and Blue (the Angry American)." *Unleashed*. Stroud, James (prod.) DreamWorks Nashville.

29. Anthony, Oliver. 2023. "Rich Men North of Richmond." Oliver Anthony Music (rec. artist) Radiowv. 2023.

30. Anthony, Oliver. 2023. "Virginia." Oliver Anthony Music (rec. artist) Radiowv. 2023.

Country Music Isn't Conservative

Andrea Conque

If we were to ask the average American whether they think country music is conservative, the answer is likely to be a resounding "yes." Most will be thinking of older tunes like Merle Haggard's "Okie from Mus-gokee"[1] and "Fightin' Side of Me"[2] in which "American values" are cherished and defended. They may have in mind "A Country Boy Can Survive"[3] by Hank Williams, Jr., or even Toby Keith's 2002 "Courtesy of the Red, White, and Blue (the Angry American)."[4] Or, they may even be thinking of more current hits like Oliver Anthony's "Rich Men North of Richmond" and Jason Aldean's "Try That in a Small Town,"[5] both of which critique elite politicians and policies that just wouldn't make sense in a rural environment full of working-class people. Yet, country music has not always been inherently conservative. With a few notable exceptions, the genre was fairly apolitical until politicians like then-presidential hopeful George Wallace and former president Richard Nixon began using it to connect to potential voters in the late '60s and early '70s.

Over the decades, artists like Merle Haggard, Hank Williams, Jr., Toby Keith, and John Rich have strengthened the relationship between conservative political beliefs and country music. However, other artists have broken out of that mold. Maren Morris's "Better Than We Found It," Kacey Musgraves's "Follow Your Arrow," and Gwen Levey & the Break-down's "Barefoot and Pregnant" show that, while there remains a heavy connection between country music and conservatism, country music isn't inherently conservative.

"Follow Your Arrow"

Before defending the claim that country isn't inherently conservative, it's worth asking: what do the terms "liberal" and "conservative" really mean? Political philosophers mark the distinction between liberal and conservative very simply—liberals want progress and change, while conservatives are happy with the *status quo*. However, there's much more to these ideological differences than we might see with just an initial glance. Let's first take a look at liberalism.

We can divide liberalism into two different camps: *classical liberalism* and *contemporary liberalism*. There are some features which these two types of liberalism have in common, but they have some important differences as well. Classical liberalism is associated with the work of the Enlightenment thinker, John Locke,[6] who maintained a very optimistic view of human beings and their nature. According to Locke, all human beings are rational, intelligent, and capable of making their own decisions because knowledge is dependent on experience. Knowledge, for Locke, is not some mysterious access to the truth with a capital "T"; instead, each person's mind is a *tabula rasa*, a blank sheet that can be written on by our experiences. In arguing these things, Locke paints a picture of human beings as individuals who can separate their own knowledge from what society believes.

Locke also agrees with the theory of "natural law." Natural law tells us that observing and understanding the natural world can reveal the laws of ethics. For Locke, because human beings are rational and capable, they can figure out how they should correctly behave and be ethical by using reason. In other words, they can access the laws of ethics just by using their own ability to think about the natural world. But using reason to determine behavior has another important consequence—if every person can use reason to discover how to act ethically, then every person is also fundamentally equal when it comes to morality. Therefore, all people must be fundamentally equal, period. This idea is called "radical egalitarianism."

Locke's understanding of human nature heavily affects his ideas about politics. Rather than depending upon some authority or tradition that had already been established (like the monarchy), Locke argues that reason should be the guiding principle of government. In this sense, the individual is more important than the society as a whole, and any government that stands in opposition to this idea is oppressive to Locke. When the government has too much power, in other words, that government is bad for the people. These ideas may seem familiar to you, perhaps because Locke heavily influenced the founding fathers of the United States as they created a new nation after the Revolutionary War. Thomas Jefferson's famous saying, "That government governs best which governs least," for instance, is straight from Locke.

The Modern philosopher Jeremy Bentham,[7] writing not quite a century after Locke, changed the way we look at liberalism and is credited with what we call "contemporary liberalism." Contemporary liberals still think people are capable, reasonable, intelligent, and equal, but they also maintain an optimistic view about how that very ability to reason can be used to bring about positive change in society. For the contemporary liberal, it is human rights (not natural law) that make us equal. Liberalism is, in fact, mainly about rights. The belief is that even though there are differences between people, there is no one person who is better or more important than any other. Therefore, everyone, simply in virtue of being human, deserves to be treated equally and fairly by others. Progressive political policies work to accomplish those goals, attempting to create fairness for workers and equality for all citizens, all based on the notion of equality expressed by liberalism and all desirous of steady change that will result in a better society for all.

Keep the Change

It's resistance to change that marks conservative political ideology, as opposed to liberal ideology. People who identify as conservative often have the very same goals as those who identify with liberal views; they both want the world to be a better place. However, they differ in how they believe that goal should be accomplished. The conservative wants to preserve life as it is—not necessarily because they believe it's the best way to live, but because they believe it is the best we've got so far. Remember how liberals in the tradition of Locke and Bentham had a lot of faith in humanity and the human ability to reason? That leads liberals to have a pretty optimistic view of human nature.

Conservatives, on the other hand, do not have as much faith in their fellow human beings to use their reason to solve the political problems that affect the entire community or nation. The conservative lacks faith in the ability of a particular society to govern itself properly through policy. Because of this, those who identify as conservative will often, instead, try to effect change as slowly and carefully as possible. A conservative person will think to themselves, "The ability of humans to think and reason is really not that strong. If that is true, then how can we really depend on human reason to solve the problems that arise in a society or in governing that society?"

Contrary to the liberal theories of John Locke, the philosopher Thomas Hobbes based his theory of government on the idea that human beings are awful people who cannot be trusted. He thought that, before government existed to help control things, people lived lives that were "solitary, nasty, brutish, and short."[8] Why was life so terrible in this state of nature? According to Hobbes, it is because human beings are more likely to be at war with one another than to cooperate, more likely to harm one another than be reasonable, and he thinks we need a strong leader to prevent people from running completely amok! Whereas liberals are much more trusting of human nature, conservatives are suspicious of it at best and mistrust it completely at worst.

Additionally, while both liberals and conservatives acknowledge that there are differences between people and their talents, the liberal will consider these to be unimportant differences, while the conservative will say they are of the utmost importance. Conservatism has been around for as long as anyone has been resistant to change in any society, but it was Edmund Burke who really systematized and explained the conservative viewpoint in any orderly fashion.[9] Burke is most famous for supporting the American Revolution (as a fight for rights already denied to the colonists as British citizens) but rejecting the French Revolution (as a struggle for new rights that had not yet been granted).

As a conservative, Burke understood people to have differences. However, he thought that those differences were not just surface-level but an indication of how society and government should be ordered. In other words, for Burke, the average person is not the person who is best suited to be in charge. Instead, those who are "rich" and "well-born" ought to lead, and those who do not possess these qualities should be happy to be ruled by those who are a part of the elite. Nothing noble, Burke maintains, can come from something unexceptional and common. However, he is quick to add that "there is no qualification for government but virtue and wisdom."[10]

So, although "virtue and wisdom" are meant to be the qualifications for Burke's leaders of government, those qualities are most likely found in the elite and educated. It might be helpful to mention that, just as liberals are divided into classic and contemporary, conservatives are often divided on whether they agree with Burke that the ruling class often is the most appropriate to rule and that they have an obligation to those beneath them to keep in mind what is best for the entire society.

Country Music and Politics

While it is true that country music is not always conservative, it has often been deeply connected to politics and political ideology. Plenty of country music fans are still angry at The Chicks (formerly the Dixie Chicks) for their political comments at a concert in London, England, in March of 2003. Upset about the involvement of the U.S. in what became the Iraq War, Natalie Maines famously said, "Just so you know, we're on the good side with y'all. We do not want this war, this violence, and we're ashamed that the president of the United States is from Texas."[11] In a more recent example, Oliver Anthony's "Rich Men North of Richmond"[12] certainly falls into the category of political protest songs in the sense that it both has an oppositional stance and addresses an important political issue—that of the working class versus the elites.

What we now call country music has its roots in the musical folk traditions that immigrants brought with them to North America from other continents like Europe and even Africa. In the early 1920s and '30s, the first wholly "country" artists began to record with Okeh and Victor records, sending what had been "hillbilly" music associated with Appalachia and "western" music (associated with cowboys from the western parts of the U.S.) into the American mainstream.[13] Around the same time, the National Barn Dance and the Grand Ole Opry began broadcasting into homes across the country, making further popular inroads for country music and country music artists.

From the late 1800s on, at least some form of country music was to be found in political campaigns. In the 19th century, many Americans, especially those in rural areas, found their entertainment in the various revivals, medicine shows, and other meetings that came to the area, and these all included music as part of the show. For example, Tom Watson, a populist who eventually ran for a seat in the Georgia House of Representatives, was also a fiddle player and used his musical prowess to attract attention to his various campaigns. Watson, and others like him, seemed more authentic to potential voters because of the way they presented themselves musically.[14] In the 1930s, there were also progressive politicians like "Big Jim" Folsom and Glen Taylor who tried to use country music to fight racism and to promote civil rights. Dedicated to the cause, Taylor was arrested in Birmingham, Alabama, for attending a meeting about civil rights at which both blacks and whites were present. "Big Jim" had no issue inviting a black member of Congress to his gubernatorial mansion but was met with death threats afterward for the act.[15]

On what would be considered the definitively "left" leaning side of early country music, we find artists like Harry McClintock (who wrote "Hallelujah I'm a Bum") heavily involved with radical organizations such as the Industrial Workers of the World and, more familiarly, Woody Guthrie who lived through and wrote songs about the tragedies of the Dust Bowl in Oklahoma, where he was from. Guthrie, in particular, had a guitar on which was written "This Machine Kills Fascists" and strongly supported unionization and workers' rights. You may recognize Guthrie's most famous song, "This Land Is Your Land." However, you may not know all the lyrics, as the song has been carefully edited over the years in an attempt to cleanse it of its original political meaning. For example, one verse that has been cut out goes like this: "There was a big high wall there that tried to stop me / Sign was painted, it said private property / But on the back side it didn't say nothing / This land was made for you and me."[16] Later, in the 1960s, what used to be this strain of country music would morph into the folk and protest singer-songwriters of the time, while others would drift farther right as the Vietnam War progressed and the counterculture movements of the time strengthened.

Thank You, Mr. President

On the side of conservatism, or of the "right" on the political spectrum, country music also had its fans. We already know that there were single politicians who used music to make themselves more relatable to voters. In the 1960s, conservative politicians began to take that connection to a much higher level. George Wallace, for example, had a country song composed for his 1968 presidential campaign called "Stand Up for America." What they have in common is an active engagement in making country music the soundtrack of conservative political views in the U.S. Although Wallace lost that presidential election to Richard Nixon, Nixon couldn't help but notice that courting country music and its fans was not a bad idea.

You've probably heard the term "Southern Strategy" before. It was Nixon's plan to try to get southern voters on his side in case he had to again face someone like Wallace in a national political contest. A big part of the Southern Strategy was to get working-class white voters in the South to shift over to Republicanism. Nixon went to great lengths to make certain that people associated the country music lifestyle with his brand of politics. In fact, in 1970, he declared October to be country music month in the U.S. and was careful to use country music and country artists to help build his political persona as an everyday kind of guy. He even invited country stars to the White House that same year. And, in 1972, the country world gave President Nixon a gift in return—a country music album made just for him titled *Thank You, Mr. President*, recorded and produced by the Country Music Association. The album paints a picture of country music and cultural pride—of hard-working people who want to fight against the elites.

The real turning point in the cultural shift of country music toward the political position with which most people associate it today was thus during Nixon's presidency. The Vietnam War was raging, and protests against it were becoming more and more common. The very existence of counter-cultural music and hippies was enough to send many country artists careening toward the right. In 1969, Merle Haggard released his now widely known "Okie from Muskogee," which resonated with working-class whites, especially those who were sympathetic to the cause of the Vietnam War and disliked the counterculture.[17]

Republican strategists at the time wanted to capitalize on the fact that many working-class whites did not consider themselves in the same moral category as those on the left; they considered themselves superior to protesters who they thought were freeloaders and unpatriotic. Unsurprisingly, an appeal to patriotism and moral rectitude in a time when working-class whites felt attacked by the countercultural movements of the late '60s truly worked well for Nixon and politicians like him.[18] Ronald Reagan's presidency cemented the core of what we consider political conservatism today—advocating Christian values, religious involvement in the law, concerns with the moral direction of the nation, and drawing battle lines between people considered the "elites" and regular, hard-working folk. The connection, thus, between country music and conservatism is not accidental; it was cultivated over time and to the benefit of both politicians and the country music industry.

"Better than we found it"

The truth of the matter is that, even though most may think of country music as inherently conservative, it simply isn't and never has been. That implication was purposefully crafted and honed by politicians for whom it was beneficial to be seen as average, everyday working-class people with certain values and morals. From the singing politicians of the early days of country music to today's chart-toppers, we can find both very liberal and conservative lyrics and ideas.

Loretta Lynn's "Coal Miner's Daughter,"[19] in which she is proud to be from a poor, hard-working family, is on the album presented to Nixon, but she also performed "The Pill"[20] in 1975 in support of the newly gained option of birth control: "There's gonna be some changes made right here on nursery hill / You've set this chicken your last time / 'Cause now I've got the pill." And, for every Hank Williams, Jr.'s "If the South Woulda Won,"[21] there's a Garth Brooks' "We Shall Be Free"[22] about diversity and inclusion.

For instance, the Drive-By Truckers' 2016 song about the deaths of Trayvon Martin and Michael Brown questions "What It Means"[23] to be "post-racial," as the group sings, "I mean Barack Obama won, and you can choose where to eat / But you don't see too many white kids lying bleeding on the street." Jason Isbell's "White Man's World"[24] delves into his understanding of privilege as a white man. Maren Morris's "Better Than We Found It"[25] asks, "But who's gonna care if I don't? / Who's gonna change if I won't? / Will we leave this world better than we found it?" suggesting a progressive position of change. And Kacey Musgraves's "Follow Your Arrow"[26] tells us that whatever you do, you'll disappoint someone, so "Kiss lots of boys (yup) / Or kiss lots of girls, if that's something you're into / Roll up a joint, or don't" is indicative of a kind of liberal tolerance. Finally, Gwen Levey and the Breakdown's 2023 "Barefoot & Pregnant"[27] asks what we do with Miss American Pie (a nod to the Don McLean song). The unfortunate answer is that we "keep her barefoot and pregnant, and down on the farm! / What does she do with her college degree? / Throw it out the window with her IUD."

Throughout its history, country music has been fairly representative of both ends of the political spectrum. We're only inclined to think of country music as conservative because that's been the aim of conservative politicians trying to get votes. So, even though people really think of country music as inherently conservative, it is not. Again, as we can see, there's no shortage of examples throughout the history of country music that demonstrate that the genre is and always has been a beautiful mixture of different, and sometimes quite strong, political opinions, and that it has never been solely conservative.

NOTES

1. Haggard, Merle; Burris, Roy Edward. 1969. "Okie from Muskogee." *Okie from Muskogee*. Merle Haggard and the Strangers (rec. artist). Owen, Fuzzy (prod.) Capitol Records.

2. Haggard, Merle. 1970. "The Fightin' Side of Me." *The Fightin' Side of Me*. Nelson, Ken (prod.) Capitol Records.

3. Williams, Jr., Hank. 1982. "A Country Boy Can Survive." *The Pressure Is On*. Bowen, Jimmy; Williams, Hank, Jr. (prods.) Elektra/Curb.

4. Keith, Toby. 2002. "Courtesy of the Red, White, and Blue (the Angry American)." *Unleashed*. Stroud, James (prod.) DreamWorks Nashville.

5. Lovelace, Kelley; Thrasher, Neil; Kennedy, Tully; Allison, Kurt. 2023. "Try That in a Small Town." *Highway Desperado*. Aldean, Jason (rec. artist). Know, Michael (prod.) BBR.

6. See Locke, John. 1959. *An Essay Concerning Human Understanding*, ed. Alexander Fraser. Dover Publications; Locke, John. 1965. *Two Treatises of Government*, ed. Peter Laslett. New American Library.

7. See Bentham, Jeremy. 1967. *Fragment on Government and an Introduction to the Principles of Morals and Legislation*, ed. Wilfred Harrison. Basil Blackwell.

8. See Hobbes, Thomas. 1962. *The Leviathan*, ed. Michael Oakeshott. Collier Books.

9. See Burke, Edmund. 1955. *Reflections on the Revolution in France*, ed. Thomas H.D. Mahoney. Bobbs-Merril.

10. *Ibid.*, 57.

11. Maines, Natalie. 2003. From the stage in London, England. Dixie Chicks Concert. March,.

12. Oliver, Anthony. 2023. "Rich Men North of Richmond." Anthony, Oliver (prod.) Self-released.

13. Cusic, Don. 2011. *The Cowboy in Country Music: A Historical Survey with Artist Profiles*. McFarland.

14. Not unimportantly, the youthful Watson fought alongside the Colored Farmers Alliance to gain the right to vote for Southern blacks. He believed that the same system that kept poor whites down also oppressed poor blacks—it was the rich elite and economic disenfranchisement that he was against. Of note, Watson's political beliefs took a complete U-turn later in life and he began to espouse anti-Semitic and racist views. See Ali, Omar H. 2010. *In the Lion's Mouth: Black Populism in the New South 1896–1900*. University Press of Mississippi, 79–80.

15. La Chapelle, Peter. 2019. *I'd Fight the World: A Political History of Old-Time, Hillbilly, and Country Music*. University of Chicago Press, 1–10.

16. Guthrie, Woody. 1944. "This Land Is Your Land." Asch, Moses (prod.) Folkways Records, 1951.

17. Haggard, Merle. "Okie from Muskogee." I should mention that there is some debate as to whether or not this song was actually satire. Merle Haggard said as much in at least one interview about the song (February 1970). However, it likely doesn't matter whether or not it was satire—many people took it seriously at the time and that is what counts. Also, the song's very title has been the cause of much serious disagreement. The term "Okie" was a derogatory term for those Oklahomans who escaped the horrors of the Dust Bowl and migrated to California. Now, it is used to describe anyone from Oklahoma, but that wasn't always the case.

18. Of course, it should be remarked that the policies of the Republicans never actually supported the working-class whites the way that the Democratic politics like the New Deal and unions did.

19. Lynn, Loretta. 1970. "Coal Miner's Daughter." *Coal Miner's Daughter*. Bradley, Owen (prod.) Decca Records.

20. Allen, Lorene; McHan, Don; Bayless, T.D.; Lynn, Loretta. 1975. "The Pill." *Back to the Country*. Bradley, Owen (prod.) MCA Records.

21. Williams, Hank, Jr. 1988. "If the South Woulda Won." *Wild Streak*. Beckett, Barry; Williams, Jr., Hank; Norman, Jim Ed (prods.) Warner Bros./Curb.

22. Brooks, Garth; Davis, Stephanie. 1992. "We Shall Be Free." *The Chase*. Brooks, Garth (rec. artist). Reynolds, Allen (prod.) Liberty.

23. Hood, Patterson. 2016. "What It Means." *American Band*. The Drive-By Truckers (rec. artist). Barbe, David (prod.) ATO.

24. Isbell, Jason. 2017. "White Man's World." *The Nashville Sound*. Jason Isbell and the 400 Unit (rec. artist). Cobb, Dave (prod.) Southeastern.

25. Morris, Maren. 2020. "Better Than We Found It." Promotional single.

26. Clark, Brandy; McAnally, Shane; Musgraves, Kacey. 2013. "Follow Your Arrow." *Same Trailer Different Park*. Musgraves, Kacey (rec. artist). Laird, Luke; McAnally, Shane; Musgraves, Kacey (prod.) Mercury Nashville.

27. Levey, Gwen. 2023. "Barefoot and Pregnant." *Not the Girl Next Door*. Gwen Levey & the Breakdown (rec. artist). Self-release.

V

The Dark Side
of Country

The Tragedy of Country Music

JOSHUA HETER

In the song "I Fall to Pieces," Patsy Cline laments the loss of composure she experiences when she sees an old flame and is forced to pretend they've never met.[1] In "I'm So Lonesome I Could Cry," Hank Williams confesses that he has "lost the will to live" due to his lack of company and feelings of isolation.[2] The lyrics to Gene Autry and Jimmy Long's "That Silver Haired Daddy of Mine" read as a tearful letter of apology from a son to a father for all the grief the son has caused the father over the many years of their relationship.[3] More contemporarily, Lady A's "Need You Now" recounts the drunken late-night exchange of defeated former lovers as they give in to their impulse to reach out to one another even though they've promised not to.[4]

These songs, along with countless other examples, demonstrate that some of the most enduring and substantive works of country music have focused on sadness and tales of woe. For as long as there has been country music, there have been country songs centered around heartache, regret, and despondency. All of this is perhaps best illustrated by an old, well-worn joke (eventually immortalized in the song "Backwards" by Rascal Flatts)[5] about the familiar subject of loss in country music that typically goes something like this. What do you get when you play a country song in reverse? You get your dog back, your truck back, your house back, your lady back, etc.

Again, as we can see, country artists (perhaps particularly) have centered a great deal of their music around melancholy. And you don't have to listen to these songs all that long to know that doing so can stir up this same type of feeling in the listener. All of this raises a fairly obvious question: why are we drawn to such depressing, mournful music? Perhaps naively, but nevertheless intuitively, feeling sorrowful and unhappy is *bad*. It's something that we take great strides to avoid. Presumably, a fair amount of what we do on a daily basis is motivated by the knowledge

132

that *not* doing those things will eventually lead to circumstances that will make us sad or mournful. Yet, at the end of the day, when we have a chance to kick back and open up a cold one, we often enough feel the urge to listen to these very country songs which (are designed to and quite frequently) lead us to feel all of those emotions we seem to want to avoid.

Of course, while this question is important to our understanding of country music and our relation to it, it is not unique to the genre. Long before artists were producing music that could reasonably be considered "country," a number of philosophers were asking essentially this same question about other pieces of art: why are we drawn to—and seem, on some level, to enjoy—creative works which serve primarily as delivery mechanisms for misery and sorrow, things which we seem to want nothing to do with in any other, normal context?[6] In what follows, we'll take a look at three unique (though potentially compatible) answers to this question, each from a different era of philosophy.

Country Catharsis

A first potential answer to the question of why we are drawn to sad country songs finds its origin in the work of the ancient Greek philosopher Aristotle, one of the most influential thinkers in Western thought. However, he is particularly noteworthy in regard to what you are now reading, because he was one of the first to take seriously the broad aim of this book: thinking critically about art and (what was essentially the) popular culture (of his day).

In his work *Poetics*, Aristotle raises a number of questions about the poetic arts in general and has a great deal to say about tragedies in particular.[7] Specifically, Aristotle considers the Athenian tragedy *Oedipus the King*, in which the titular character unknowingly kills his father and marries his mother, Jocasta, who bears him four children. When all of this eventually comes to light, Jocasta hangs herself, while Oedipus laments the birth of their children, blinds himself, and wanders as a hermit for the rest of his life as a form of self-punishment. Such an unpleasant, discomforting tale makes the country songs mentioned at the opening of this essay almost sound cheerful. As such, it was only natural for Aristotle to wonder why anyone would subject themselves to such a seemingly distasteful story.

His explanation of this mystery is that experiencing fictional or dramatized tragedies (such as that of Oedipus) allows us to purge our souls of certain unwanted emotions such as pity and fear. These uncomfortable, perhaps painful emotions may be buried deep within us, and consuming tragic storytelling can, in its own way, help us expel them. The term Aristotle uses to describe this experience is "*katharsis*" which is the root of the modern term "catharsis": "the process of releasing strong feelings, for example, through plays or other artistic activities, as a way of providing relief from anger, mental pain, etc."[8]

With this in mind, it seems clear how Aristotle might explain why we listen to sad country music. Someone who has recently experienced a breakup, for instance, might be afflicted with painful feelings, such as regret or loss, which they wish to purge or remove from themselves. Unfortunately, try as we may, we can't simply change the way we feel through sheer force of will; we can't just *choose* to remove those unwanted emotions. But, if we listen to just the right, mournful country song (such as Hank Williams's "Wedding Bells,"[9] in which the singer learns of the impending nuptials of a former love he had previously intended to marry or Dolly Parton's "I Will Always Love You"[10] about someone expressing their affection for their partner despite the fact that they know they must let them go) we may be able to purge those emotions from our soul (or mind, or body). At the risk of using a crude metaphor, anyone who has "had a good cry" brought on by this type of music will likely tell you that there can be something pleasurable about the experience which is comparable to the pleasurable feeling we might get after expelling something unwanted from the body by vomiting (making a sad country song analogous to a spoonful of ipecac syrup).

So, Aristotle offers us an interesting (if not reasonable) account of why we are drawn to the sorrowful side of country music: by having a second-hand experience of the sadness found in certain country songs, we can expel those same feelings that lurk deep within us.

Transformative Beauty

A second potential explanation of the mystery of why we enjoy depressing country songs finds its origin in an essay from the Scottish modern philosopher David Hume. Long after Aristotle explored the topic of pleasure derived from tragedy in the *Poetics*, Hume raised more or less this same issue: why do audiences enjoy experiencing through art that which would otherwise be thought of as horrible, unpleasant things? In "Of Tragedy," published in 1757, Hume points out that

> It seems an unaccountable pleasure which the spectators of a well-written tragedy receive from sorrow, terror, anxiety, and other passions, that are in themselves disagreeable and uneasy ... [these spectators are] pleased in proportion as they are afflicted, and never are so happy as when they employ tears,

sobs, and cries to give vent to their sorrow, and relieve their heart, swoln with the tenderest sympathy and compassion … [and yet it] is certain that the same object of distress, which pleases in a tragedy, were it really set before us, would give the most unfeigned uneasiness.[11]

Put differently, we have no desire to watch some of the scenes in tragedies like *Oedipus the King* unfold in real life. It would be truly horrifying to watch someone *actually* hang or blind themselves. However, for whatever reason, when these types of events are displayed before us in an artistic medium, they bring us pleasure or at least enjoyment.[12] Again, it is only natural to wonder how we might account for this.

Initially, it appears as if Hume's answer will essentially be no different than Aristotle's as Hume describes spectators giving "vent to their sorrow" and being able to "relieve their heart." However, Hume's explanation is at least somewhat unique. According to Hume, negative feelings, emotions, or "passions" can be converted into positive feelings when they're expressed through beautiful or artful displays. As Hume puts it,

The impulse of vehemence, arising from sorrow, compassion, indignation, receives a new direction from the sentiments of beauty. The latter, being the predominant emotion, seizes the whole mind, and convert the former into themselves, at least tincture them so strongly as totally to alter their nature. And, the soul, being, at the same time, rouzed by passion, and charmed by eloquence, feels on the whole a strong movement, which is altogether delightful.[13]

In other words, when audiences experience an artful display of tragedy, they are moved in two distinct ways. The predominant movement is caused by the positive feelings of appreciating the beauty of the artful display. The subordinate movement is caused by the negative feelings that come from the more unpleasant aspects of the dramatized tragedy. However, the mixing of these two movements (as made inevitable by a beautiful display of tragedy) forces the subordinate movement to be overtaken by the predominant movement.

This overtaking doesn't merely mask or hide the negative feelings of the subordinate movement; it actually transforms them into positive feelings. And, as it causes us to be "rouzed by passion" and "charmed by eloquence," we find this conversion process to be "altogether delightful." The inclusion of intensely negative emotions isn't a bug; it's a feature. As Hume points out, should the same beautiful work be paired with something mundane (as opposed to something tragic), we would find the whole display odd and unworthy of our attention. It is the intermingling of the beautiful with the macabre that has an intensifying effect (through the transformation of the macabre into something beautiful) that truly makes for enjoyable, satisfying art.

To illustrate this, Hume offers a number of examples, citing Shakespeare's *Othello* in the process. However, had he been writing in the U.S. in the 21st century as opposed to 18th-century Scotland, he could have just as easily used any number of country songs. For instance, consider Kris Kristofferson's "Sunday Mornin' Comin' Down,"[14] a ballad with a subdued melody, punctuated by backing vocal harmonies at the chorus. The song's leisurely pace and organ track almost make it sound like an old spiritual, perhaps conveying the gospel message. But this is not what the song is about; it's about a man suffering through a hangover as he wanders the streets of his town. As he passes a number of folks along his way with something productive or meaningful to do with their Sunday morning, he is overcome with loneliness and wishes (to the Lord) that he were stoned.

In the listener, the predominant movement is caused by the appeal of the loveliness of the tune itself and perhaps the cleverness of the rhyming structure of the lyrics. The subordinate movement is brought on by the sorrow that we feel at the actual content of those lyrics. It is the combination and juxtaposition of those two things that convert the subordinate movement into something positive and make the whole experience of listening to the song more intense and pleasurable.

Admittedly, Hume's theory may leave some things to be desired. For instance, it is not at all obvious (and Hume does not really explain) exactly *how* the negative feelings are "converted" into positive feelings. Relatedly, while we may feel negative emotions more viscerally when they are conveyed through an artful medium, some may find it a stretch to say that they are transformed into anything positive. It is the wallowing in *negative* things like loneliness, heartache, and despair that so many listeners (for whatever reason) seem to enjoy.

Nevertheless, there *is* something here. It does seem as if there is an intensifying effect born out by the mixing of the beauty of an artful piece of music and the sorrow of its subject matter. Had Kristofferson used the music of "Sunday Mornin' Comin' Down" to recount something more pedestrian, such as the tale of a man simply picking up donuts on his way to church, the song might not be as enjoyable despite retaining the part of it which is thought to be positive.

Friends in Low Places

According to Aristotle's account of tragedy, we may be drawn to sad country songs because listening to them allows us to purge our souls of the same negative emotions contained in those songs. According to the theory proposed by David Hume, the reason could be somewhat different;

we listen to sad country songs not in order to purge negative feelings but because the beauty of the songs in question can convert negative feelings into positive feelings and because this process makes the whole experience of listening to the song more enjoyable overall.

However, with all of this in mind, let's take a look at one final potential explanation for the draw that the mournful side of country music seems to have on us. Contemporary philosophers Mario Attie-Picker, Tara Venkatesan, George E. Newman, and Joshua Knobe have proposed (what we might call) a relational theory of the value of sad music. According to Knobe et al.,

> the value of sad music resides in the connection it creates through the expression of sadness and other complex emotions. The musical expression of emotion gives rise to an experience of connection that is hard to articulate but easy to recognize … and it is an experience we can understand by analogy to that present in conversations.[15]

This is to say that the value of sad music generally resides in its ability to make connections between the performer and audience, which may be relevantly similar to the type of connection two people can experience by conversing with one another about something important to them.

With little doubt, one of the more important aspects of a well-lived, happy life (at least for most of us) is having deep, meaningful connections with other people. And, at the risk of stating the obvious, one method for cultivating these types of relationships with those other people is by *talking to them*. Because of this, it should be of little surprise that we find pleasure in those modest but significant interactions which allow us to make or sustain such connections.

Of course, not all conversations are equal in this regard. Small talk (e.g., chatting about the weather or traffic, inane observations about work, etc.) is the elevator music of conversation. It's fine in small doses here and there. But if these were the only types of conversations we had, our lives would be truly pitiful. The conversations in which we find true connection, and that (as a result) we often find most pleasurable, are those which are about something meaningful.[16] If I share a sad story from my life, and my conversation partner empathizes by sharing a similar tale of woe from hers, the resulting connection can be literally therapeutic (and thus, on some substantive level, enjoyable).

Knobe et al. hypothesize that we experience something similar when we listen to sad music, which (for our purposes) would, of course, explain why we are drawn to sad country songs. In Charley Pride's "Where Do I Put Her Memory,"[17] the singer is going through the regrettable but necessary process of removing from his life all of the things left behind by a recently lost love. However, the one thing he can find no place for, the thing that can't simply be stored away, he laments, is the *memory* of his former love. When we listen to a song such as this, we feel a connection to the artist who is, in a way, opening up about his deep, intimate feelings. And the connection we experience is likely only bolstered as we reflect on the times in our lives when we've gone through something similar, when we've taken every step we can to turn the page after a loss, but we are unable to dispose of one last thing that still burdens us: the memory of that which we have lost.

If the analogy between the connection we experience in conversation and the connection we seem to experience as the audience of musical artists is apt, enjoying sad country songs is exactly what we should expect. Just as we can feel a stronger sense of connection when in conversation about issues of deep importance to us (which often enough results in a more pleasurable experience), it is only natural that we are drawn to songs with weighty, personal themes. Conversely, we wouldn't expect to be drawn as strongly to songs with lyrics about trite or inconsequential matters.[18]

Of course, there is an obvious objection here. Unlike conversations, listening to sad music is typically a one-way street. The artist may be able to (in some sense) unload their emotions on the listener, but the listener is rarely (if ever) in a position to reciprocate. And, unless the audience is listening live in a small, intimate venue, they are isolated and detached from the artist in a way that we aren't typically isolated or detached from our conversation partners. That said, it could be argued that the analogy mustn't be stretched so far to account for this fact in order for it to explain the draw of sad music. Even if the experience of listening to sad country songs isn't idealized in regard to building connections as it might be in a conversation between two close friends sitting face-to-face, listeners of sad music may still be able to benefit from the same *type* of (feeling of) connection as close conversation partners enjoy. And this may be additionally supported by the phenomenon that we can achieve this sort of feeling of connection by simply reading someone's diary or personal account of something significant to them such as their experience of lost love (which might otherwise be communicated through a sad country song).[19]

A Crestfallen Crescendo

We began this essay with something of a mystery: why is it that we are drawn to sad country songs? Why do we enjoy wallowing in music that seems to make us feel (or a least focus our attention on) emotions that we seem to otherwise want to avoid? However, as we can see, there is no shortage of potential explanations. Sad country songs seem to have a cathartic quality to them. The combination of a beautiful song and a mournful theme may have an intensifying effect on our overall enjoyment of the song. And listening to sad country songs may deliver us a therapeutic sense of connection not unlike the connection we feel in meaningful conversations.

Admittedly, it would be difficult to adjudicate this matter more thoroughly. Which of these explanations is actually correct? It's hard to say; they all seem to have their own intuitive appeal. Beyond this, it's not at all obvious that (or at what points) these theories conflict with one another. Perhaps sad country songs could (for instance) allow us to purge negative emotions from our soul while at the same time delivering us a mode for connecting with others which is enjoyable in its own right. Whatever the case, this may be something to reflect on the next time you are listening to your favorite mournful country ballad. With that in mind, let's do what we alluded to toward the start of this essay: open up a cold one, put on our favorite sad country tune, and have a good cry.

NOTES

1. Cochran, Hank; Harlan, Howard. 1961. "I Fall to Pieces." *Showcase.* Cline, Patsy (rec. artist). Bradley, Owen (prod.) Decca Records.

2. Williams, Hank. 1949. "I'm So Lonesome I Could Cry." B-side to "My Bucket's Got a Hole in It." Williams, Clarence (prod.) MGM Records.

3. Autry, Gene; Long, Jimmy. 1932. "That Silver Haired Daddy of Mine." Long, Jimmy (prod.) Perfect Records.

4. Scott, Hillary; Kelley, Charles; Haywood, Dave; Kear, Josh. 2009. "Need You Now." *Need You Now.* Lady Antebellum (rec. artist). Worley, Paul; Lady Antebellum (prod.) Capitol Records Nashville.

5. Chagnon, Marcel Francois; Mullins, Tony. 2006. "Backwards." *Me and My Gang.* Rascal Flatts (rec. artist). Lyric Street Records.

6. This (type of) question has been raised in regard to a wide variety of pieces of popular culture, including a good deal of popular music. See Littmann, Greg. 2022. "The Filth and the Fury." *Punk Rock and Philosophy: Research and Destroy.* Heter, Joshua, and Greene, Richard (eds.) Carus Books; Lott, Micah. 2009. "Why Such Sad Songs?" *Radiohead and Philosophy: Fitter, Happier, More Deductive.* Forbes, Brandon W., and Reisch, George A. (eds.) Open Court.

7. Aristotle. 1997. *Poetics.* Heath, Malcolm (trans.) Penguin Classics.

8. Oxford University Press. 2024. "Catharsis." *Oxford Living Dictionary.*

9. Boone, Claude. 1949. "Wedding Bells." Hank Williams with His Drifting Cowboys (rec. artist). Rose, Fred (prod.) MGM Records.

10. Parton, Dolly. 1974. "I Will Always Love You." *Jolene.* Ferguson, Bob (prod.) RCA Records.

11. Hume, David. 2001. "Of Tragedy." *Four Dissertations and Essays on Suicide and the Immortality of the Soul.* St. Augustine's Press.

12. Littmann.

13. Hume.

14. Kristofferson, Kris. 1969. "Sunday Mornin' Comin' Down." *Have a Little Talk with Myself.* Ray Stevens (rec. artist). Monument Records.

15. Attie-Picker, Mario; Venkatesan, Tara; Newman, George E.; Knobe, Joshua. 2024. "On the Value of Sad Music." *The Journal of Aesthetic Education*. University of Illinois Press, 46–65.

16. *Ibid.*

17. Weatherly, Jim. 1979. "Where Do I Put Her Memory." *Burgers and Fries/When I Stop Leaving (I'll Be Gone)*. Pride, Charley (rec. artist). RCA Records.

18. Knobe et al.

19. *Ibid.*

Why Do We Drink, Smoke, and Cheat on Those We Love Most?

ALEXANDER CRIST

While country music often affirms certain values that are thought to lead to a life of happiness or living well (e.g., God, family, and country), some of the most moving and appealing country songs lament a life of trouble, vice, rowdiness, or uncontrollable desire. This represents what Ken Burns, in his PBS documentary on country music, refers to as the "Saturday night/Sunday morning" juxtaposition that has been at the root of country music since at least the Carter Family and Jimmie Rodgers.[1]

Though this phenomenon is often depicted in the Christian context of the sin of Saturday night debauchery and the repentance or righteousness of a Sunday morning church service, it can likewise be cast in more secular terms; in order to properly understand a life of virtue and flourishing, one also needs to know about a life of vice and corruption. Perhaps the most well-known philosopher in the Western tradition to articulate such a robust notion of virtue, vice, and what it ultimately means to live a good life is the Ancient Greek philosopher Aristotle. Aristotle considers a good life to be one of virtue, which means cultivating various character traits that make a person an excellent human being (e.g., courage, temperance, patience, etc.). Yet Aristotle likewise recognizes that any discussion of human flourishing must include an explanation of someone in the opposite condition, that is, someone with a vicious character.

While there are many vices which correspond to the many virtues in his account, Aristotle spends a substantial amount of time focusing on the vice of intemperance. The person with an intemperate character is someone who has cultivated bad habits over a long period of time, especially as it relates to bodily pleasures and appetites. However, Aristotle thinks that some people are simply incontinent (*akratic*). This is to say, it's not that they developed bad habits over time, but that they are weak-willed or overwhelmed by certain appetites. While the intemperate person is more or less responsible for his or her vicious lifestyle, the incontinent person seems to have no say in the matter.

Aristotle's distinction between intemperance and incontinence offers us a helpful way of thinking about the tradition of country music that often represents the difficult and tumultuous lives of those who are not living well. When we listen to songs about not living the good life, what is the nature of the singer's unhappiness? Has the singer chosen a life of bad habits, or were the circumstances always out of his or her hands? This distinction indicates two different sub-genres of country music: the intemperate and the incontinent. Two classic country music hits from the 1970s represent these genres well: Hank Williams, Jr.'s, "Family Tradition"[2] and "The Midnight Oil"[3] by Barbara Mandrell. Intemperate songs like "Family Tradition" show us that living an unhappy life is often something that we affirm and justify to ourselves and others, while incontinent songs like "The Midnight Oil" show us that sometimes we are not in control of the unhappy life we might be living.

Aristotle on Happiness, Virtue, and Vice

In order to understand the role of intemperance and incontinence in "Family Tradition" and "The Midnight Oil," it's important to first understand some of the basics of Aristotle's account of happiness, virtue, and vice in his text the *Nicomachean Ethics*.[4] His explicit focus in this text is to investigate the highest good, end, or purpose of all human activity. This is what he calls *eudaimonia*: happiness, living well, doing well, or flourishing. Now, general notions of happiness, such as pleasure, contentment, or satisfaction, are part and parcel of popular country music. Think, for instance, of "Pontoon"[5] by Little Big Town or "Toes"[6] by the Zac Brown Band, both of which extol a life of rest, relaxation, and a good amount of wholesome beer drinking with friends. Another common notion of happiness which appears in country music is one of achieving material and professional success. We hear this in songs such as "Rhinestone Cowboy"[7] by Glen Campbell or "I'm Gonna Be Somebody"[8] by Travis Tritt. Both songs elevate notions of hard work, sacrifice, and determination in order to make it to the top and to accomplish one's goals.

While Aristotle does not consider these notions of happiness to be inherently immoral or unworthy of pursuit (to a certain degree), he does not take them to constitute genuine happiness. For Aristotle, the highest good of human activity requires us to ground all of our pursuits in an appropriate disposition and moral education, namely, in the virtues. In straightforward terms, a virtue is that which makes something an excellent version of whatever it is. What Aristotle calls moral virtues or virtues of character, such as courage, temperance, and patience, make us excellent at being a human being. Such virtues are first a matter of habituation and cultivation. We must ingrain these virtues into our character through practice, training, and the repetition of the exercise of the virtue.

The only way we can become brave or courageous is by performing many acts of bravery over and over again. For Aristotle, we must also begin this kind of virtuous education at an early age: "It is not unimportant, then, to acquire one sort of habit or another, right from our youth. On the contrary, it is very important, indeed all-important."[9] The necessity of this kind of early moral education is another common theme in country music. In Merle Haggard's "Mama Tried,"[10] the singer reflects from his prison cell on his own failure to heed his mother's advice and habituate himself properly at a young age. In his song "I Washed My Hands in Muddy Water,"[11] Stonewall Jackson describes his trouble with the law as a result of falling in with "bad companions" at an early age, which cultivated vice instead of virtue. Both of these songs also raise some interesting questions about whether some individuals are simply immune to a virtuous education.

For instance, "Mama Tried" indicates that a virtuous upbringing for the singer was seemingly impossible. While he displays a remarkable honesty in accepting his own responsibility for his failure, all of the positive influences of church and family values had no effect on his rebellious spirit. In "I Washed My Hands in Muddy Water," the singer's father, locked away in jail, advises his son to "keep his hands clean," and it appears that the singer genuinely tries to heed this advice. However, the singer also appears easily corrupted by the world he grows up in. Part of what makes this early virtuous education difficult to accomplish involves the delicate balance of learning how to hit the mean or intermediate point between the two extremes of deficiency and excess.

A deficiency related to courage, for instance, would be cowardice, and an excess related to courage would be rashness or overzealousness. As Aristotle points out, the virtuous (and happy) person is then disposed toward feelings, emotions, pleasures, and pain "at the right times, about the right things, toward the right people, for the right end, and in the right way."[12] The mark of vice or a vicious character is someone who demonstrates a deficiency or excess in relation to this mean, and as Aristotle tells us, it is all too easy for us to miss the mark.

Intemperance and Incontinence (Akrasia)

The virtue of character which corresponds to how we are disposed toward bodily pleasures and appetites is the virtue of temperance. Temperate people can enjoy such pleasures in the right way, at the right time, and to the right degree. The intemperate person is then someone who enjoys such pleasures to excess.[13] For Aristotle, such a person engages in eating, drinking, and sexual pleasures to such a degree that it undermines their ability to live well. Furthermore, the intemperate person is someone who considers their decisions and actions to be correct and proper. As Aristotle tells us, "the intemperate person acts on decision when he is led on, since he thinks it is right in every case to pursue the pleasant thing at hand."[14] When the intemperate person walks into a bar, his character has developed in such a way that he desires to drink to excess. In this way, his character determines his desire, which determines the particular end to be pursued. In this case, drunkenness is the desired end, and the intemperate person exercises his rational faculty to deliberate about the best means toward this particular end. This person's decision is precisely the conclusion of his deliberation. For instance, after deliberation, this person decides to drink domestic bottles all night because they are on the happy hour special, and he only has a limited amount of cash to spend that night. Such an individual deliberates on the best way to get drunk but does not deliberate about the desired goal of drunkenness as the right and proper aim to pursue. For this reason, Aristotle considers the intemperate person to be incorrigible and someone who has no regrets about achieving his intemperate ends.

The incontinent person, on the other hand, is full of regret precisely because he acts against his rational deliberation and decisions. The incontinent person may have a virtuous desire and an end he wishes to pursue, he may deliberate well, and he may come to a correct decision about the virtuous mean as it relates to bodily pleasures and appetites. However, for whatever reason, the incontinent person is overwhelmed by these very pleasures or appetites, and he acts against his decision. The incontinent person walks into the bar and decides that two beers is the correct amount for him to enjoy himself, be convivial, support his local dive bar, and engage in merriment and friendship with those around him. However, the incontinent person is overwhelmed by the pleasure he experiences in his first few sips of beer and cannot help but continue to drink to excess. The incontinent person knows this is incorrect and not a virtuous end to pursue, but he is seemingly unable to do otherwise. The incontinent person then lives a life of regret, as he is torn between what he knows to be the correct action to take in order to live well and the fact that he simply cannot will himself to act in this way.

Aristotle's distinction between the intemperate and incontinent person offers a clarifying perspective on the country songs we enjoy for the very reason that they narrate an unhappy life of regret and the perpetual struggle with our baser passions and appetites. Yet when we listen to these songs, are we hearing the story of someone who has developed a vicious and intemperate character and who vouches for the intemperate aims that he achieves, or are we hearing the story of someone who wishes he could do the right thing, but simply cannot help himself? Are we listening to a story that justifies indulgence and the excess of pleasure, or a story that cries out with the pain of endless regret?

"Family Tradition" and Intemperance

For Hank Williams, Jr., carrying on the family tradition is more than just being a country music singer-songwriter. While Hank Williams, Sr., is on the short list of the most influential country artists of all time, he is just as well known for his struggles with alcohol and drug addiction, as well as dying at the age of just 29. For many years after his father's death, Hank Jr. made a career out of playing covers of his father's music until he decided to break out on his own. Yet along with this turn in musical style came a turn toward his own struggles with alcohol and drug use. His country hit from 1979, "Family Tradition," plays on the tense relationship he has with the influence of his father and functions as a response to those who disapprove of his change in musical and lifestyle direction.

This tension is what makes "Family Tradition" a perfect example of what we might call the "intemperate" genre of country music. The first and unmistakable quality of the song is Hank Jr.'s unrepentant and unapologetic tone. It's a song about drinking, smoking, and not giving a damn about what others think about it. He's sick and tired of the more clean-cut country music establishment criticizing him for what they consider to be a deviation from his father's legacy, as indicated by the repeated questioning throughout the song. They want to know why he drinks and smokes so much, and why he feels the need to actually live the intemperate life he describes in his music.

His response to this line of questioning is simply that it's a family tradition. What Hank Jr. inherited from his father is not just a collection of songs for him to cover, but the spirit of authenticity in one's music, namely, that one's music should be a manifestation of the life one lives. If Hank Jr. is going to sing about drinking and smoking, it's because he drinks and smokes. What's more, this is a life he has considered and a life he affirms. In responding to the naysayers in his song, it is clear that he has no regrets about the decisions he makes and the ends he pursues.

While there is a rebellious charm to "Family Tradition" that can stir the soul of any listener, it is undeniable that it's a song that likewise affirms an intemperate excess. It's one thing to engage in Bacchanalian revelry every once in a while during certain celebratory occasions, but intemperance implies that such occasions have become repetitive and habitual to the point that it has become ingrained in one's character. Intoxication has become the end that one deliberates about and pursues. For Aristotle, one of the reasons why intemperance is a vice and not a virtue is that instead of contributing to our well-being, it detracts from it. Hank Jr. even alludes to this toward the end of the song when he describes a visit to the doctor's office. He tells the doctor about his passion for women and whiskey, and how both of these things almost took his life several years ago. The doctor then asks him how he ended up in such a poor state, to which Hank Jr. replies that, once again, he is simply continuing a family tradition.

Simply by virtue of being in a doctor's office, having to explain how his life almost ended due to a life of excess indicates that such a lifestyle has impeded him in his ability to live well. Yet Hank Jr.'s response to the doctor is not one of regret or the moral concern of an incontinent person. There is an almost joyful and nostalgic tone in his voice as he explains to the doctor how he almost died due to his intemperate lifestyle. With his nonchalant response to the "Sawbones," he justifies his lifestyle with yet another reference to his family tradition.

The idea that he is carrying on this tradition even indicates that he is acting out of his own sense of duty, obligation, or responsibility. While Hank Jr. may be speaking in a tongue-in-cheek manner, the justification of "family tradition" for his life of excess is very much in line with the tradition he was brought up in, as his father and many other country artists lived a vicious and intemperate lifestyle. While Hank Jr. and others who affirm this version of family tradition might make great country music, it's much harder to make the claim that they are pursuing a life of happiness or flourishing.

"The Midnight Oil" and Incontinence

If "Family Tradition" affirms a life that does not lead to happiness, Barbara Mandrell's 1973 hit, "The Midnight Oil," is full of incontinent regret. Instead of drugs and alcohol, the singer is caught up in the stranglehold of infidelity as she lies to her presumed husband every night (while sleeping with another man). This is not a song in which the singer is asserting her independence or trying to escape an abusive relationship. There is no suggestion that her husband is likewise cheating on her or that she is attempting to break out of a loveless marriage. In fact, the refrain indicates just the opposite: "While I'm puttin' on my makeup, I'm puttin' on the one that really loves me."[15]

Unlike "Family Tradition," the singer does not offer any kind of justification for her actions and does not consider the aim of her desires to be noble. There is a powerful sense of self-awareness in this regard with the play on the phrase, "to put on," whereby the application of her makeup at the same time represents an act of deception toward someone who genuinely cares about her. This act of applying makeup provides a captivating internal/external image for the listener. Acting upon oneself is at the same time an act that affects the other in a profound way. What we do to ourselves, we do to another. In this case, the seemingly innocent act of putting on her makeup simultaneously indicates a moral transgression she commits against the one who loves her. This repeated image in the song's refrain turns into a symbol of conscious regret. She knows unequivocally that what she is doing is wrong and that her actions have the potential to cause great pain to someone very close to her.

This painful recognition speaks to the incontinent nature of the singer. She knows very well that going out again to cheat on her husband is not the best means toward the end of living a happy or flourishing life. What's more, she knows that she will continue to do so: "And tonight I'll cheat again and tomorrow I'll be sorry."[16] When we hear Mandrell sing these lines, her voice crescendos in a way that one would otherwise associate with a sense of triumph, but it is immediately understood to be a sorrowful cry of acquiescence to the fact that she is not in control: "God knows his dream would shatter if he knew the devil had me and won't set me free."[17] Notice here that she does not say that her husband's life would be ruined by finding out that she is cheating on him, but in finding out that she is cheating *and* that she cannot stop herself from doing so! While a reference to the devil here may not be literal, it is undoubtedly an expression of a lack of agency or strength of the will to overcome the passions. Happiness or living well is not a matter in this case of adjusting one's habits away from vice and toward virtue, as it might be with the intemperate person. No amount of practice or character (re)formation will change the narrator's predicament. At least in this situation, she is not sovereign over herself and is in the hands of seemingly external forces. To be released from this condition requires something beyond her own faculties.

Honesty and Self-Examination in Unhappy Country Songs

While there are some clear and important distinctions between intemperate and incontinent country songs, both genres prompt us to consider our own trials and tribulations with passionate desire and whether we are genuinely pursuing a life of *eudaimonia*. What makes a song like "Family Tradition" or "The Midnight Oil" a *great* country song is its capacity to speak to a universal truth about the human condition. For instance, questions related to the definition of happiness and whether we are living a happy life are questions that never have and never will go out of style.

Whether we have these conversations in the classroom, around the dinner table, or at the local dive bar, they often involve a discussion about how to navigate the internal struggle with passion, desire, and the excess of pleasure. This is why, I would argue, many of us continue to enjoy intemperate and incontinent country music songs. It's not necessarily because we want to affirm a life of intemperance or incontinence, but because they are conversation starters, whether that conversation is an internal dialogue with ourselves or one we have with others. They nudge us toward a crucial reflection about whether we are living well and to what degree we are actually in control of our own happiness.

Hank Williams, Jr., affirms an unhappy life of drinking and smoking, while Barbara Mandrell must wait for "the devil" to set her free from the chains of infidelity. There is a remarkable honesty in both songs which indicates why these philosophical conversations and reflections are often difficult or restricted to a certain degree. While it's one thing to discuss the nature of happiness on an abstract level, it's another thing entirely to engage in a sincere assessment of one's own actions and the kind of life one lives. What does it mean to live well? Are *you* living well? Country music calls all of us not only to consider these questions as a matter of intellectual curiosity but to engage them with an honest and uncompromising examination of our own lives. This, of course, is the old Socratic wisdom, that "the unexamined life is not worth living."[18]

NOTES

1. Burns, Ken. 2019. *Country Music: A Film by Ken Burns*. "Episode One." Public Broadcasting Service (PBS).

2. Williams, Hank, Jr. 1979. "Family Tradition." *Family Tradition*. Williams, Hank, Jr. (rec. artist). Bowen, Jimmy (prod.) Elektra/Curb Records.

3. Mandrell, Barbara. 1973. "The Midnight Oil." *The Midnight Oil*. Mandrell, Barbara (rec. artist). Sherrill, Billy (prod.) Columbia Records.

4. Aristotle. 2019. *Nicomachean Ethics*. Irwin, Terence (trans.) Hackett.

5. Little Big Town. 2012. "Pontoon." *Tornado*. Little Big Town (rec. artist). Joyce, Jay (prod.) Capitol Nashville.

6. Zac Brown Band. 2009. "Toes." *The Foundation*. Zac Brown Band (rec. artist). Brown, Zac, and Stegall, Keith (prod.) Atlantic/Home Grown/Big Picture.

7. Campbell, Glen. 1975. "Rhinestone Cowboy." *Rhinestone Cowboy*. Campbell, Glen (rec. artist). Lambert, Dennis and Potter, Brian (prod.) Capitol.

8. Tritt, Travis. 1990. "I'm Gonna Be Somebody." *Country Club*. Tritt, Travis (rec. artist). Brown, Gregg (prod.) Warner Bros. Nashville.

9. Aristotle, 1103b/23–26.

10. Haggard, Merle, and the Strangers. 1968. "Mama Tried." *Mama Tried*. Haggard, Merle (rec. artist). Nelson, Ken (prod.) Capitol.

11. Jackson, Stonewall. 1965. "I Washed My Hands in Muddy Water." *Trouble and Me*. Jackson, Stonewall (rec. artist). Law, Don and Jones, Frank (prod.) Columbia.

12. *Ibid.*, Aristotle, 1106b/21–23.

13. Aristotle thinks that individuals who are deficient in temperance "are not found very much" and he considers such a person to be "far from being human" (*Ibid.*, Aristotle, 1119a/7–11).

14. *Ibid.*, 1146b/23–25.

15. Mandrell.

16. *Ibid.*

17. *Ibid.*

18. Plato. 1997. "Apology." In *Plato: Complete Works*. Cooper, John M. (ed.) Grube, G.M.A. (trans.) Hackett. 38a.

What's Wrong with the Good Old Days?

Keith Dromm
and Heather Salter Dromm

"Take me back to yesterday," sing the Judds in their song "Grandpa (Tell Me 'Bout the Good Ol' Days)."[1] He can't literally take them back, but he can "paint" them a "picture" with his words about a time when things weren't so "crazy." What could they *do* with such a picture? They could look at it. It's pleasant to look at pictures we like, such as photos from family vacations. That could satisfy some of their feelings of nostalgia, and if the Judds were especially ambitious—and extremely nostalgic—they could try to recreate what they see in the picture. That could be difficult, but just looking at pictures of places you'd rather be is not entirely satisfying. That's a problem with nostalgia. It is a longing for something, but since that something can't be had—it is long gone or far away—it can't really be fulfilled.

Yet, we often become nostalgic, willingly so, and country music is notorious for making us feel that way. Country artists often sing about better days or better places, ones that are typically far away or in the past. But not only do they sing about nostalgia; their music *is* nostalgic. Country music originated from the vernacular music of the United States. It was discovered in the early part of the 20th century that people liked listening to this "old-timey" music, and they were willing to pay or listen to advertisements for the pleasure of doing so. Large numbers of people were migrating across America at the time. Southerners, especially, were moving in large numbers away from their homes.[2] This music likely reminded them of where they used to live and their earlier years.

But it didn't bring them back home. And there are other problems with nostalgia beyond the fact that it gives us longings which cannot be satisfied. In what follows, we'll discuss these very problems while we also consider some of the benefits of being nostalgic.

But First, What Is Nostalgia?

The word nostalgia was originally coined in 1688 by a Swiss medical student, Johannes Hofer. It combines the words for returning to one's native land (*nostos*) and pain (*algos*). He coined the term to refer to what was, at the time, regarded as a disease, one that had both physical and mental symptoms. It was believed to be caused by intense longing for a place, particularly one's home.[3] Hofer believed that persistent mental pictures, like the ones the Judds try to get Grandpa to help them create, provoked the sometimes debilitating symptoms of this extreme form of homesickness.[4] Patients suffered from sadness, sluggish heart rates, and poor digestion, and some were thought to have even died from nostalgia. Treatments, besides simply being sent home, included opium and leeches.[5] It reached epidemic status, particularly among soldiers, and even inspired cases of feigned nostalgia.[6]

The meaning of "nostalgia" has since expanded to include longing for a lost time, not just a place, as part of its meaning. In fact, it is now more commonly associated with longing for some time in the past, though that time might also be associated with a particular place. We also no longer consider it a disease. Many consider it benign; some even think it's beneficial.[7] For country artists, it could be a mark of authenticity. A country artist who lived in or sang about the joys of living in the big city, or whose songs were about life in an optimistic future, would not be very popular. Such an artist might not even be considered to be *genuinely* country. Yet, singing about wanting to return to the small town or country farm that one grew up on seems like a theme almost unique to country music.

The nostalgia of country music is about both time and place. Its name refers to the place. Rural and small-town America is consistently portrayed in country music as superior aesthetically, morally, and in other ways, to urban America (as well as every other part of the world). In "Chicken Fried," the Zac Brown Band sings about a humble home filled with love where they could enjoy the simple life and not be concerned with expensive cars and clothing.[8] Darius Rucker, in "Wagon Wheel," longs for his Southern home, which he associates with love and nurture, singing, "Rock me, mama, like a southbound train."[9] In "Meanwhile Back at Mama's," Louisiana native Tim McGraw, accompanied by his wife, Mississippi native Faith Hill, sings about living in a big city and missing the slow pace of small-town life and "catching a Southern breeze." As in the Judds' song, McGraw and Hill sing that the modern big city is a "world gone crazy" and make plans to buy a "three-acre lot" back home near Mama's house.[10]

But country artists also express nostalgia for a time. The Judds want Grandpa to tell them about some time in the past, apparently a time they can't recall, or before they were born, but a time witnessed by their grandfather (and great-grandfather, or father and grandfather; it's not clear since a mother-daughter duo is doing the singing). The country artists are often not specific about what time. In his song, "Are the Good Times Really Over (I Wish a Buck Was Still Silver),"[11] Merle Haggard does not pinpoint an exact time for these alleged good times, only that they were "back before Elvis and before the Vietnam War came along" and when "a girl could still cook."

Beyond nostalgia in regard to time and place, there are some other distinctions we can draw, and these apply to both of those types. First, nostalgia can be *personal*. One could be longing for a time in their past or a place they lived. Alternatively, it can be *historical*.[12] Someone could long for a time in the past, but it need not be their own past, and it could even be a time before they were born. The 1950s are often a target of nostalgia. Most of the people today getting nostalgic about the '50s weren't even born yet. Both types of nostalgia are caused by the perception that something has been lost, but in the case of historical nostalgia, it is the loss of the opportunity to live in a certain time. Country artists sing about both types. An example is Tim McGraw, in "Back When," singing about listening to his favorite records and radio stations when he was younger but also lamenting the loss of "the old and dated way of life."[13]

Nostalgia is about loss, but we can be nostalgic about things that we haven't lost yet. This has been called *anticipatory* nostalgia.[14] It is caused by the anticipation of a future loss. It has been described as the "premature missing of what is still present."[15] It is not merely anticipating that loss, but actually feeling it now.[16] Some country artists have sung about it. In their song "The Good Old Days," The Abrams sing about making memories last and living in the moment because one day in the future, "we're gonna say these were the good old days."[17] Tim McGraw warns in "Louisiana" that "the moment you're living right now / Will soon become your past."[18]

Some believe that the past about which they are nostalgic is not lost forever. Of course, we cannot go back in time, but maybe we could make things like they used to be. Svetlana Boym calls this "restorative nostalgia."[19] She associates it with some recent religious and political movements. We can also find it in country music. Merle Haggard answers the question in his song's title, "Are the Good Times Really Over?" and tells us that they "ain't over for good." Which should come as a relief, because the alternative is us "rolling downhill like a snowball headed for Hell," according to Haggard. Yet, restoring his good times does not seem like an easy task (or a desirable one, as we will soon discuss); it's much more difficult than giving McGraw and Hill their "three-acre lot." "Reflective nostalgia" is content with just thinking about the past, even if doing so does make one sad; it is either opposed to or ambivalent about restoring the past. The Judds only talk about pictures, not about resurrecting the "good old days." They may regret their loss, but they're not directly calling for a return, through restoration, of that "prelapsarian moment"[20] before everything went "crazy."

But besides all these distinctions, what more precisely is nostalgia? We've talked about it as a feeling, also as a longing. We think it is best characterized as an emotion. As with any emotion, there is a cognitive component to it, in particular, a belief.[21] For comparison, when we experience fear, we are not just feeling something; we are also believing something, in particular, that we are being threatened by something (e.g., the sheriff, an angry partner, damnation, etc.). Similarly, when you are feeling nostalgic, you don't merely have this sensation of longing for the past or some place; you are also believing that that time or place is superior to the one you occupy now. The Judds are nostalgic about the past because they believe it was the "good old days," implying that the current days are not so good.[22] Merle Haggard is more explicit, citing all the reasons why he thinks the past is better than the present. It is that belief that causes most of the problems with nostalgia.

What's Wrong with Nostalgia?

We think there are at least three types of problems with nostalgia that are well illustrated by country music. Since nostalgia is so prevalent in country music, as we have seen, these are also problems with country music. We distinguish between epistemic, political, and aesthetic problems.

As to the epistemic problems, nostalgia often gets the past wrong. We tend to romanticize the past. We are particularly prone to do this if we are dissatisfied with our present. That can make the past seem to us even better than it really was. Since nostalgia is an emotion, consisting partly of a longing for the past, our perception of it can be skewed, as when hunger can make something otherwise unappetizing seem like it would be delicious.

As we saw previously, for contemporary America generally, including country music, the '50s (before Elvis and Vietnam), are the frequent target of nostalgia. But our nostalgia exaggerates the positive aspects of that time and ignores a lot that was wrong with it. For example, while the Judds want to be reminded of a time in which couples stood with one another no matter what troubles come their way, the 1950s were not that time. As Stephanie Coontz reports in her book *The Way We Never Were: American*

Families and the Nostalgia Trap, "Between one-quarter and one-third of the marriages contracted in the 1950s eventually ended in divorce," and "2 million legally married people lived apart from each other."[23] While that is slightly below today's divorce rate, there were many couples at the time who married and remained married, even if unhappy, to avoid being labeled psychologically unsound or socially deviant.[24] Many women needed to stay in these marriages because there was no other way for them to support themselves and their children. And in order to stay in these loveless marriages, many had to conform to roles that they felt were constraining. They "could still cook," as Merle Haggard says, but many would have been happier doing other things instead.

There were others whose freedom was curtailed; so many, in fact, that it may be a characteristic of the time. Jim Crow laws were still prevalent in the South, which denied African Americans access to many businesses, schools, and other public facilities. They were also still denied the right to vote in most of the South, through poll taxes, literacy tests, and just outright intimidation. And they were being killed. Lynchings were still happening.[25] Emmett Till, fourteen years old, was murdered in 1955 for allegedly flirting with a white woman. Nostalgia can induce amnesia in us about the less savory aspects of the past, but we shouldn't let it. Perhaps Jason Aldean did not have in mind lynchings when he recorded "Try That in a Small Town," but the song is a clear endorsement of vigilante justice.[26] However, when he filmed the video for it in front of the courthouse where lynchings of black citizens used to occur, he implicitly endorsed that specific kind of vigilante justice, even if that was not his intention. Relatedly, when people express historical and restorative justice by chanting things like "Make America Great Again," they should be specific about what parts of the past they want to bring back, as well as what past. But if they, or the Judds and others, are looking even further back than the 1950s, things don't get better in the aspects we've been discussing; in fact, they get worse.

When it comes to the place that country music is nostalgic about, rural or small-town America, it can be factually wrong about it, or just ignore its problems. There are familiar problems such as the lack of cultural, economic, and educational opportunities. But some lesser-known ones are that substance abuse is an epidemic in many rural parts of America.[27] Gun deaths are higher in rural parts of America than elsewhere, including big cities.[28] You're also just more likely to die violently, in any number of ways, in the country than elsewhere.[29] And agriculture, the biggest and, in many places, the only industry in rural America, is one of the worst polluters. For example, more people die from emissions from animal agriculture than from coal power plants.[30]

We've been focusing mostly on what country artists sing about, but as we have mentioned, the sound of country music is nostalgic. Its historical roots are in the efforts to preserve some of the nation's oldest musical songs and sounds. The culture of country music remains inclined toward conserving its sound. While country music listeners, like everyone else, enjoy music that sounds fresh and new, it at the same time needs to sound familiar. Artists in other genres do not have to worry as much about achieving that balance. They can experiment much more. Innovation in country music consists most often of reintroducing older sounds and styles of itself. So, country music's nostalgia may be inhibiting its development.

Nostalgia can have an analogous impact on politics. Maybe some things were better in the past, and we should bring them back. But we should not let nostalgia guide our political decisions, in either its restorative or reflective modes. The latter can keep us disengaged from the present. The former can lead us to bring back things that were not good about the past, like oppressive forms of social organization. Nostalgia blinds us to the past's negative aspects. It makes us tell stories about the past that exaggerate their positive aspects. But much of the past was not very good, for most people. Our politics should be guided by ideals, and even other emotions like hope, compassion, and so on, but not by myths.

Nostalgia: Not All Bad

While there are those types of problems with country music's nostalgia, they also point toward the promise of country music. Country should not abandon nostalgia, but refine it and redirect it.

There are some epistemic benefits to preserving old sounds. They enhance our understanding of music, and that understanding is best acquired by listening to recent performances, especially live ones, rather than old, sometimes inferior, recordings. Performing that music also encourages interest in it, without which there would not be that epistemic benefit. And to make the point about the aesthetic benefit here, those old sounds just *sound* good. So, if nostalgia motivates us to preserve music, then nostalgia can be epistemically and aesthetically beneficial. Also, rather than always limiting innovation, attention to the past can give artists direction. It tells them what's been done, what's been successful and not so successful, what hasn't been tried yet, and so on.

Historical nostalgia can foster community. As Lori Holyfield and her fellow researchers put it, "nostalgia [has] the potential to create positive affect and solidarity for community in the present" and "music and song are the ideal conduit for nostalgia."[31] Communities are good. They protect us from various dangers and help us recover from disasters. They allow us to pursue goals collectively, including goals that would be out of reach if we acted individually. For example, they help us remember things by preserving them in books, monuments, and songs. But as we've seen, songs can get the past wrong. Yet, while they may be unreliable sources of knowledge about the past, our nostalgia for the music can bring us together, helping us to form and maintain communities.

But bringing people together is good only so far as the people are good. Bringing together members of the Klan, for instance, is not good. And nostalgia is often associated with authoritarian political movements, whose political models are usually derived from some mythical past. So, communities are not always good, and they are never absolutely good, because their members can be bad or have bad ideas. But even if the people brought together are good, we don't want them excluding other people from their community for arbitrary reasons (which would actually detract from their goodness).

Country music has been accused of being exclusionary. Specifically, it's been said that country music is too white. That fact belies the history of country music, whose early musical influences span the entire spectrum of American races and identities. It emerged not only from folk songs from the British Isles but just as much from blues and gospel music made by African Americans, as well as Mexican and indigenous musical traditions, among other influences.[32] Its instruments, which have lent it its characteristic sound, have similarly diverse origins; for example, the banjo is from Africa and the steel guitar is from Hawaii. Artists that represent more of this history are increasing in prominence and popularity, including Darius Rucker, Vincent Neil Emerson, Rhiannon Giddens, and Charley Crockett. Yet, prior to them were Charley Pride, Linda Martell, Herb Jeffries (the first black singing cowboy), and several more that we have a chance to rediscover. There is an opportunity for country music to create a broader community, one that looks as American as it sounds.[33]

A Final Reflection

There probably wouldn't be country music were it not for nostalgia. That emotion motivated the efforts that made the country sound, and it gave material to its artists to sing about. But their lyrics are probably not historically accurate, nostalgia might be stifling musical innovation, and the past is not a good source for political ideas or social models. Still, those old sounds are very much worth preserving; the past can inspire and direct musical innovation, and communities (of the right sort and made of the right people) are good things. Country music is really music for a large and diverse community. Perhaps if country artists stop singing about things like vigilante justice, then they can create that community.

Notes

1. O'Hara, Jamie. 1986. "Grandpa (Tell Me 'bout the Good Ol' Days)." *Rockin' with the Rhythm*. The Judds (rec. artist). Maher, Brent (prod.) RCA Records.

2. Gregory, James. 2022. "Mapping the Southern Diaspora Part II." *America's Great Migrations Project.*

3. Landwehr, Achim. 2018. "Nostalgia and the Turbulence of Times." *History and Theory*. Wesleyan University, 251–268.

4. *Ibid.*, 254.

5. Boym, Svetlana. 2007. "Nostalgia and Its Discontents." *Hedgehog Review*. University of Virginia, 7–18.

6. *Ibid.*, 8.

7. See Juhl, Jacob, et al. 2010. "Fighting the Future with the Past: Nostalgia Buffers Existential Threat." *Journal of Research in Personality*. Elsevier, 309–314, and Abeyta, Andrew, et al. 2020. "Combating Loneliness with Nostalgia: Nostalgic Feelings Attenuate Negative Thoughts and Motivations Associated with Loneliness." *Frontiers in Psychology*. Frontiers, 1–15.

8. Brown, Zac; Durrette, Wyatt. 2008. "Chicken Fried." *The Foundation*. Zac Brown Band (rec. artist). Brown, Zac; and Stegall, Keith (prod.) Atlantic Records.

9. Dylan, Bob; Secor, Ketch. 2013. "Wagon Wheel." *True Believers*. Darius Rucker (rec. artist). Rogers, Frank (prod.) Capitol Records Nashville.

10. Douglas, Tom; Johnston, Jaren; Steele, Jeffrey. 2014. "Meanwhile Back at Mama's." *Sundown Heaven Town*. McGraw, Tim; Hill, Faith (rec. artists). Gallimore, Byron (prod.) Big Machine Records.

11. Haggard, Merle. 1982. "Are the Good Times Really Over (I Wish a Buck Was Still Silver)." B-side to "I Always Get Lucky with You." Epic Records.

12. Bäckryd, Emmanuel. 2023. "The Benefits and Risks of Nostalgia: Analysis of a Fictional Case with Special Reference to Ethical and Existential Issues." *Philosophy, Ethics, and Humanities in Medicine*. Georgetown University Medical Center, 1–7.

13. Lynch, Stan; Smith, Stephony; Stevens, Jeff. 2004. "Back When." *Live Like You Were Dying*. McGraw, Tim (rec. artist). Gallimore, Byron (prod.) Curb Records.

14. Batcho, Krystine I. 2020. "When Nostalgia Tilts to Sad: Anticipatory and Personal Nostalgia." *Frontiers in Psychology*. Frontiers Media, 1–8.

15. *Ibid.*, 2.

16. So, it is different from *anticipated* nostalgia. See Chung, Wing-Yee. 2023. "Anticipated Nostalgia." *Current Opinion in Psychology*. Elsevier, 1–8.

17. Lyda, Jacob; Stegall, Jen; Abrams, John; Abrams, James; Mac, Kevin. 2019. "The Good Old Days." *Reminder*. The Abrams (rec. artist). Warner Music.

18. Davidson, Dallas; Lindsey, Hillary; McCormick, Jim. 2017. "Louisiana." *McGraw: The Ultimate Collection*. McGraw, Tim (rec. artist). Curb Records.

19. Boym, 13.

20. *Ibid.*, 15.

21. This is known as the cognitive theory of the emotions, among other similar names. See Nussbaum, Martha. 2001. *Upheavals of Thought: The Intelligence of the Emotions*. Cambridge University Press.

22. In a specifically moral way. The past was a time when "the line between right and wrong didn't seem so hazy."

23. Coontz, Stephanie. 1992. *The Way We Never Were: American Families and the Nostalgia Trap*. Basic Books.

24. Coontz, 34–35.

25. These are sometimes called "extra-judicial killings," and while they were certainly illegal, they were often done by or with the complicity of law enforcement.

26. Lovelace, Kelly; Thrasher, Neil; Kennedy, Tully; Allsion, Kurt. 2023. "Try That in a Small Town." *Highway Desperado*. Aldean, Jason (rec. artist). Michael Knox (prod.) Bad Boy Records.

27. Lambert, D.; Gale, J.A.; Hartley D. 2008. "Substance Abuse by Youth and Young Adults in Rural America." *Journal of Rural Health*, 221–8. doi: 10.1111/j.1748-0361.2008.00162.x. PMID: 18643798. See also CDC Rural Health. 2024. *Public Health Strategies for Opioid Overdoses Policy Brief*.

28. Bendix, Aria; Murphy, Joe. 2023. "Map of Gun Deaths Across the U.S. Show That Cities Have Lower Rate Than Rural Counties." *NBC News*.

29. Not only homicide, but all types of violent (including accidental) deaths. See Walsh, Bryan. 2013. "In Town vs. Country, It Turns Out That Cities Are the Safest Places to Live." *Time*.

30. Kaplan, Sarah. 2021. "Air Pollution from Farms Leads to 17,900 Deaths U.S. Deaths Per Year, Study Finds." *The Washington Post*.

31. Holyfield, Lori; Cobb, Maggie; Murray, Kimberly; Mckinzie, Ashleigh. 2013. "Musical Ties That Bind: Nostalgia, Affect, and Heritage in Festival Narratives." *Symbolic Interaction*. The Society for the Study of Symbolic Interaction, 457–477.

32. Dayton, Duncan; Burns, Ken. 2019. *Country Music: An Illustrated History*. Knopf.

33. Such country music already exists—although deserving of more recognition—consisting of artists like Orville Peck, Shaboozey, Alison Nichols, Cody Hibbard, Gabe Lee, Brandy Clark, and others.

VI

Country Music Values

Puzzles About Prayer

Jonathan Reibsamen

Prayer is as ubiquitous in country music as songs about pickup trucks, patriotism, heartache, and drinking on Saturday night. Country artists seem to pray (or at least sing about praying) about almost everything and in nearly every context. There are country songs about "Prayin' in a Deer Stand,"[1] praying on a "dirt road,"[2] and going "Down to the River to Pray."[3] Some country songs are about "Praying for Rain,"[4] "for Peace,"[5] "for Me,"[6] "for You,"[7] or just praying "about Everything."[8] Other songs recount the prayers of specific types of folks such as the "Hobo's Prayer,"[9] the "Drunkard's Prayer,"[10] the "Housewife's Prayer,"[11] the "Farmer's Prayer,"[12] the "Cowboy's Prayer,"[13] the "Good Ol Boy's Prayer,"[14] and even "The Outlaw's Prayer."[15] So, it isn't difficult to see that, for probably a variety of reasons, country artists have focused a fair amount of their music on (the subject of) calling out to God through prayer and supplication.

As it turns out, perhaps unbeknownst to many of the country greats who penned these songs, there is another group that has paid at least as much attention to the topic of prayer (albeit in their own unique way): philosophers of religion. Long before anyone penned a note of music that would become known as "country," philosophers were asking deep and probative questions about the practice. Continuing into the present day, they've sought to understand what prayer is and why people pray. They've raised the question of whether praying to God is ever a rational thing to do or, to put it crudely, whether praying even *makes sense*. You might think that philosophers question the rationality or efficacy of prayer because they doubt the existence of God, but even religious philosophers have raised concerns about prayer. Perhaps prayer *doesn't* make sense (or at least believing that prayer has any actual effect on God or the world doesn't make sense) even if God is real.

People pray for all sorts of reasons: to express thanks, to give praise, to worship, to confess sins, and to make requests of God.[16] Philosophical puzzles that concern prayer are usually born out of the idea that God (to whom all those country artists seem to be praying) is the God of what has been called *traditional monotheism*. According to traditional monotheism, God is omnipotent (all-powerful), omniscient (all-knowing), and omnibenevolent (all-good). Most mainstream branches of Judaism, Christianity, and Islam fall under the umbrella of traditional monotheism. Since country music has historically had close ties to Christianity, it seems that whatever puzzles about prayer exist for traditional monotheism also exist for the conceptions of God and prayer that exist in these country songs and for the artists who wrote them.

If those who pray to God believe that he is omniscient, omnipotent, and omnibenevolent, then a number of puzzles arise about prayer. For instance, if God already knows everything before someone prays to Him, what could be the point of confessing a sin or revealing one of our desires to Him? And, if God is completely good, what could be the point of requesting something from Him? If we ask for something bad, wouldn't his goodness preclude Him from giving us what we ask for? Conversely, if we ask for something good, wouldn't His goodness require Him to give it to us even if we hadn't asked? Again, all of these puzzles raise the general worry: could it be that all of those country artists, the fans who sing along with them, or any of the millions of believers who pray are engaged in a fundamentally misguided activity?

Why Inform an Omniscient God?

Traditional monotheists believe that God is omniscient—that is, that God knows everything that can be known. So, why tell God that "I can't do this on my own," as Carrie Underwood sings in "Jesus, Take the Wheel"?[17] God already knows she can't do it on her own. Why should Lauren Alaina tell God that her sixteen-year-old brother has been "playing with fire," as she sings in "Dirt Road Prayer"? God already knows what her brother has been up to. Why tell God what he already knows? Do we pray to inform God about what is going on in our lives and the lives of our loved ones? The early Christian philosopher and theologian Augustine of Hippo (AD 354–430) pondered this question in his commentary *On the Sermon on the Mount* when he asked, "What need is there for prayer itself, if God already knows what is necessary for us?"[18]

Augustine's answer is one that has often been repeated by traditional monotheist thinkers: the reason for praying to God is not to inform Him of things that God doesn't already know but, rather, to change something in *us*. Augustine suggests that the act of praying is, in a sense, therapeutic:

it makes our hearts and minds more receptive to the spiritual blessings that God wishes to give us. Indeed, some empirical studies suggest that prayer can have psychological benefits, such as reducing anxiety.[19] So, there can be reasons to pray, even if prayer is not informing God of things that God doesn't already know. The practice of prayer itself may have psychological and spiritual benefits for those who engage in the practice.

However, there is more to prayer than apparent or attempted information sharing, and more is desired from prayer than personal therapeutic effects. Prayers are often *petitionary*—that is, they are requests asking God for things or to do things for us and others. To pray, "Jesus, take the wheel" is to petition Jesus, not merely to inform Him. Prayers that are petitionary rather than merely informative give rise to further puzzles.

Why Petition a Perfectly Good God?

Traditional monotheists also believe that God is omnibenevolent—that is, that God is perfectly good and that this perfect goodness means that God has goodwill toward everyone. Some philosophers have pointed out that the practice of petitionary prayer to a perfectly good God is also puzzling. Actually, there are at least three related but distinct puzzles related to petitioning God. First, if God already knows and wills what is best, as a perfectly good God would, then how could our requests possibly have any effect on God's actions?[20] Let's call this the *puzzle of effective prayer*. Second, even if it is somehow possible for our prayers to have an effect on God's actions, should we want our prayers to have that effect?[21] Let's call this the *puzzle of desiring effective prayer*. Third, even if it is possible for our prayers to have an effect on God, and it is not irrational for us to desire this, how could we ever know that our prayers were answered? That is, even if something we requested did happen, how could we be justified in believing that it happened *because of* our prayers?[22] Let's call this the *puzzle of believing in answered prayer*.

The Puzzle of Effective Prayer

In "Praying for Rain," Don Henley sings (in the persona of a farmer experiencing extreme drought), "Lord, I've never been a prayin' man / But I'm saying one tonight / I'm praying for rain."[23] If God brings rain because[24] of this prayer, then that prayer was *efficacious*; that is, it had an effect on God's action in the world. Some philosophers have puzzled over how any prayer could possibly be effective, given the assumption that God is perfectly good.[25] If God is perfectly good (so this line of thought goes), then God will always do what is best. So, if Henley's farmer's request for rain is what is actually best, then God will do it. But God would have done it anyway, even if it hadn't been requested, since God *always* does what is best. If rain isn't what is actually best, then God won't do it, even if it is requested. So, the request seems superfluous to any action of God's and, consequently, cannot have any actual effect on what happens.

Other philosophers, however, have pointed out that this line of reasoning makes some assumptions that shouldn't be accepted. One assumption is that there is only one "best" outcome of any situation that someone might pray about. Suppose that there are a number of equally good outcomes that God could bring about. In that case, perhaps God would take into account a prayer requesting one outcome over another that was equally good from God's (omniscient) point of view. In that case, the prayer could make a difference in what God does.[26]

Related to this, and perhaps more compelling, is the possibility that the goodness of certain events may depend upon those events being answers to prayer.[27] Note that another assumption of the skeptical reasoning described above is that the fact that something is requested in prayer doesn't affect the goodness of its coming to pass. But why think that? It could be that bringing rain wouldn't be best for God to do if Henley's farmer didn't request it, but it becomes the best *because* it is requested. Suppose, for example, that God desired to strengthen the farmer's faith in God's goodness, and the best way (or at least a good way) for this to happen was for God to answer the request for rain. Then, even if rain was not otherwise the best, it might become the best and, therefore, be brought about by God. In fact, there might be many good things that a perfectly good God desires, and prayer uniquely provides them. If this is so, then God's perfect goodness is no barrier to God's answering at least some petitionary prayers.

The Puzzle of Desiring Effective Prayer

But, even if petitionary prayer is possibly efficacious, should we desire to influence God's actions in the world through prayer? Should Henley's farmer even want to influence God to bring rain? Some philosophers have argued that it seems misguided for us to want God to answer our prayers.[28]

Suppose that anything we request from God is either good, neutral, or bad. Of course, we should not desire God to bring about what is bad, and a good God wouldn't do that, anyway. If it's good, then God doesn't need us to request it. If it's neutral (either neither good nor bad, or perhaps equally good with other possible outcomes, as described in the previous section), then even if our prayers could make a difference, why should we want them to? Philosopher Allison Thornton compares our making requests of God to giving musical composition advice to Johann Sebastian Bach. Given the theme of this book, we can change the example a bit. Suppose you had the chance to hang out with Hank Williams[29] (yes, time travel would have been involved, but let's set that complexity aside). Would you try to influence his songwriting? Or would you recognize that whatever he comes up with would be at least no worse than whatever ideas you might have, given how much better of a songwriter he is than you? Now consider how much greater the difference is between mere human beings and the all-good, all-wise God of the universe. Shouldn't you leave it up to God and not seek to influence His actions?

Consider Garth Brooks's song "Unanswered Prayers," in which he remembers a high school crush and how "each night I'd spend prayin' that God would make her mine."[30] Years later, he says, "Sometimes I thank God for unanswered prayers," since (in the song) he is now married to someone he believes to be a much better match for him than his high school crush would have been. The point Brooks makes in this song generalizes: we know so little compared to God that we can rarely, if ever, be confident that our requests are for what is actually good or best in the grand scheme of things. Since this is so, it seems that we shouldn't desire our prayers to be effective in making a difference in what God does.

However, even granting God's surpassing wisdom and goodness along with our own limited (to say the least) wisdom and goodness, there may be reasons to desire effective prayer. Consider the suggestion above that there might be many good things that efficacious prayer uniquely provides. One kind of such a good may be relational. According to Christian theology, God desires to be reconciled with humanity.[31] But suppose that for reconciliation to happen, forgiveness of the offenses that ruptured the relationship must be requested by the offending party.[32] If that is the case, it is certainly reasonable to desire that our prayers for forgiveness are effective in making a difference in what God does—that is, by forgiving us rather than not forgiving us.

But perhaps the case of forgiveness is unique and one of the only kinds of prayer that we can know is a request for what is best. What about cases in which we admit we don't really know what is best? Should we not desire to influence God in any of those cases? The answer may depend on what we believe about God's desires for humanity, and that may depend on our particular religious traditions. We have already seen that a Christian idea of God's desires with respect to humanity would lead Christians to expect that prayers for forgiveness are efficacious. Christian theology, however, doesn't stop at reconciliation; the mainstream of Christian theology holds that the greatest good for any particular person is to be in as close a loving relationship with God as possible.[33]

Suppose, as Christians have also thought, that this closeness involves cooperating in world-building; that is, that God seeks to work out His will in the world in and through the activities of humans. One way that this cooperation could happen is through God allowing Himself to be influenced by us to act in the world in certain ways and at certain times; that is, that God wants to engage in joint action in the world with us.[34] One way to do this is for God to request us to do things, such as loving our neighbors, but another way to do this is for God to respond to our requests for Him to do things in the world. Believing this could give a person a reason to desire that petitionary prayer in general is efficacious, even if that same person may not know whether particular requests are for what is best or not. But Christians, following Jesus' teaching about prayer, do typically start with the proviso, "Thy will be done,"[35] before proceeding with particular requests.

The Puzzle of Believing in Answered Prayer

Let's consider one more puzzle related to petitionary prayer, this time an epistemic one.[36] Can we ever be justified in believing that a petitionary prayer has been answered? Suppose the day after Henley's farmer prays for rain, an unexpected downpour occurs, and the drought is broken. Could the farmer legitimately claim to know that God answered his prayer? Consider also the song "Prayed for You" by Matt Stell. In the song, Stell proclaims that he is a "believer," and, like many believers, he testifies that God has answered his prayers. He sings that he prayed every day, "For someone to love me like you do / Baby you're perfect / I guess the Good Lord heard it."[37] Is Stell justified in believing that God heard and answered his prayer for someone to love him? Or would such a belief be an example of the *post hoc* logical fallacy?[38]

As we noted earlier, for a prayer to be efficacious, it actually has to make a difference. In other words, prayers are *answered* only if the thing asked for happens *because of* the prayer. Just because the thing requested happened after the request was made does not mean that it happened because of the request. If you pray today that the sun will come up tomorrow, and the sun does come up tomorrow, could you claim that it came up *because* you prayed that it would? If it would have come up anyway, then it seems that your request wasn't answered, even if what you requested happened. Now, consider again that God knows so much more than we do and, therefore, presumably has access to many reasons to bring about or not to bring about things that are beyond what we know or perhaps even could know. So, for anything we might request in prayer, God may have all kinds of reasons besides our prayers to bring it about. Consequently, for anything that happens, it seems that, for all we know, it would have happened anyway, regardless of whether or not we prayed for it. Therefore, we cannot claim to know that what happened was an answer to prayer just because it happened after we prayed that it would.

If the preceding line of reasoning is correct, then believers who claim to know that God has answered their prayers are mistaken; that is, they may be right that God answered their prayer, but they are mistaken to claim that they *know* God answered their prayer. Instead, according to this line of thought, they should be agnostic about whether or not their prayers are answered.[39]

There is, however, something to be said in defense of Stell and others who testify to know of answered prayers. To say that God does something "because" it was requested in prayer does not need to imply that the prayer is God's most significant or weightiest reason for bringing it about. To see why, consider how good human parents react to their children's requests. Even if they do not give their children everything they ask for, the fact that a beloved child asks for something does give the parents a reason. Suppose that a child asks for something the parent knows is good for the child, wants to give to the child, and was already planning to give to the child when the child requested it. When the parent does give the child the requested thing, would we say that the child's request wasn't granted, since the parent would have given it to the child even if it wasn't requested? If it seems that the child's request was still granted, then perhaps we should say, also, that receiving something requested from God in prayer should count as an answer to prayer, even if God had already had sufficient reasons to bring it about aside from the prayer. If that is so, then perhaps Stell is justified in believing that his prayer for someone to love him was answered. After all, he knows that he made the request and that he now has what he requested. If he also knows that God's love toward him is such that his desires and requests give God a reason (even if it's not the only reason), then perhaps it is reasonable for him to believe that God answered his prayer.

"Let's go down to the river to pray"

The practice of prayer, and petitionary prayer in particular, can be puzzling. But it is important to note that none of the puzzles themselves imply that the practice of prayer is to be avoided. The philosophical puzzles discussed here have to do with how we think about God and humanity and the relationship between God and humanity that is manifested in our practices of prayer. Reflecting on these puzzles should not discourage prayer itself but can, perhaps, help us to avoid thinking of prayer as a way to manipulate God into fulfilling our desires, or thinking too highly of our own desires relative to God's governance of the entire world, or being overly confident in claiming to know why God does what God does. But, by all means, keep praying, and keep singing about praying.

Notes

1. Bryan, Luke; Gaylon, Nicolle; Robbins, Jimmy. 2022. "Prayin' in a Deer Stand." *Prayin' in a Deer Stand*. Stevens, Jeff; Stevens, Jody (prods.) Capital Records Nashville.

2. Gaylon, Nicolle; Geesbreght, April. 2011. "Dirt Road Prayer." *Wildflower*. Alaina, Lauren (rec. artist). Gallimore, Byron (prod.) Mercury Nashville.

3. Allan, George H. 1867. "Down in the River to Pray." *Slave Songs of the United States*. A Simpson & Co. The song is an old spiritual or Christian folk hymn whose origin is unknown. George H. Allan was the first to contribute to a publication. It has also gone by the name "Down to the River to Pray."

4. Henley, Don; Lynch, Stan. 2015. "Praying for Rain." *Cass County*. Capital Records.

5. McEntire, Reba. 2015. "Pray for Peace." *Love Somebody*. Sisemore, Doug (prod.) Nash Icon Records.

6. Crosby, Rob; Shamblin, Rob. "Pray for Me." *Steam*. Herndon, Ty (rec. artist). Scaife, Joe (prod.) Epic Records.

7. Stell, Matt; Veltz, Allison; Bowers, Ash. 2019. "Prayed for You." *Everywhere but On*. Arista Nashville.

8. Stevens, Jeff. Regan, Bob. "Pray About Everything." *I'll Stay Me*. Stevens, Jeff (prod.) Capitol Records Nashville.

9. Stuart, Marty. 1999. "Hobo's Prayer." *The Pilgrim*. MCA Nashville.

10. Bergquist, Karin; Detweiler, Linford. 2005. "Drunkard's Prayer." *Drunkard's Prayer*. Back Porch Records.

11. Lambert, Miranda. 2011. "Housewife's Prayer." *Hell on Heels*. Pistol Annies (rec. artist). Liddell, Frank (prod.) Columbia Nashville.

12. Bruce, Ed. 1963. "A Farmer's Prayer." *Six Days on the Road*. Dudley, Dave (rec. artist). Golden Wing Records.

13. Clark, Badger. 1906. "A Cowboy's Prayer." *Sun and Saddle Leather*. The Gorham Press.

14. Hays, Fordie; Kennedy, John. 2024. "Good Ol Boy's Prayer." Childers, Chas (prod.) Blue Arch Music Publishing.

15. Sherrill, Billy; Sutton; Glenn. "The Outlaw's Prayer." *Armed and Crazy*. Paycheck, Johnny (rec. artist). Sherrill, Billy (prod.) Epic Records.

16. Davison, Scott A. 2021. "Petitionary Prayer." *The Stanford Encyclopedia of Philosophy*. Zalta, Edward N. (ed.).

17. Lindsey, Hillary; Sampson, Gordie; James, Brett. 2005. "Jesus, Take the Wheel." *Some Hearts*. Underwood, Carrie (rec. artist). Bright, Mark (prod.) Arista Nashville.

18. Augustine. 1888. *On the Sermon on the Mount*. Findlay, William (trans.) *Nicene and Post-Nicene Fathers*, First Series, Vol 6. Philip Schaff, Philip (ed.) Christian Literature Publishing Co.

19. Upenieks, Laura. 2023. "Unpacking the Relationship Between Prayer and Anxiety: A Consideration of Prayer Types and Expectations in the United States." *Journal of Religion and Health* 62: 1810–1831.

20. For one of many examples of this problem being discussed, see Basinger, David.

1983. "Why Petition an Omnipotent, Omniscient, Wholly Good God?" *Religious Studies* 19: 25–41.

21. Thornton, Alison Krile. 2024. "Petitionary Prayer: Wanting to Change the Mind of the Being Who Knows Best." *Faith and Philosophy* 39 (2): 227–242.

22. Davison, Scott. 2009. "Petitionary Prayer." *The Oxford Handbook of Philosophical Theology.* Flint, Thomas P.; Rae, Michael (eds.), 286–305. Oxford University Press.

23. Henley.

24. It's not easy to say just how to understand this "because," but we will have to set aside a discussion of the different senses of the term. Just think of it as the fact that the prayer was made has a place in a true causal explanation of why the thing requested happened when and where it did. There's no need to think of it forcing God to act.

25. For example, see Basinger, David. 1983. "Why Petition an Omnipotent, Omniscient, Wholly Good God?" *Religious Studies* 19, 25–41.

26. For example, see Reibsamen, Jonathan. 2019. "Divine Goodness and the Efficacy of Petitionary Prayer." *Religious Studies* 55 (1): 131–144.

27. *Ibid.*

28. Thornton, Allison Krile. 2022. "Petitionary Prayer: Wanting to Change the Mind of the Being Who Knows Best." *Faith and Philosophy* 39 (2): 227–242.

29. The reader should feel free to substitute for Hank whoever it is that you believe to be the greatest of the great country music songwriters.

30. Brooks, Garth; Bastian, Larry; Alger, Pat. 1990. "Unanswered Prayers." *No Fences.* Brooks, Garth (rec. artist). Reynolds, Allen (prod.) Capitol Nashville.

31. For example, see 2 Corinthians 5:16–21.

32. For a defense of this view, that reconciliation requires a request for forgiveness, see Geivett, R. Douglas. 2012. "Forgiveness." *Being Good: Christian Virtues for Everyday Life.* Austin, Michael W.; Geivett, R. Douglas (eds.), 204–241. Wm. B. Eerdmans.

33. Both Augustine of Hippo (aka "Saint Augustine") and Thomas Aquinas held this view. See Augustine *Confessions* X.xxii and Thomas Aquinas, *ST* I–II, Q3, A8.

34. Reibsamen.

35. See Matthew 6:8–13.

36. "Epistemic" means, roughly, having to do with knowledge and justified belief. Epistemology is the branch of philosophy concerned with the nature of knowledge and whether and how we know the things we take ourselves to know.

37. Stell, et al.

38. The *post hoc* fallacy gets its name from the Latin phrase *post hoc ergo propter hoc,* which means "after this, therefore because of this."

39. For other presentations of the epistemic puzzle, see Davison, Scott A. 2021. "Petitionary Prayer." *The Stanford Encyclopedia of Philosophy.* Zalta, Edward N. (ed.), section 5, and Davison, Scott A. 2022. *God and Prayer,* Cambridge University Press, Chapter 4.

True Country as the Art of Self-Deprecation

Benjamin Hutchens

What is my worth as a person? What is the good I am "for"? What am *I* good for? These questions, as old as ancient Greek thought,[1] resonate strongly in American country music. What elicits these questions, and what confounds them, is the hardship of life itself: failure and loss, abandonment and poverty.

Often more pensive and even mournful than it is given credit for, country music is remarkably honest in its confrontation with this collision between the demand for meaning in life and the challenges that can seem to render it meaningless. Whereas a number of other genres of popular music seek to exalt and motivate the self in a vacuum, country music strives to describe the basic rhythms of life itself in an undeniably real social realm. It often takes an audience where no other form of music can: the depths of anxiety and depression, sometimes remedied only by drinking, cheating, and brawling. Country music is about fallen people, though not entirely godless ones. They do not know the mettle of their own pasture.[2]

The challenge for country music is not to take the vainglory of a good drinkin', screwin', and fightin' Saturday night seriously as a solution to life's problems; but by the same token, it is not to give in to the despair of the desperately failing life. Country music is an art of self-deprecation when it strives to offer a reasonable and appropriate understanding of the individual's own self-worth. Being mainly good and "living right" are largely normative matters that satisfy the expectations of a community. Despite its high-minded values, the subject of true country often fails to meet its own needs. And it may, on occasion, find consolation for this failure in the violent imagery of revenge.

"True country" is the implicit ideal of all country music. It is incarnated in the good ol' boy (e.g., "them Duke boys"). It is less the labor, the piety, and the fidelity that defines the good ol' boy as the charms of his play and the irrationally defiant stance he takes in adversity. What is needed is a stable sense of an identity, encoded in culture and motivational in life, an equilibrium of virtue that fosters equanimity of mind. What is needed is that active, persisting and reliable virtue that is a deep feature of a person. Its acquisition and exercise are not unlike that of a skill.[3]

Traditionally known as "humility," the virtue in question here suggests a reasonable understanding of one's own worth, a mean between the brazen and vacuous self-promotion of the mainstream consumer subjectivity and the rootless despondency and atomic individualism of modern nomadic life. What is needed is an assertion of social defiance that issues from the depths of the culture itself, one tempered by a modesty concerning the significance of one's own life.

Vainglory

In order to understand the role of humility in country music as an art of self-deprecation, we should turn to the vainglory celebrated so commonly in popular culture. The vice opposed to the virtue of humility has often been thought to be vainglory, which is an inordinate desire for the kind of pleasure that only public approval of one's actions can provide. We might notice an interesting dynamic within the concept of vainglory: on the one hand, one glorifies (and seeks the glorification of) what one does, which is "vain" in the sense of vanity, and on the other, one's self-glorification is "in vain," as in futile or useless. Self-glorification is inherently discombobulating: in itself, it is without rule or order and in effect it disorganizes life. The vainglorious person talks a big game with a confident smirk on his face, but inwardly, he is a disorganized mess, driven by a lack of order that produces more disorder. The open-endedness of alcoholism and nomadism are attractive natural responses to the failures of the vainglorious life.

Now, although humility and vainglory are opposites, some thinkers, such as the ancient Greek philosopher Aristotle and those he influenced, including the medieval thinker Thomas Aquinas, regard vainglory as having another opposite virtue as well. Magnanimity (in Greek, *megalopsuchia*), greatness of soul, is extremely important for Aristotle in his *Nicomachean Ethics*. Since the public should honor most of those things that are honored by the gods, he says, a great person will perform those deeds that are most honored. In that sense, they are magnanimous.

Moreover, as Aristotle says, a great person does great things and knows he does so.[4] He is mainly concerned with honors and dishonors. He will receive a moderate pleasure by being honored by respectable people but no pleasure at all when being honored by those who are not respectable.[5] Aristotle distinguishes the "conceited" person who believes he is great when he is not, and the "lowly" or pusillanimous person (*micropsuchia*, small souled) who does not even believe he could perform great deeds—and for that reason will not. The problem with this "lowly" person is simple: he may deserve better than he has, may be able to achieve more than he does, but "deprives himself of the advantages he deserves," thereby appearing to have some defect, specifically of not even knowing his own quality.[6]

In terms of Aristotle's famous theory of the "mean," the magnanimous man is virtuous because his claims to greatness are correct (the mean), while the conceited man is non-virtuous because he has a greater sense of self-worth than he deserves (excess) and the pusillanimous man is non-virtuous because he lacks even enough self-worth to strive for greatness (deficiency). What may be most interesting for us in the last type of person is that he falls short twice over: short of his own merit (he defectively does not know it) and short of the standard set by the magnanimous person. We should be aware that both the magnanimous person and the vainglorious person seek public approbation, the latter to earn renown for its own sake, the former for the sake of something greater. But it is personal glory, in the end.

Humility in Descartes, Spinoza, and Kant

In order to understand the nature of self-deprecation in country music, it would be helpful to survey philosophical views of humility. We will take a quick look at the views of Descartes, Spinoza, and Kant.

René Descartes, regarded as the first modern philosopher, authored a short work on psychology entitled *The Passions of the Soul* in 1649. In it, he offered an intriguing approach to the subject of humility. We are moved by wonder when something we perceive is different from what we perceive it to be. We might hold what surprises us in esteem or in contempt, depending on whether we regard it as valuable or insignificant. When we turn this back on ourselves, we may respond by being either magnanimous or vain, if we regard ourselves as valuable, or otherwise humble or abject if we think of ourselves as insignificant.[7]

For Descartes, there is only one proper reason to esteem ourselves, and that is if and when we exercise our free will and control our choices. The wise person understands that only this freedom truly belongs to him, and thus he should only be blamed or praised for his use of this freedom. Descartes describes this as generosity, which prevents us from having contempt for others. The wise person "generously" acknowledges that others often make mistakes through ignorance, a lack of knowledge about how to properly use free will. Such a person is generous toward human frailty, such that he does not feel particularly inferior to those who are more fortunate, or very superior to those who are less so.[8] Descartes then makes a distinction between humility as a virtue and the vice of abjectness. In the former, we do not "prefer ourselves" to others because others may use their free will as well as we do. We acknowledge our common "infirmity" of nature as well as the wrongs we have committed and those we will continue to commit.[9] Descartes argues that abjectness consists in a state of weak confusion in which we perform regretful actions or realize we are dependent on things in the control of others.[10]

We might take note of the reliance on external goods (e.g., wealth, property, fame, etc.) whose acquisition depends, not solely on our own free will but on the provisions of others. So, the wellness of one's being is dependent on factors beyond personal control. Couple this with a sense that we lack the proper use of our free will, as we discourage ourselves from the outset from doing with it what we may, and the result is a certain abjection. The world is unlikely to provide what I need, and I may lack the means to get it anyway. Such people tend to debase themselves before those from whom they expect advantages, while at the same time lording it with contempt over those who can give nothing.[11] Ultimately, there is movement in the "soul," as Descartes understands it, which produces humility, a movement made up of wonder, sadness, and self-love mingled with a certain internalized hatred for all those faults that give rise to self-contempt.[12]

How can we characterize this movement? We turn to the philosophy of Baruch Spinoza, who focused on the power and powerlessness of this movement in Book III of his famous *Ethics* (published in 1677). Humility, he declares, is "pain arising from a man's contemplation of his own impotence, or weakness."[13] To this, he opposes self-abasement (*abjectio*), which is "thinking too meanly of oneself by pain."[14] To explain this, let us look at his earlier propositions. In Proposition 53 we learn

> when the mind regards its own self and its power of activity, it feels pleasure, and the more so the more distinctly it imagines itself and its power of activity.[15]
>
> pleasure and power enhance one another. Moreover, it follows that: The mind endeavors to think only of the things that affirm its power of activity.[16]

He explains in the "proof" of this proposition that the mind is empowered when it affirms what it is. The more powerful it is, the more it has the ability to affirm that power; the more it affirms that power, the more powerful is the idea it has of itself. However, what of the absence of power or the thought of it?

When the mind thinks of its own impotence, by that very fact it feels pain.[17]

In other words, when the mind seeks to empower itself by thinking of its power and thinks only of its impotence instead, it feels pain instead of the pleasure it would feel if it had succeeded. And pain is increased if the sense of impotence is associated with blame by others.[18] And in the Scholium to this Proposition, Spinoza explains that when this pain is accompanied by the idea of our own impotence, the result is humility (*humilitas*).

Self-abasement is opposed to humility. When a person regards himself as powerless, he may think others blame or despise him for being so. Consequently, in believing he lacks power, he does lack it, and thus may fail to boldly try to do what he should. In this way, self-abasement arises from humility. Why? Because the original painful awareness of actual impotence gives rise to thinking of oneself as deserving to be in pain because of powerlessness.

What may be most remarkable about Spinoza's view of humility is his conclusion about it in Book IV. There, he flatly declares that humility is not a virtue, but a mere passive emotion. It springs from an emotion-laden self-perception, not rational activity of mind. One may learn lessons from being humble, but it is not a virtue.[19] Since humility is not in keeping with self-empowerment, it is as incompatible with a healthy, rational life as self-abasement.

Immanuel Kant offers another approach to humility. In his *Metaphysics of Morals* (1797), he presents a dual understanding of the human being. On the one hand, as a natural animal, human beings have a merely "ordinary value" (*pretium vulgare*). Emphasizing human understanding and rationality gives such human beings an "extrinsic value" as someone useful (*pretium usus*). One human being is more valuable, if more useful, than another. Such human beings have what he calls a "price," an exchange value. On the other hand, when a human being is autonomous, an "end in itself," then it is a person above price. It thus possesses a "dignity," an absolute inner moral worth. All rational human beings owe each person respect because of this dignity. Consequently, human beings then have a low value, as sensible beings, and a high value, as morally intelligible beings.

What is most important for us here is this: if we seek the favor of others so much that we belittle ourselves in order to get it, then we do not acknowledge and act from the absolute inner moral worth we have. This he calls "false humility," putting oneself down for the purpose of material advantage as a merely sensible being, contrary to what we acknowledge as dignified individuals. True humility, however, comes from understanding that, at one's best, as a dignified person, one is under the "law" that makes it possible for one to be so. We may kneel before the ideal of our own reason, being dignified and acknowledging one's own dignity, but not to any idol of our own making.[20] Kant offers the inspiring notion that the rational person should submit only to the moral law, not to anything that is incompatible with its dignity.

Humility: The Fine Tuning of the Self in Country Music

What will we find in country music? Vainglory or magnanimity? Humility or abjection? True humility (under the moral law) or false humility under some idol?

From ol' Hank's laments to Jamey Johnson's "That Lonesome Song,"[21] true country speaks to the isolation of real people surrounded by others and awash in the familiar expectations of their culture. Without explicitly moralizing, true country explores the responses of real people seeking, and often losing, the equilibrium of humility, in a challenging world. We can see this in fighting songs, songs about aging and poverty, and those about complete despondency.

We might start with the defiance of fighting songs. As the sun goes down ("Low down leaving sun") and the subject has worked hard, he cannot help but go out gambling and fighting under the neon lights, in Waylon Jennings' "Honky Tonk Heroes."[22] In Loretta Lynn's "You Ain't Woman Enough"[23] and "Fist City,"[24] she will fight for her man, no holds barred. In Merle Haggard's "Fightin' Side of Me,"[25] the subject is angered by disloyalty to shared norms, with fighting the only solution to dissent. In Toby Keith's "As Good as I Once Was,"[26] time distances the subject from his glorious bar fightin' days. At best, the misery of the failing man's life can only be addressed by drinkin' and fightin', as in Waylon Jennings' "I Ain't Living Long Like This"[27] or George Jones' "If Drinkin' Don't Kill Me."[28] But, of course, for a grown man to resolve his problems and assert his competence through brawling is self-defeating, and even drinking cannot kill bad memories, as in Merle Haggard's "The Bottle Let Me Down"[29] and George Jones' "Still Doin' Time."[30] In each of these, we hear a lack of magnanimity, in Aristotle's sense. And abjection in Descartes and Spinoza's senses is all too apparent.

There is a certain vainglorious defiance in country music. In Tyler

Childers' "Whitehouse Road,"[31] a drug user vaingloriously boasts of his life and the freedom to "run these roads" even though the holler life he has made for himself is hard. Such a man may cruise back and forth to the Tasty Freeze in Brooks & Dunn's "Hillbilly Deluxe,"[32] but he ends up crying at a back table in "Neon Moon."[33] Hank Jr. would like to spit tobacco in a mugger's eye, but can't because he lives in the backwoods. In Townes van Zandt's "Waitin' Around to Die,"[34] the subject gambles, drinks, and robs so as not to "wait around to die," but is actually just experiencing a living death. Amusingly, in Toby Keith's "Red Solo Cup,"[35] the subject has lost his home to foreclosure (Freddie Mac can kiss his ass), but what matters to him is that men who prefer to drink from glasses have no testicles (he makes values even as he loses everything). When failing, the country subject often loses itself in irrational abandon (at least I can...). We can see the failure of the conceited man lapsing into abjection.

The subject of aging, ignored by most other popular genres of music, is an important aspect of the country subject's life. In Hank Sr.'s "Pictures from Life's Other Side"[36] and Jamey Johnson's "In Color,"[37] memory is a problem for aging people. One can hear the pensiveness in Hank Jr.'s acknowledgment that his friends no longer "rowdy on down." Times have changed, memory cannot recover the past, and drinking shapes the future, as in Haggard's "Are the Good Times Really Over"[38] and George Jones' "Who's Gonna Fill Their Shoes."[39] In Jennings' "Amanda,"[40] the subject looks in the mirror to an "awful awakening" and realizes he does not deserve his wife. Keith's "Don't Let the Old Man In"[41] shows that aging men should get outside and stay active, but the struggle is inward. In Jones' "Same Ole Me,"[42] his aging hands tremble, but his love is steady. In Trace Adkins' "You're Gonna Miss This,"[43] a father realizes that, as his daughter is growing up, time is accelerating and memory cannot preserve it. And in Kenny Chesney's "There Goes My Life,"[44] a young man thinks that fatherhood has ruined his life, only to discover life in fatherhood itself. In these cases, we can see some humility, in Descartes and Kant's senses. But, in a cruel twist, in Miranda Lambert's "Mama's Broken Heart,"[45] a distraught daughter disavows her mother's advice to collect herself after a breakup, refusing to heed her wisdom. Generational repudiation of the past is something that the fatherly subjects of Adkins and Chesney's songs might go on to experience.

Poverty is seen very clearly by female subjects in country music. In Bobbie Gentry and Reba McEntire's "Fancy,"[46] a teenager is sent out to be an escort by her own mother, who is dying, abandoned, and cannot feed her baby. In Dolly Parton's "Coat of Many Colors,"[47] a young girl is proud of the coat her mother made of rags, only to be ridiculed by kids at school. And in Loretta Lynn's "The Pill,"[48] a woman is liberated from a succession of pregnancies and from an unloving husband. One senses the failures of husbands and fathers behind the scenes. One might grasp Spinoza's sense of the absence of pleasure and power in these examples.

Country music may be at its best when it is honest about the subject's limitations, often revealed in despondency. Helpless, desperate men are out of control. They remain in a prison of their own making. For Merle Haggard in "Mama Tried," even his mother knew she would fail to raise him right and that he would fall into degeneracy and crime (morality under the law). Men who dream of being competent masters of life (Keith's "Should've Been a Cowboy")[49] struggle to provide for their families (Haggard's "Workin' Mans Blues").[50] These are men who are subjected to infidelity and live in the ruins of their marriages, as in Jones' "The Grand Tour."[51] The subject of Jones' "These Days (I Barely Get By)"[52] knows physical pain, a meaningless job, an absconding wife, and imminent unemployment. Toby Keith's "Who's That Man"[53] takes the listener on a drive to the house where another man is leading his family.

Perhaps no writer of country music follows the desperate subject into the depths better than Billy Joe Shaver. In "Willy the Wandering Gypsy and Me"[54] and "Ride Me Down Easy,"[55] a lonely, failing drifter imagines a high life (vainglory), but acknowledges a life of defiant failure (abjection). In his "Ole Five and Dimers Like Me,"[56] the subject measures his esteem against the expectations of others and overestimates it such that he has his own cruel awakening that his life wholly consists of his unimpressive speech and actions. We hear a man who has found the relationship between ideas, pleasure and power in Spinoza, and his realization suggests that now, finally, he has found humility under the moral law.

Defeating Abjection

True country aims to describe the troubled lives of decent, hardworking people in their actual social world. Yet it must maintain a fine equilibrium. When times are good, and one feels empowered and happy, it is easy to be swept up into vainglory. But the hardship of life (abandonment and poverty, failure and loss) can drag one down below a proper threshold of the self-perception of one's own genuine worth.

In many of the songs mentioned in this essay, true country follows the subject down into Descartes or Spinoza's abjection, warning the listener of the dangers of giving into the helpless "old man" in every cheerful "good ole boy." The drinkers and brawlers, the men who abandon family, can only "get by" in a state of abjection. Female victims of this abjection have little choice but to find their own way. The false sense of empowerment they have complicates Spinoza's theory, and finding refuge in the moral law (work, providing, preserving) keeps genuine humility possible. And in living by this law, a certain measure of magnanimity can be achieved; however, achieving it must not be the aim of the endeavor, since the product could be a disappointed vainglory that plunges one into abjection. True country suggests solutions (fidelity, diligence, sexual continence) by often describing those who could not find them. Its subject is not in a vacuum, but in a family, a community, a tradition that, although imperfect, finds security in conventional forms of living: remain faithful to your spouse, raise your kids well, find a career and improve it. Neither vainglorious dismissal nor abject surrender of these options will be empowering, as it is never enough for the subject to "get by." Hard-won humility and happy living enhance one another.

Notes

1. Adams, Robert Merrihew. 2006. *A Theory of Virtue: Excellence as Being for the Good.* Oxford: Clarendon, 15–23.

2. Shakespeare. 1599. *Henry V,* Act 3, scene 1, line 28.

3. Annas, Julia. 2011. *Intelligent Virtue.* Oxford: Oxford University Press, chapters 2 and 3.

4. Aristotle. 1976. *Nicomachean Ethics.* Trans. J.A.K. Thomson. New York: Penguin (NE 1123b), 93.

5. *Ibid.* (1124a5–10), 95.

6. *Ibid.* (1125a20), 96.

7. Descartes, René. 1985. "The Passions of the Soul" in *The Philosophical Writings of Descartes.* Trans. J. Cottingham, R. Stoothoff and D. Murdoch. Cambridge: Cambridge University Press, sections 53–4, 350. See also 149–151, 383–4.

8. *Ibid.* (153–4), 384.

9. *Ibid.* (155), 385.

10. *Ibid.* (159), 386.

11. *Ibid.*

12. *Ibid.* (160), 387

13. Spinoza, Baruch. 1982. *The Ethics and Selected Letters.* Trans. Samuel Shirley. Ed. Seymour Feldman. Indianapolis: Hackett (Explication 26) page 146.

14. *Ibid.* (Explication 29), 147.

15. *Ibid.* (Proposition 53), 136.

16. *Ibid.* (Proposition 54), 136.

17. *Ibid.* (Proposition 55), 136

18. *Ibid.* (Corollary to Proposition 55), 137.

19. *Ibid.* (Proposition 53), 184. See also Scholium to Proposition 54, 185.

20. Kant, Immanuel. 1996. *The Metaphysics of Morals.* Trans and ed. Mary Gregor. Cambridge: Cambridge University Press, section 11, page 186. See also Kant, Immanuel. 1997. *The Groundwork of the Metaphysics of Morals.* Trans and ed. Mary Gregor. Cambridge: Cambridge University Press, 4:435–6, 42–43.

21. Johnson, Jamey. 2007. "The Lonesome Song." *That Lonesome Song.* Cobb, Dave (prod.) Mercury Nashville.

22. Shaver, Billy Joe. 1973. "Honky Tonk Heroes." Honky Tonk Heroes. Jennings, Walyon (rec. artist; prod.) RCA Victor.

23. Lynn, Loretta. 1966. "You Ain't Woman Enough (to Take My Man)." *You Ain't Woman Enough*. Bradley, Owen (prod.) Decca Records.

24. Lynn Loretta. 1968. "Fist City." *Fist City*. Bradley, Owen (prod.) Decca Records.

25. Haggard, Merle. 1970. "The Fightin' Side of Me." *The Fightin' Side of Me*. Nelson, Ken (prod.) Capitol Records.

26. Keith, Toby; Emerick, Scotty. "As Good as I Once Was." *Honkytonk University*. Stroud, James (prod.) Dreamworks Nashville.

27. Crowell, Rodney. 1979. "I Ain't Living Long Like This." *What Goes Around*. Jennings, Waylon (rec. artist). Albright, Richie (prod.) RCA Victor.

28. Sanders, Harlan; Beresford, Rick. 1981. "If Drinkin' Don't Kill Me (Her Memory Will)." *I Am What I Am*. Jones, George (rec. artist). Sherrill, Billy (prod.) Epic Records.

29. Haggard, Merle. 1966. "The Bottle Let Me Down." *Swinging Doors*. Merle Haggard and The Strangers (rec. artist). Nelson, Ken; Owen, Fuzzy (prods.) Capitol Records.

30. Heeney, Michael P.; Moffatt, John. 1981. "Still Doin' Time." Still the Same Ole Me. Jones, George (rec. artist). Sherrill, Billy (prod.) Epic Records.

31. Childers, Tyler. 2017. "Whitehouse Road." *Purgatory*. Simpson, Sturgill; Ferguson, David R. (prods.) Hickman Holler Records; Thirty Tigers.

32. Crisler, Brad; Wiseman, Craig. 2006. "Hillbilly Deluxe." *Hillbilly Deluxe*. Brooks & Dunn (rec. artist). Brooks, Kix; Brown, Tony; Dunn, Ronnie (prods.) Arista Nashville.

33. Dunn, Ronnie. 1991. "Neon Moon." *Brand New Man*. Brooks & Dunn (rec. artist). Cook, Don; Hendricks, Scott (prods.) Arista Records.

34. Van Zandt, Townes. 1969. "Waitin' Around to Die." *Townes Van Zandt*. Eggers, Kevin; Malloy, Jim (prods). Poppy.

35. Beavers, Brett; Beavers, Jim; Warren, Brad; Warren, Brett. 2011. "Red Solo Cup." *Clancy's Tavern*. Keith, Toby (rec. artist; prod.) Show Do-Universal.

36. Traditional. 1951. "Picture's from Life's Other Side." *The Drifter*. Williams, Hank (rec. artist). Rose, Fred (prod.) MGM Records.

37. Johnson, Jamey; Miller, Lee Thomas; Otto, James. 2008. "In Color." *That Lonesome Song*. The Kent Hardly Playboys (prod.) Mercury Nashville.

38. Haggard, Merle. 1981. "Are the Good Times Really Over (I Wish a Buck Was Still Silver)." *Big City*. Merle Haggard and the Strangers (rec. artist). Epic Records.

39. Seals, Troy; Barnes, Max D. 1985. "Who's Gonna Fill Their Shoes." *Who's Gonna Fill Their Shoes*. Jones, George (rec. artist). Sherrill, Billy (prod.) Epic Records.

40. McDill, Bob. 1979. "Amanda." *Greatest Hits*. Jennings, Waylon (rec. artist; prod.) RCA Records.

41. Keith, Toby. 2019. "Don't Let the Old Man In." *Greatest Hits: The Show Dog Years*. Buenahora, Arturo, Jr.; Shippen, F. Reid (prods.) Show Dog-Universal.

42. Overstreet, Paul. 1981. "Same Ole Me." *Still the Same Ole Me*. Jones, George (rec. artist). Sherrill, Billy (prod.) Epic Records.

43. Gorley, Ashley; Miller, Lee Thomas. 2007. "You're Gonna Miss Him." *American Man: Greatest Hits Volume II*. Adkins, Trace (rec. artist). Rogers, Frank (prod.) Capitol Nashville.

44. Thrasher, Neil; Mobley, Wendell. 2004. "There Goes My Life." *When the Sun Goes Down*. Chesney, Kenny (rec. artist). Cannon, Buddy (prod.) BNA Records.

45. Clark, Brandy; McAnally, Shane; Musgraves, Kacey. 2011. "Mama's Broken Heart." *Four the Record*. Lambert, Miranda (rec. artist). Liddell, Frank; Worf, Glenn; Ainlay, Chuck (prods.) RCA Nashville.

46. Gentry, Bobby. 1990. "Fancy." *Rumor Has It*. McEntire, Reba (rec. artist). Brown, Tony (prod.) MCA Records.

47. Parton, Dolly. 1971. "Coat of Many Colors." *Coat of Many Colors*. Ferguson, Bob (prod.) RCA Victor.

48. Allen, Lorene; McHan, Don; Bayless, T.D.; Lynn, Loretta. 1975. "The Pill." *Back to the Country*. Bradley, Owen (prod.) MCA Records.

49. Keith, Toby. 1993. "Should've Been a Cowboy. *Toby Keith*. Larkin, Nelson; Shedd, Harold (prods). Mercury Records.

50. Haggard, Merle. 1969. "Workin' Man's Blues." *A Portrait of Merle Haggard*." Nelson, Ken (prod.) Capitol Records.

51. Wilson, Norro; Taylor, Carmol; Richey, George. 1974. "The Grand Tour." *The Grand Tour.* Jones, George (rec. artist). Sherrill, Billy (prod.) Epic Records.

52. Jones, George; Wynette, Tammy. 1974. "The Days (I Barely Get By)." *The Best of George Jones.* Sherrill, Billy (prod.) Epic Records.

53. Keith, Toby. 1994. "Who's That Man." *Boomtown.* Larkin, Nelson; Shedd, Harold (prod.) PolyGram/Polydor Nashville.

54. Shaver, Billy Joe. 1973. "Willy the Wandering Gypsy and Me." *Honky Tonk Heroes.* Jennings, Waylon (rec. artist; prod.) RCA Victor.

55. Shaver, Billy Joe. 1973. "Ride Me Down Easy." *Honky Tonk Heroes.* Jennings, Waylon (rec. artist; prod.) RCA Victor.

56. Shaver, Billy Joe. 1973. "Old Five and Dimers (Like Me)." *Old Five and Dimers Like Me.* Kristofferson, Kris (prod.) Monument Records.

Dolly Parton

Reluctant Feminist but Definite Woman!

CINDY MUENCHRATH SPADY

When you first see Dolly Parton, the last thing you might think is "There goes a feminist." But why? She chose and carefully cultivated her look over the last 70-plus years. She has used her look, her wisdom, and her savvy to build an empire, and she has fought for her right as a woman to be who she is and who she wants to be. This, in turn, has empowered many women (and men), not only in country music but throughout the world. So, if Dolly isn't deserving of the title "feminist," who is?

There might not be a better example of a pop culture icon who has transcended both her genre and the cultural expectations set before her. Dolly's audience is as diverse as almost any other. Just consider her Q Score. In marketing, a Q Score is calculated based on familiarity and the appeal of a brand or celebrity, among other aspects of popular culture. Dolly has the highest Q Score among all musicians and one of the highest scores overall, with a wide range of media consumers having the least negative and the most positive views of her.[1] Dolly, it seems, is for everyone (or at least almost everyone). This is not by accident. Dolly's strategy has been to create a relatable image and persona that are also a force to reckon with. She does this not in a spurious way but in a fully authentic fashion.

She began her career as a country singer/songwriter, though she quickly crossed over to other genres and media, including television and film. Over the last seven decades, Dolly has superseded outside expectations of a young, poor woman from the hills of Tennessee. Early in her career, she was put in a box intended to limit her identity, but Dolly would have no such thing. And she has proven this again and again with her music as well as the way she lives her life.

In this essay, we'll look deeper into and defend the claim that Dolly is indeed a feminist. This is noteworthy at least in part because there has been pushback against this claim, some of which has come from Dolly herself. However, part of the more recent pushback has been based on the idea that Dolly's beloved song "Jolene" is actually *anti*-feminist, as it has been contrasted with Beyoncé's more contemporary reimagining of the song.[2] That is, Beyoncé's version has been bestowed as a feminist anthem in *contrast* to Dolly's original version.[3] However, in what follows, we'll take a critical look and respond to this line of reasoning. In the end, it will be made clear that Dolly isn't *just* a feminist (though she very much is one!); she's an icon for women and feminism generally.

Burning Bras

Before making the case for Dolly's feminist credentials, the term "feminist" needs to be defined, both how it has been used historically along with some variations of it. Dolly has been frequently asked if she's a feminist, and she's often been reluctant to accept the moniker. The burning of bras and the hatred of men are two images that emerge for those who have a negative connotation of feminism, and Dolly herself seems to have adopted this negative and skewed understanding of the concept. "I think of myself as a woman in business. I love men. I write a lot about men. That word 'feminist' everyone goes to extremes. I don't believe in extremes. To me, when you say the word 'feminist' it means I hate all men."[4] So, for Dolly, appreciating women *and men* at the same time, or in the same respect, seems counter to the crux of feminism. And, of course, if that were at the core of feminism, then it would be problematic. But, to be sure, there are other ways to understand the concept.

Feminism has held a variety of meanings for different people and groups throughout history; it is often traditionally and broadly defined as the desire to change women's position in society. The fight for legal and financial equality, justice in the workplace and freedom for women to have equal opportunities in all aspects of life are all at the center of feminism.[5] Note that there is nothing innately anti-men in any of these pursuits. Yet many assume that if one is pro-women, they must or will inevitably be anti-men. But, again, that is simply a misunderstanding of the feminist movement at its core. There may be particular individuals who claim to be feminists and have those personal opinions, but an anti-men stance isn't any sort of fundamental part of feminism. One needn't be anti-men to identify as a feminist.

Dolly's initial understanding of feminism is not unique to her and may very well be in part a product of her generation and place of origin. Yet, if we look at Dolly's accomplishments, actions, and discography (not to mention her filmography), the feminist label seems to fit whether she embraces it or not. As feminism scholar Rosalind Delmar puts it, "If feminism is a concern with issues affecting women, a concern to advance women's interest, so that anyone who shares this concern is a feminist, whether they acknowledge it or not, then the range of feminism is general, and its meaning is equally diffuse."[6] Hence, though there may not be a single, unified way to define "feminist," Dolly's life's work should lead us to conclude that, for her, the title is surely fitting.

As we previously alluded, some of Dolly's songs have been at the center of controversy and have even been labeled by some to be anti-feminist, the primary example being "Jolene" (a claim we'll explore in depth in the next section of this essay). However, even *if* the point were conceded, it seems at least as equally relevant to the case (that Dolly is a feminist) that many of her songs have been dubbed and are undeniably feminist anthems. Two important examples are "9 to 5" and "Just Because I'm a Woman." "9 to 5," of course, is the theme to the movie of the same name in which Dolly stars.[7] The movie raises a number of issues that women have faced in the workplace throughout history and in interactions with men more generally. Both the song and the movie highlight the struggle women have working in a "man's world."

In a similar fashion, "Just Because I'm a Woman," a song from earlier in Dolly's career, has striking feminist undertones.[8] The song points out the double standards put on women as the refrain, "No, my mistakes are no worse than yours just because I'm a woman," rejects women being treated differently, especially in relationships, simply because of their gender. And, of course, these are just two examples of many of Dolly's songs that explore the plight of women and the unique struggles they have to deal with.

Perhaps because of these songs, Dolly has actually revised her answer at times to the question of whether or not she is a feminist when a different definition of feminism is presented to her. "I mean, I must be if being a feminist means I'm all for women, yes. But I don't think I have to march, hold up a sign or label myself. I think the way I have conducted my life and my business and myself speaks for itself. I don't think of it as being feminist. It's not a label I have to put on myself. I'm just all for the gals."[9] One song in her catalog, which highlights her appreciation of other gals, is one of her most famous, "Jolene."

"Jolene, Jolene, Jolene, Jolene"

How can a song practically begging another woman not to steal her man be considered in any way feminist? Wouldn't that kind of vulnerability and defeat be counter to the principles of feminism as traditionally understood? Perhaps, but again, this is only the case if we accept a very narrow understanding of feminism or what it means to be a feminist.

The two-part story behind "Jolene" is almost as famous as the song itself. At an autograph signing, Dolly met a little girl with auburn hair; "You sure are pretty." Dolly remarked, "What's your name?"[10] The little girl's name was Jolene. Dolly went on to tell Jolene that she would some-day write a song with that name. Years later, her husband Carl was flirting with a red-haired woman at the bank. The rest is history.

Dolly's "Jolene"[11] is a particular type of song, perhaps most common in country music, often referred to as an "other women" song.[12] Her focus is not on the cheating man but on the other woman he's with, a common theme in the subgenre. Dolly compliments Jolene before she essentially pleads with her not to steal her partner, and she makes it known that she is vulnerable and that keeping her man is very important to her. This is different than the majority of songs of this sort; most call out the other woman, and many do so in a manner that's not so nice. However, in contrast, Dolly doesn't vilify Jolene. Rather, she almost exalts her for having the power to take her man.[13] On first listen, it might be easy to understand why some have called out Dolly's version of the song for being anti-feminist, but this again depends on one's understanding of feminism.

In contrast to Dolly's "Jolene," recall that a recent reimagining of the song by Beyoncé has been lauded as pro-woman, feminist, and the "correct" way one should handle the woman her man is cheating with. Beyoncé does mention Jolene's appearance but not necessarily in a complementary way. Rather than flattering Jolene, Beyoncé points out that it takes more than looks to come between a happy man and his loving family.[14] Instead of begging (to not take her man), Beyoncé's version contains warnings and threats to Jolene.

There have actually been over 100 recorded covers of "Jolene," but none really diverted from the meaning and mood of Dolly's original version as much as Beyoncé's. For many fans, Beyoncé's retelling is a refreshing and needed upgrade to the story. Others make the case that she ruined the song, having missed the point entirely. However, a common thread in the discussions of these two versions of the song is that one has clear feminist undertones, and the other simply does not. Yet not everyone agrees on which one is which.

Perhaps the loudest voice in the debate has been daytime talk show host, Joy Behar, who made it clear that she believes Dolly's "Jolene" has always been clearly anti-feminist, while Beyoncé's version empowers women to respond to Jolene-types in the right way. "Because the original thing with Dolly Parton is so, like, anti-feminist, worrying about some good-looking woman taking your man. If it's so easy to take your man, then take him."[15] Behar praises Beyoncé for her guts and call to action. Apparently, to Behar, threatening another woman is a feminist act.

This raises the question, what is the proper way for someone living out feminist ideals to respond to a Jolene-type? If we simply focus on the lyrics of both renditions, the singers recount two very different responses. Dolly compliments and pleads; Beyoncé warns and threatens. Again, which reaction adheres to feminist ideals? Only one of them? Both? Neither? Are either of them even trying to support a feminist agenda? Isn't that asking a lot of a pop song?

In contrast to Behar, conservative talk show host Megyn Kelly has a less favorable take on Beyoncé's cover: "I have to say, I don't find this empowering at all…. There's something strange about what's happening with the modern-day definition of what a strong woman is. You can't have any vulnerabilities or insecurities. You have to be this badass b–h who's threatening, 'f–king a, you mess with my man.'"[16] What Kelly is suggesting is that Beyoncé's approach is actually wrong and doesn't show women at their best. She proclaims that the definition of a strong, empowered woman is skewed not only in Beyoncé's "Jolene," but in our culture overall.

In Kelly's critique, some fair questions linger. Why are insecurities not part of being a woman? Why is vulnerability not an acceptable reaction of a feminist? Isn't threatening another woman just another way to live out one's insecurities? Aren't there many ways to be a woman and a feminist? One thing is for sure, neither rendition holds the man accountable. Answering these questions goes well beyond the scope of this essay, but they are nevertheless worthwhile questions to ponder.

Perhaps we can say that Dolly's "Jolene" is not the ideal feminist anthem that some of her previously mentioned songs are. Dolly wrote "Jolene" as a creative piece of art. It wasn't necessarily a statement of her understanding of womanhood, and it would be unreasonable to expect every song of even an ardent feminist to explicitly or perfectly champion feminist ideals. Even feminist icons may have vulnerabilities they wish to express through song. That said, all things considered, Dolly seems to understand that there are many ways to be a woman, and it is clear that her songs do not have a singular perspective and tone. And why would they? Dolly has created her identity and transcended basic understandings and expectations of what it means to be a woman.

Dolly's Transcendence

With the understanding that there are indeed many ways to understand feminism and live out feminist ideals, we can now examine Dolly's life and artistry through the lens of feminist philosophy. Ultimately, we'll see that the claim that Dolly is not a feminist is altogether indefensible. The philosopher best situated to help us in this discussion (who has a great deal to say about importantly relevant concepts such as authenticity and transcendence) is Simone de Beauvoir. Beauvoir is clear that each human is free to choose the direction of their life through the choices they make and the identity they create.[17] However, she does not deny that we all have aspects that we do not necessarily choose that are part of who we are and that influence the choices we make.

Beauvoir calls these elements one's *facticity*, given facts about each individual. These include a particular past, a certain place of origin, the way one is viewed by others, and certain physical properties.[18] For Dolly, we know all of these; her roots as a poor young girl in Tennessee and her body have been key spurs to inspire her music and her choices. Beauvoir goes on to say that although we create ourselves through choices, women, unfortunately, often accept the identity that culture thrusts upon them, especially in regard to their bodies.[19]

As we dive deeper into Beauvoir's existentialist feminist philosophy, we encounter two terms essential to our exploration of Dolly: immanence and transcendence. Immanence, for Beauvoir, is the state most women assume and/or have forced upon them.[20] Immanence is having goals thrust upon oneself from outside forces and societal expectations. Many women, especially in the time of Beauvoir, simply accepted this state. Transcendence, on the other hand, naturally occurs for most men.

Transcendence, especially for men, is being able to create one's own goals and identity.[21] But thankfully, for Beauvoir, women are not always stuck in immanence, and there is hope for transcendence, the best version of life. In *The Ethics of Ambiguity*, a tome furthering her existentialist feminist philosophy, Beauvoir adds that both realities are valuable, and because of our ambiguous nature, everyone, male and female, experiences both.[22] Also relevant to the discussion, Beauvoir includes the proclamation that one *becomes* a woman rather than simply being born one, and to live authentically, one must create their own life. As we apply this feminist philosophy to Dolly, these ideas are made readily apparent.

Yes, Dolly, like all of us, had to deal with her facticity. But she clearly both used and shaped it to her advantage. Dolly has transcended what society, her roots, and country music said a woman had to be. At the time Dolly was an up-and-coming star, society said that a woman had to have a strong man holding her up. Interestingly, for Dolly, this wasn't necessarily her longtime husband, Carl, to whom people were referring, but rather her singing partner, Porter Wagoner.

Wagoner called her his "girl singer" and the "finest little thing" and tried very hard for years to keep her in his shadow, even when it was clear she was the true star in their professional relationship.[23] She famously broke away from Wagoner in 1974, as she began creating her musical and pop culture empire. Beauvoir might also say that she transcended and became more of a woman throughout the years through her various pursuits and how she claimed her identity and used her facticity to her advantage. Some of these actions include owning all of her songs and publishing rights, crossing genres, and entering the mainstream television and film arenas, not to mention her extensive philanthropic efforts. She dictates what she does, who she associates with, and how she impacts the culture and the world. If those aren't feminist ideals in action, it's hard to imagine what would be.

An exploration of Dolly and how she created her own identity cannot conclude without addressing the image she puts out to the world, particularly her literal image (i.e., her look). Ironically, her physical appearance has been one of the things her doubters (of her feminist credentials) point to to prove how Dolly buys into cultural expectations of who a woman is supposed to be, immanence, and that she therefore doesn't embrace feminist ideals. The truth is that her very cultivated look is one of the ways she has transcended traditional notions of womanhood. Her voluminous bosom, various blonde wigs, and her surgically sculpted face have been fodder for the negativity toward Dolly's persona and body. But the joke is on them. She *chose* her look and even embraces humor concerning it. "She calls her 'look'—exaggerated makeup, big wigs, plastic nails, elaborate costuming including five-inch heels—'fake' a gimmick to gain attention and then capture audiences with her songs, but simultaneously asserts her underlying genuineness and 'realness.'"[24]

Inspiring the World with Her Authenticity

Dolly's transcendence has not only served her well but has inspired generations of people to find their own authenticity and path in life. Call her a dumb blonde. Call her an anti-feminist. Call her a joke. Whatever empty criticisms are thrown at her, they do not diminish Dolly's true identity, her confidence in that identity, and her impact on the world. She has used her facticity, her understanding and love of self, and her authenticity to not only further the genre of country music but also affect the world in many ways. As historians Mary Bufwack and Robert Oermann put it: "As Parton often advocated for social justice, including women's rights, racial equality and gay rights, her statements are striking for how she anchors them in her own discourses of authenticity, perhaps making them seem more genuine to some audiences by framing them in terms of her sincerity as well as her rural, working-class background."[25]

Dolly's influence has spanned the globe and taken her well beyond her country music roots. She is the "real deal" and a force to be reckoned with. The last thing anyone should want to do is underestimate her.

NOTES

1. Abumrad, Jad. 2019. "Sad Ass Songs." *Dolly Parton's America*.

2. Parton, Dolly. 1973. "Jolene." *Jolene*. Parton, Dolly (rec. artist). Ferguson, Bob (prod.) RCA Victor.

3. Parton, Dolly; Beyoncé; Andrews, Denisia; Coney, Brittany; Gesteelde-Diamant, Terius. 2024. "Jolene." *Cowboy Carter*. Beyoncé (rec. artist). Vickery, Alex; Rochon, Jack; Tyler, Khirye (prods.) Parkwood; Columbia Records.

4. Abumrad.

5. Delmar, Rosalind. 2005. "What Is Feminism?" *Feminist Theory*, 2nd ed. Kolmar, Wendy and Bartkowski, Frances (eds.) McGraw Hill, 31–34.

6. *Ibid.*, 30.

7. Parton, Dolly. 1980. "9 to 5." *9 to 5 and Odd Jobs*. Perry, Greg (prod.) RCA Nashville.

8. Parton, Dolly. 1968. "Just Because I Am a Woman." *Just Because I Am a Woman*. Ferguson, Bob (prod.) RCA Victor.

9. Freeman, Hadley. 2019. "Dolly Parton on Sexual Politics: I've Probably Hit on Some People Myself!" *The Guardian*, 3.

10. Smarsh, Sarah. 2020. *She Come by It Natural*. Scribner, 78–79.

11. Parton, Dolly, and Robert Oermann. 2020. *Dolly Parton Song Teller*. Chronicle Books, 117.

12. Abumrad, Jad. 2019. "The Only One for Me, Jolene." *Dolly Parton's America*.

13. Abumrad, "The Only One for Me, Jolene."

14. Rossignol, Derrick. 2024. "How Are Beyoncé's Jolene and Dolly Patron's Original Version Different." *Uproxx*, 2.

15. Nolfi, Joey. 2024. "Joy Behar Says Dolly Parton's 'Jolene' is 'Anti-Feminist,' Prefers Beyoncé." ew.com.

16. Patton, Tess. 2024. "Megyn Kelly Mocks Kamala Harris, Michelle Obama for Praising Beyoncé's 'Cowboy Carter': 'We Have to Pretend She's the Second Coming.'" *The Wrap*.

17. Stone, Alison. 2007. *An Introduction to Feminist Philosophy*. Polity Press, 175.

18. *Ibid.*

19. *Ibid.*, 177.

20. Beauvoir, Simone, de. 1949. *The Second Sex*. Borde, Constance; Malovany-Chevallier, Sheila (trans.) Alfred Knopf, 16–17.

21. *Ibid.*

22. Stone, 197. Beauvoir, Simone, de. 1949. *The Ethics of Ambiguity*. Frechtman, Bernard (trans.) Citadel Press.

23. Burns, Ken. 2019. "Music Will Get Through." *Country Music: A Film by Ken Burns*. PBS.

24. Edwards, Leigh H. 2023. "Dolly Parton's Netflix Reimagining." *Whose Country Music?* Bishop, Paula; Watson, Jada (eds.) Cambridge University Press, 137.

25. Bufwack, Mary A., and Robert K. 2003. Oermann. *Finding Her Voice: Women in Country Music, 1800–2000*. Country Music Foundation Press / Vanderbilt University Press, 362.

Loyalty and Its Limits

Casey Rentmeester

Tammy Wynette's 1968 hit, "Stand by Your Man," is one of the more controversial songs in the history of country music. The song provides a common narrative in the genre: a good woman is one who stands by her man, even when he is "doing things that you don't understand."[1] Released as a single at the peak of the countercultural hippie movement, the song became a crossover hit that couldn't help but be met with ridicule by some at the time, given the culture wars that took place in the late '60s. The traditional "just put up with him, and love him anyway" sentiment stood in stark contrast to the free love the hippies were spreading during the Summer of Love which emphasized sexual experimentation over monogamous loyalty. The song and its message also seemed to be at odds with the women's liberation movement at the time, whose motto, "the personal is political," underscored how the experience of women in the home was reflected in patriarchal societal structures more broadly, thereby questioning the traditional gender-normative cultural values that "Stand by Your Man" affirms.

Ultimately, Wynette's song is not an anti-feminist ballad but rather an ode to loyalty, which she made clear in her 1979 autobiography.[2] We get a similar tribute to loyalty in the genre decades later with Tracy Lawrence's 2006 hit single, "Find Out Who Your Friends Are," in the context of friendship rather than marriage.[3] And, of course, there are numerous patriotic country songs encouraging loyalty to one's country, perhaps most prominently Merle Haggard's "The Fightin' Side of Me," which was released during the baby boomer culture wars and caused a similar indignation from the counterculture as "Stand by Your Man."[4] What, though, does it really mean to be loyal and when is it time to break loyalty to another, whether that be a spouse, a friend, or even a country? The American philosopher Josiah Royce dedicated a 400-plus page treatise to the concept of loyalty and ultimately argued that persons need a sense of loyalty to live a good life since loyalty provides unity to life, as well as a sense of meaning beyond oneself. The primary goal of this essay is to outline Royce's argument and show how loyalty is a common value in some of country music's signature songs. However, we'll also see that loyalty has its limits as a virtue by exploring Aristotle's virtue ethics.

Stand by Your Man (If He Walks the Line)

Josiah Royce was a professor of philosophy at Harvard University who made significant contributions in the realms of philosophy, history, psychology, and religion in the late 19th and early 20th centuries. He was a colleague of Charles Sanders Peirce and William James, the philosophers who founded and popularized pragmatism, the signature philosophical movement of the United States. Toward the end of Royce's career, he became deeply interested in loyalty and its importance in living a meaningful life as he saw more and more people living lives dedicated to individualism, often to the detriment of their own well-being.

In *The Philosophy of Loyalty*, one of his later works, Royce defines loyalty as "the willing and practical and thoroughgoing devotion of a person to a cause."[5] As he unpacks this concept, he notes the three main features of being loyal: (1) a cause to which one is loyal; (2) a willing and thorough devotion to the cause; and (3) a sustained and practical commitment to that devotion. By its very definition, loyalty is not a fleeting sort of thing: it requires a practical commitment that one will "stand by" someone or something, to use Wynette's language, regardless of the sacrifice it may impose upon oneself or the pain and suffering that one will endure as a result of that steadfast stance. Royce makes it clear that loyalty is never mere emotion since we often restrain our natural instincts out of respect for loyalty, nor is loyalty merely about one's own pleasure or self-advantage since the loyal cause is always outside of oneself and might not align with one's own self-interest. And yet, despite its lack of self-regarding nature, loyalty is so important to a well-lived human life that Royce does not think we can answer very basic philosophical questions like "What do we live for? What is our duty? What is the true ideal of life? What is the true difference between right and wrong? [and] What is the true good which we all need?"[6] without appealing to it.

The overarching message of "Stand by Your Man" is that a woman should remain loyal to her man, even if the man can't live up to his ideal self "'cause after all, he's just a man." That narrative of giving a man some grace epitomizes the reputation of perhaps the greatest country artist of all time, Johnny Cash, who has been aptly hailed as "a saint" and "a bad man" all at the same time by his biographer.[7] "I Walk the Line," the smash hit from 1956 that was written while the young Cash was on tour, consists essentially of a public vow of loyalty to his first wife, Vivian, that Cash will "walk the line" and maintain his fidelity to her despite the steady stream of nubile temptations that presented themselves to him while on the road.[8] As it turned out, Cash was only "human, all too human," to use Nietzsche's phrase, and couldn't always "walk the line," especially when it came to his love affair with June Carter.[9]

The song and the factual context of Cash failing to walk the line provides a fitting encapsulation of one of the issues with remaining loyal to anything: eventually, life is going to throw you curveballs that test your loyalty. Royce explains this phenomenon as a conflict between your ideal self and your actual self: "the plan or ideal of life comes to stand over against your actual life as a general authority by which each deed is to be tested."[10] For Cash, the ideal husband is the one who finds himself "alone when each day's through" while on the road out of loyalty to his wife. But Cash's *actual* self faced too many lustful allurements to uphold that ideal. These sorts of moments of conflict, for Royce, are a steady companion to any human life, which might be why so many of us are drawn to Cash as a musician and as a person since he clearly exemplified the conflict of character that we all inevitably face at some point in life's trajectory. As Cash himself put it, "Sometimes I am two people. Johnny is the nice one. Cash causes all the trouble. They fight."[11] While most of us do not have such drastic extremes in our own character, there is a bit of Dr. Jekyll and Mr. Hyde in all of us, leading to conflicting interests and intentions.[12]

In navigating life's conflicts, Royce makes it clear that "the individual retains the inalienable duty ... to decide wherein his own loyalty lies."[13] For Cash, the initial loyalty to Vivian shifted decidedly to June Carter after they fell into the "Ring of Fire" so famously captured in the 1963 Cash hit purportedly written by Carter to signify her love for him.[14] In terms of country music values, there seemed to be more leeway for men to break loyalties to women than the other way around during this era. "Stand by Your Man," for instance, was followed by the massively successful "Good Hearted Woman" by Waylon Jennings and Willie Nelson in the early 1970s that applauds the woman who "loves me in spite of my wicked ways that she don't understand."[15] Another staple of that era, "She's Actin' Single (I'm Drinking Doubles)" by Gary Stewart tries to elicit the sympathy of the listener by chronicling the sorrow of a man whose wife regularly seeks attention from others with the lyrics "while she pours herself on some stranger / I pour myself a drink somewhere."[16] In this era of country music, it seems that men can "have their fun," but women aren't generally provided similar latitude.

By 2000, however, the "inalienable duty" to decide one's own loyalties and therefore the licensure to break them—even in the realm of marriage—is culturally bestowed upon women as well in the genre through the Dixie Chicks, who released the single "Goodbye Earl" with a B-side cover of "Stand by Your Man" to signal that there are some situations in which it is no longer appropriate to "stand by your man."[17] The song chronicles the story of Mary Anne, who settled in her small town by marrying the chronically abusive Earl, eventually resulting in a beating so damaging that she winds up in intensive care. Mary Anne calls her best friend Wanda who immediately flies in on the red eye, and they concoct and execute a plan to kill Earl by poisoning his black-eyed peas at dinner since, as the song tells us, Earl needed to die.[18] The song not only turns "Stand by Your Man" on its head but also demonstrates the type of loyalty best friends can have for one another, a loyalty in which you are there for your friend at a moment's notice, if necessary.

"You find out who your friends are"

In order to unpack the type of friendship the characters Mary Anne and Wanda must have had, it is helpful to explore the philosophy of Aristotle, as he spent two of the ten books in his *Nicomachean Ethics* on the topic of friendship and its importance to a good life. Aristotle argues that there are three types of friendship: those based on utility, on pleasure, and on virtue. Importantly, Aristotle states, "those who love because of utility love because of what is good *for themselves*, and those who love because of pleasure do so because of what is pleasant *to themselves*, and not because of who the loved person is but in so far as he is useful or pleasant."[19] True loyalty to another is found only in friendships based on virtue, as the other types of friendships are really formed out of reasons of self-regard. If, for instance, I hang out with someone funny when I'm feeling down as a pick-me-up, I'm using that person as a means to feel better. Or, if I have a friend who loves the same band as I do and we go to concerts together, that friendship is based on pleasure. Neither the person of comic relief nor the concert partner needs to be friends based on their virtue—they serve a different purpose in that the means for friendship is self-regarding in nature.

We see these types of friendship in "All My Rowdy Friends Are Coming Over Tonight," by Hank Williams, Jr., which became well-known nationally by serving as the theme song for Monday Night Football from 1989 to 2011. The friends solicited in the song seem to be based on pleasure and utility at the same time. In the refrain, Williams asks, "Do you wanna drink / Hey do you wanna party?" and assures that old Hank is "ready to get the thing started."[20] It is clear that Hank is ready to have a good time and needs to find some raucous friends who are in a similar sort of mood. These friends need not be the sort of friends who would be there in a heartbeat when you're in a time of need in the sense that Mary Anne and Wanda are friends: they simply need to come out and let loose with Williams to fulfill their role as his rowdy friends.

Aristotle makes it clear that it is not as if such drinking buddies aren't "real" friends; it is rather that such relationships are "easily dissolved,"[21] because once their utility is gone or once they are no longer pleasant, one has no need for them. Thus, their friendship is not the highest form of friendship for Aristotle. In the context of Royce's concept of loyalty, we can say that there is no true or genuine loyalty to the other *as such* since the cause for friendship is self-regarding (e.g., having fun with others), rather than other-regarding (e.g., being there for another for another's sake).

On the other hand, the highest form of friendship, namely, friendship based on virtue, is the truest form, such that "the true friend ... is he who is worth choosing for his own sake."[22] When we do things for the sake of the other and not for ourselves—or even *in spite of ourselves*, to use the language of John Prine[23]—we are displaying an other-regarding characteristic that aligns with virtue, which both Aristotle and Royce recognized as essential to a good life. Indeed, Aristotle even argued that "without friends no one would choose to live, though he had all other goods."[24] In stating this, Aristotle seems to agree with Royce that loyalty to another forms an especially meaningful aspect of life.

The country song that provides a fitting homage to the importance of loyalty in friendship is Tracy Lawrence's "Find Out Who Your Friends Are," which features fellow country superstars Tim McGraw and Kenny Chesney. The song chronicles the sorts of hardships we inevitably come upon in life—being stranded by a stalled car in the middle of nowhere, falling on a rough patch where we need a place to stay, etc.—and the importance of having a friend who will "never stop to think 'What's in it for me?' / They just show on up / with their big old heart."[25] It is in these moments of desperation or adversity that true friends step up to help without any regard for themselves, and this lies at the heart of loyalty. Aristotle states that "misfortune reveals those who are not true friends but keep our company for utility's sake."[26] Similarly, Royce claims that even though "danger is everywhere ... anybody who has friends may devote his life to some cause which his friendship defines for him and makes, in his eyes, sacred."[27] For the true friend, there is a sacred bond to remain loyal to each other, even when it does not benefit oneself to do so. In the song, you find out who your friends are when you are not your best version of yourself, and your friends remain loyal anyway.

Of course, since we are "human, all too human," we are not always capable of living up to the expectation of *always* being there for one another. Therefore, the expectations that accompany the sanctity of loyalty may at times turn out to be too high. The failure of living up to one's ideal of a true, loyal friend is explored in Johnny Cash's cover of the Nine Inch Nails' song "Hurt" from 2002. In the song's harrowing refrain, Cash asks what he's become and laments that, in the end, everyone he knows has gone away which leads him to the realization that, ultimately, "I will let you down / I will make you hurt."[28] Cash's version of the song elicits the sense that the pain inflicted upon the friend is shared as deeply by the person narrating the lyrics whose actual self was unable to meet the expectations of the ideal self, which, in this case, meant being a true friend. This aligns well with Royce's notion that loyalty "tends to unify life, to give it center, fixity, stability."[29] When we don't live up to our own expectations of loyalty to others, we lose this sense of unity in ourselves since that commitment to loyalty forms a significant part of our identity—in this case, the identity of being a good friend. At the end of the song, when Cash urges that you can have his whole "empire of dirt," it is clear that the unity that loyalty once bound has unraveled, thus causing the deep suffering so well expressed by Cash's gravelly bass-baritone voice. "Hurt" gives us a fitting sense that our own failure to live up to the loyalties we've vowed to "stand by" can lead to our own torturous agony.

"The fightin' side of me"

Thus far, we've seen that one way of framing loyalty has to do with molding an ideal self with expectations of loyalty that one's actual self tries to strive toward. In the context of other people, whether it be a significant other or a friend, those expectations of loyalty can be made explicit and mutual. We do, however, form loyalties beyond individual human beings, some of which are insignificant but others of which form important aspects of our identities. Trivially, we may be a fan of a certain sports team and become invested in their success or failure. Regardless of how much of a "diehard" fan we may be, our actions likely have little to no impact on the team's actual performance, since the relationship is not built as strongly on reciprocity as relationships between unique persons. If, for instance, we stop following a team, there are plenty of others who will continue to be fans. Thus, this type of loyalty seems to work differently than loyalty between individual persons. At the same time, however, there are loyalties that do play a significant role in our lives, so much so that we may be willing to die for a loyal cause.

This sort of loyalty is explored in Toby Keith's "American Soldier," which chronicles the soldier who knows sacrifice well, noting he doesn't want to die but "if dyin's asked of me / I'll bear that cross with honor / 'cause freedom don't come free."[30] That narrative is also expressed in Trace Adkins' "Arlington," which tells the story of the fallen soldier who "can rest in peace" since "this is what it cost to keep us free."[31] In the case of the soldier who is willing to sacrifice his or her life to protect the freedoms of others, there is a deep sense of loyalty to a cause. This sort of loyalty can exist even if the person doesn't know the others for whom he or she is fighting for since the commitment is based on defending principles, freedoms, or a way of life that the person values so strongly that it forms part of his or her identity. Royce thinks that this type of loyalty is crucial to living a meaningful life: "Unless you can find some sort of loyalty, you cannot find unity and peace in your active living. You must find, then, a cause that is really worthy of the sort of devotion that the soldiers, rushing cheerfully to certain death, have felt for their clan or for their country."[32] It is these types of deep loyalties that center our lives in Royce's philosophy of loyalty.

Merle Haggard's "The Fightin' Side of Me" is a good example of the sort of mentality we might find in someone who is frustrated with fellow citizens who do not honor the sacrifice of members of the military. Haggard defends freedom of speech in the song and a person's right to stand up for the things they believe in, thereby honoring that inalienable duty to choose one's loyalties of which Royce spoke, but Haggard draws the line with those who dishonor the sacrifice of others by "runnin' down a way of life our fightin' men have fought and died to keep."[33] Haggard's song was written during the time of the Vietnam War when soldiers would return from the war to anti-war protesters from the hippie countercultural movement. His point was not that people can't stand up for their principles, whether that be pacifism or protesting the dubious reasons the United States entered the war in this case, but that it is wrong to be hypocritical by loving "our milk an' honey" while simultaneously preaching "about some other way of livin'" that would not even be possible without those willing to defend the country and thus the right to live freely.

The year after the release of "The Fightin' Side of Me," John Prine thought through legitimate reasons to protest the actions of one's country in "Your Flag Decal Won't Get You Into Heaven Anymore." In the song, Prine attacks the hypocrisy governments sometimes show in engaging in war using bogus religious reasons to justify their cause, noting "Jesus don't like killin' no matter what the reason's for," thus discouraging persons from supporting the "dirty little war."[34] Patriotism is surely a sign of loyalty to one's country and should be celebrated at times, but Prine shows us that blind patriotism is problematic since loyalty should have limits.

"Love you anyway"

On the whole, whether it be to a spouse, a friend, or a country, loyalty ultimately comes down to devoting oneself to another or a cause beyond oneself, even if that devotion leads to significant hardship on oneself. True loyalty seems to be well expressed in Luke Combs' 2023 hit, "Love You Anyway," when he says "even if I knew the day we met you'd be the reason this heart breaks / Oh, I'd love you anyway."[35] Combs provides a fitting analogy of loyalty operating "like a compass needle needing its true North," thus demonstrating how loyalty is worth the risk of commitment since it centers our lives. Although there are legitimate reasons to break loyalty to another—if a man doesn't walk the line, if a friendship you thought was built on virtue was actually built on utility for the other and you find out who your friends are, or if a country is needlessly sending soldiers to a dirty little war—ultimately, loyalty is a virtue since it provides a meaningful center to our lives and helps us to understand what is worth living (and dying) for.

NOTES

1. Wynette, Tammy. 1968. "Stand By Your Man." *Stand By Your Man.* Sherrill, Billy (prod.) Epic.

2. Wynette, Tammy, and Dew, Joan. 1979. *Stand By Your Man: An Autobiography.* Simon & Schuster.

3. Lawrence, Tracy. 2007. "Find Out Who Your Friends Are." *For the Love.* King, Julian; Lawrence, Tracy (prod.) Rocky Comfort Records.

4. Haggard, Merle. "The Fightin' Side of Me." *The Fightin' Side of Me.* Nelson, Ken (prod.) Capitol Records.

5. Royce, Josiah. 1908. *The Philosophy of Loyalty.* Macmillan.

6. *Ibid.*

7. Michael Streissguth. 2006. *Johnny Cash: The Biography.* Da Capo Press.

8. Cash, Johnny. 1956. "I Walk the Line." Phillips, Sam (prod.) Sun Records.

9. Nietzsche, Friedrich. 1994. *Human, All Too Human: A Book For Free Spirits.* Hollingdale, R.J. (trans.) Penguin Classics.

10. Royce.

11. Cash, Johnny. *Johnny Cash: The Life in Lyrics.* Little, Brown.

12. Robert Louis Stevenson. 1991. *The Strange Case of Dr. Jekyll and Mr. Hyde.* Dover.

13. Royce.

14. Cash, Johnny. 1963. "Ring of Fire." *Ring of Fire: The Best of Johnny Cash.* Law, Don; Jones, Frank (prod.) Columbia Records. I use "purportedly" since Cash's first wife argued that Cash himself wrote the song but gave credit to Carter since she was in need of money.

15. Jennings, Waylon; Nelson, Willie. 1972. "Good Hearted Woman." *Good Hearted Woman.* Light, Ronny; Davis, Danny (prod.) RCA Nashville.

16. Stewart, Gary. 1975. "She's Actin' Single (I'm Drinkin' Doubles)." *Out of Hand.* Dea, Roy (prod.) RCA Victor.

17. Dixie Chicks. 2000. "Goodbye Earl / Stand By Your Man." Chancy, Blake; Worley, Paul (prod.) Sony Music Entertainment.

18. "Goodbye Earl" opened up a whole sub-genre of female revenge country, including

Underwood, Carrie. 2005. "Before He Cheats." *Some Hearts*. Bright, Mark (prod.) Arista Nashville; Lambert, Miranda. 2009. "White Liar." *Revolution*. Liddell, Frank; Wrucke, Mike (prod.) Columbia Nashville.

19. Aristotle. *Nicomachean Ethics*. Ross, David (trans.) Oxford University Press.

20. Williams, Hank, Jr. 1984. "All My Rowdy Friends Are Coming Over Tonight." *Major Moves*. Bowen, Jimmy; Williams, Hank, Jr. (prod.) Warner Bros.

21. *Ibid.*

22. Aristotle. *Eudemian Ethics*. Kenny, Anthony (trans.) Oxford University Press.

23. John Prine. 1999. "In Spite of Ourselves." *In Spite of Ourselves*. Rooney, Jim; Prine, John (prod.) Oh Boy.

24. Aristotle. *Nicomachean Ethics*.

25. Lawrence.

26. Aristotle. *Eudemian Ethics*.

27. Royce.

28. Cash, Johnny. 2002. "Hurt." *American IV: The Man Comes Around*. Rubin, Rick; Cash, John Carter (prod.) American Recordings.

29. Royce.

30. Keith, Toby. 2003. "American Soldier." *Shock'n Y'all*. Keith, Toby; Stroud, James (prod.) Dreamworks.

31. Adkins, Trace. 2005. "Arlington." *Songs About Me*. Hendricks, Scott (prod.) Capitol Nashville.

32. Royce.

33. Haggard.

34. Prine, John. 1971. "Your Flag Decal Won't Get You Into Heaven Anymore." *John Prine*. Mardin, Arif (prod.) Atlantic.

35. Combs, Luke. 2023. "Love You Anyway." *Gettin' Old*. Combes, Luke; Matthews, Chip; Singleton, Jonathan (prod.) Columbia Nashville.

On Being
Authentically Country

Hollywood with a Touch of Twang

Theodore Gracyk

Country fans understand that country music is a commercial product, yet they also regard it as a natural, spontaneous product of American culture. The philosopher John Dyck observes that country fans value music that "comes from pure self-expression, not commercial interests."[1] At the same time, this self-expression should be rooted in community and tradition. When hip-hop artist Post Malone recorded a country album in 2024, his appearance at the Grand Ole Opry was carefully framed to defuse fan suspicion that he was an outsider or interloper. His Opry introduction stressed that he was, in fact, Southern: a "gentleman" from Texas! Although country music is not the only genre of popular music to emphasize authenticity grounded in community and shared values, country fans are clearly suspicious of commercialization that will dilute or pollute it.

Jason Aldean's hit song "Crazy Town" comes right out and says it: the "dreams" associated with country music are often manufactured in the "Hollywood"-derived system of Nashville.[2] The working-class struggles of the typical country fan occupy a different world from the stars and business moguls of the country music industry. "Crazy Town" references Hank Williams, getting drunk in honky tonks, and struggling to make payments on your truck, but it's not really about those things. The song is about how "you gotta" sing about those things, and give it the right twang if you want to please "the record man" and make a living in country music. The song is unusual for calling attention to the way that Nashville manufactures a product, while also implying that the ideology promoted by this product is, like any ideology, a story told that covers up the true operations of the prevailing system. But Aldean was not the first to make this point. A generation earlier, the same issues and critique informed Waylon Jennings' song, "Are You Sure Hank Done It This Way."[3]

It's not a coincidence that both songs reference Hank Williams to make their point. You can't worry that "Hollywood" and "Nashville" produce inauthentic music unless you can contrast industry commercialization with an earlier, purer form. Williams was a great popularizer of country music after World War II, sending 12 singles to the top of the country music charts between 1949 and his untimely death in 1953. He set the standard for what we now consider to be "classic" country, so his name has long been shorthand for the core of country purity.

Of course, Williams didn't invent country music. The honky-tonk sound of his major hits adopted one of the popular styles of his time, and it was audibly different from its forerunner, the "hillbilly" music that the industry rechristened "country & western" and eventually just "country." Williams was all about pleasing "the record man," but that had been true of country music from the very start. Country music was an invented product of a commercial music industry, always mediated by technology, and always guided by the quest for profit. Yet, ever since the era of Hank Williams, country fans have told themselves that the music isn't like that and that the entertainment industry is somehow a threat to the music's purity and authenticity.

What are we actually looking for when we look for authenticity in what is so obviously a commercial product?

"Cash on the barrelhead"

Music production was commercialized by business interests long before the emergence of the genre we know as country. Country music was always a commercial product. It had to be. There was no way it could become so popular—virtually overnight, coast-to-coast and then internationally—without the use of recording and broadcast technology. The record companies and radio stations expected a return on their investment in all that technology. Hank Williams was no less immersed in, and in active partnership with, the entertainment technology and industry of his time than a contemporary hitmaker like Taylor Swift. But we can push this point back further, to the so-called "big bang" of country music, the recording sessions conducted by Ralph Peer in Bristol, Tennessee, from July 25 through August 5, 1927.[4] Although some similar musicians had been recorded earlier, the importance of the Bristol sessions was that Peer scouted regional "hillbilly" musicians on their home turf for mass-market distribution by the Victor Talking Machine Company. His two major discoveries were the Carter Family and Jimmie Rodgers, who together established the template for early country.

Victor's surprisingly strong sales of these artists led other labels to scout and promote White Southern musicians, sometimes advertising them as "old-time music." As with most advertising, the joke was on the audience. Understanding how money flows through the music industry, Peer had no interest in anything that was genuinely "old-time." The big money was to be found in the copyrights, and he required the musicians to bring him original songs. As a condition for recording them, Peer then paid the musicians a small fee to purchase the copyrights and subsequent publishing revenue.[5] They could only record older songs if they were rewritten enough to justify copyright protection. In practice, this sometimes meant that the musicians were plagiarizing more obscure artists, especially Black artists whose music was not familiar to the larger audience of country music.[6]

Technology, Rootlessness, and Inauthenticity

Country music fans value authenticity grounded in communal values. However, the philosophical thought of Martin Heidegger warns that communal values can undermine the very authenticity we seek. His writings also contain important ideas about technology and its relationship to authenticity. Or, more precisely, he has an original thesis about the *idea* of technology. We find various tools as far back as we can find a record of human beings. Indeed, in many cases, we know of the early spread of humans because we find the remains of durable technologies. It is interesting to note that among the oldest tools are musical instruments: flutes. Archaeologists have found "flutes made from bird bones and mammoth ivory—over 100 uncontroversial specimens," including ones that are at least 40,000 years old.[7] In one sense, every tool is a piece of technology. However, Heidegger proposes that the industrial proliferation of tools has led to a revised understanding of technology.

Using his typically cryptic language, Heidegger argues that "the essence of technology is by no means anything technological."[8] He means that we directly encounter this or that tool or machine (e.g., interacting with a smartphone app or flipping a light switch when entering a dark room) without ever directly encountering the essential element that unites all these things as technology. He then offers a surprising proposal: the true essence of all technology and manufacturing is "a way of revealing" the world around us.[9] Collectively, our technology shows us something that is otherwise concealed, namely, that everything in nature is a source of energy, power, and unexpected value. The vast plains can be plowed under, and the nutrients in the soil transformed into an endless sea of cash crops, and when the nutrients are gone, the same petroleum that fuels the farm machinery can be transformed into nitrogen fertilizers to keep the land productive. Land that cannot be farmed can be torn open for mineral deposits. Modern technology reveals that every aspect of nature is a hidden resource for human exploitation, and every object is a "standing reserve" or resource.[10]

At the same time, modern technology is a global system. Previously, when human labor was more common than machines, a woodcutter worked for those nearby, responding to local needs. Today, the worker who fells the trees is supplying an international market, perhaps to supply paper for use in another part of the world. To update Heidegger's example, an orphaned teen in the Democratic Republic of Congo spends her days digging in the riverbank for stones whose cobalt is used in Chinese-manufactured smartphones sold in Europe and North America. The smartphone revolution has revealed the value of what is hidden in the mud along the Congo River, and the teen's working life is now dictated by the global adoption of a specific technology.[11]

Modern technology in its global organization does not stop with nature: every human is a potential resource, as well. We created technology, yet it unlocked a relationship to the world (and to each other) that we did not foresee or choose; technology has a logic and scale that has put it beyond control and containment. We have brought forth a system that transforms human beings into units of standing reserve.

To put it bluntly, modern technology is dehumanizing. We generally pretend it's just a set of tools serving our needs. However, in some sense, we all know that it shapes modern life to such a degree that we end up serving it. It is often said about digital technologies that the user is not the customer; the user is the product. Technology dehumanizes all of us.

Applying these ideas to the Bristol recording sessions, Ralph Peer's genius was to see that recording technology unlocked the standing reserve of itinerant and regional musicians—but not *merely* the musicians. In conjunction with record sales, songs themselves became objects transformable into commercial assets. Much like river rock containing cobalt, an old ballad found in a remote West Virginia holler might contain the germ of a "new" song to feed the growing commercial music industry, generating corporate profits for decades to come.

Today, some or all of the above may seem obvious. But keep in mind that it wasn't obvious in the 1950s when Heidegger originated this analysis. When country fans worry about "Hollywood" values polluting the music, these worries dovetail with Heidegger's analysis. Additionally, it's worth keeping Heidegger at the forefront of the discussion because his proposed antidote is relevant here. We retain a power to resist technology's dehumanization. We retain a power for self-examination, and we have a non-technological tool for remaining aware that we are not reducible to our potential contribution to the global economy. That power, says Heidegger, is disclosure through art.[12] It is our great reminder that the world is too rich to reduce everything to its utility and commercial value.

Authenticity and Humanity

Like several other 19th- and 20th-century European philosophers, Heidegger explored the relationship between dehumanization and inauthentic living. A human being leads an authentic life by being self-directed: the Dixie Chicks faced enormous backlash when they openly criticized President Bush and the invasion of Iraq in 2003. Inauthenticity comes from socially-enforced conformity, such as eating meat and drinking alcohol as natural behaviors because everyone around you does so. This doesn't mean that the authentic life requires the *rejection* of all social norms, but it does require that any embrace of social expectations is accompanied by the self-awareness that one has the option to do otherwise. It might seem, then, that the Ricky Skaggs song "Don't Get Above Your Raising" has a man telling his girlfriend that she should forget authenticity; she should just accept her "country" raising and not strive for anything more.[13] However, the song is richer than that. The singer is concerned that she is pretending to be someone she's not, acting as if she has a social standing that places his status beneath hers. He is warning her, in other words, that she is being inauthentic by pretending to have a social position that she does not really inhabit. She is the captive of social norms. As a result, she no longer allows herself or him to be the persons they (authentically) could be.

This is merely one example of a theme that runs through the lyrics of country music. It is present in one of the genre's earliest recordings, the Carter Family's version of the traditional "Single Girl, Married Girl."[14] It's a surprisingly proto-feminist song, "a critique of female subjugation under marriage."[15] It more or less proclaims that no woman entrapped by social expectations of marriage and child-rearing has the independence needed for authenticity, self-realization, and happiness. A more recent example would be Brandy Clark's "Girl Next Door."[16]

The great irony here is that authenticity is frequently equated with its mirror opposite, social conformity. Musicologist Nadine Hubbs observes that many fans are "authenticity seekers."[17] These fans want the audience and the musicians to be members of a shared tradition that is untainted by outside forces. The authentic is established by reference to tradition and past practice. For some fans, this means the distant past. They "reject modern commercial country and its market-driven anything-goes stylistic idiom, idealizing past artists and purist notions of a genuine folk idiom."[18] These authenticity seekers seem to be highlighting the concern that commerce is a tradition-destroying technology in Heidegger's sense of the term. Or, perhaps not. Seeking a past that's untainted by commerce and mass media, their nostalgia is for "a socially agreed-upon construct in which the past is to a degree misremembered."[19] Country music has always been fabricated, crafted, and sold to the audience in the form of commercialized mass media. Recall the earlier discussion of Hank Williams as the cornerstone of country tradition. In fact, Williams didn't record until country music's third decade.

Consequently, the fans who reject commercialism are not all that different from the ones who see no problem with it. They merely emphasize different decades. Love it or hate it, our access depends on technology and commerce, which also requires shared musical tastes—a musical community—that is large enough to serve as a stable commercial market for record companies and streaming services. The social uniformity of each segment of the commercial audience is, in turn, celebrated as an authentic community. Anyone from outside that community is almost certainly *not* authentic. A case in point: (born in New Zealand and raised in Australia) Keith Urban is essentially the only country star from anywhere but the United States or Canada. Conversely, a singer with bona fide community ties might get a free pass. Because she is Johnny Cash's daughter, Rosanne Cash could make a record that was unabashedly commercial, drawing more on British pub rock and new wave than country, sending it to the top of the *Billboard* country album chart.[20]

Judgments about shared community can be more important than how the music sounds. A classic example is the appearance of the rock band The Byrds at the Grand Ole Opry in 1968. They were responsible for one of the greatest psychedelic rock hits, "Eight Miles High," yet their roots were folk music, and country-tinged tunes are present on all their albums.[21] The Opry audience didn't accept them as country musicians, and country radio wouldn't play them. Coming from the other direction, many rock fans rejected the album they were promoting, *Sweetheart of the Rodeo*, because it was too country. Too country for some people, not country enough for others; who you are can matter more than what you sound like.

Musicologist Allan Moore has proposed that this kind of thinking is typical when it comes to popular music. His key point is that "authenticity" does not refer to any objective property of popular music.[22] Audience approval is the only standard for deciding what's authentic: authenticity is nothing more than audience authentication, which may be any of three things endorsed by fans. It can be authenticity of expression, where fans perceive a performance as a genuine communicative act, not as mere show. (Keep in mind that "perceived" sincerity is not always sincere.) There can be authenticity of experience, where the fan feels that it illuminates or validates their own experiences. An example would be a queer fan who recognizes themselves in Brandi Carlile's "Party of One."[23] Finally, there is authentication of execution, which is the kind Hubbs mentions. The twang of the music, the drawl of the voice, and the black 10-gallon hat of Tim McGraw are appreciated as symbolic links to a larger, established community.

Ironically, all of this can be manufactured. Everything "country" is subject to commercial manipulation. The cowboy hat became "country" thanks to the Hollywood careers of Gene Autry and Roy Rogers. In any given case, audience authentication generally reflects style familiarity, which reflects media conditioning—another case of dehumanization.

Glimpses of Authenticity

There is a potential irony here. Heidegger suggests that the things fans consider most authentic can make their relationship to the music inauthentic. Moore's model of subjective authentication identifies three ways that fans validate country music without necessarily calling it "authentic." They're essentially judgments of how the music feels to the listener, which may or may not align with personal authenticity as found in Heidegger's philosophy. Accepted uncritically, *any* signifier of country authenticity will function as a "Hollywood" product, undercutting personal authenticity.

Most of the time, we live our lives without concern for personal authenticity. Most of the time, we're content with the social conformity that validates going along to get along. "Inauthenticity is no unqualified blemish," observes Heidegger scholar Michael Inwood. "It is the normal condition of most of us for most of the time, and without it, we could not make decisions at all."[24] We need community—the same community that contributes to inauthenticity. So, generally, we are unconcerned with authenticity.

However, art is different. We look for authenticity in art—including music—because artistic activity is the one arena of human action that remains essentially connected to original (and thus authentic) disclosure. Certainly, in practice, most art is clichéd, especially popular art. Because clichéd music feels comfortable, we feel at home with our favored genres and styles, and we often authenticate it in Moore's sense. Yet at the same time, we are open to—and hoping for—something more.

It often appears in surprising places. David Allan Coe scored his first hit by doing his version of the (self-proclaimed) "perfect country and western song"—a parody of country songwriting that strung together random phrases about prison, mama, trains, drinking, and pickup trucks.[25] At the same time, the song's joke requires a display of self-reflection that blunts any charge of lazy inauthenticity. It works by parodying the genre's endless recycling of clichéd topics and familiar chord progressions. In doing so, it ridicules what happens when music is produced and marketed by the technologies of the entertainment industry. Yet, as subversive art, it delivers a glimpse of what fans unconsciously desire: those moments of self-realization that disclose the perennial possibility of authenticity.

In other words, we live in a world that dehumanizes audiences, artists, and art. That situation is just how it is. We've all "fallen" into that world at birth.[26] Music might even get worse as the music industry adopts the technology of artificial intelligence. So, yes, country music fans all know that the latest country hit is probably just Hollywood with a touch of twang.

Nonetheless, we sometimes get the real thing. Although Heidegger dismisses most modern art as inauthentic, he identifies a tactic that allows art, even commercialized art, to challenge inauthenticity. Many people think that music is valuable for expressing emotion, but emotion can be faked. Instead, true art reaches us by offering an "unfamiliar" insight, a glimmer of something that eludes the familiar categories and concepts that dominate our thoughts and discourse. However, it makes us work for those insights. It offers specifics that anchor it in the everyday, but these are placed in tension with elements that are vague or merely suggested, inviting the respondent to engage in active interpretation. The meaning is not closed off but rather something "slumbering within" that provokes our thinking.[27]

Art of this kind goes beyond prevailing social conventions and ideas. It goes beyond simple authentication. When we engage with it, we see a glimpse of the possibilities of authentic action in a space not yet conquered by technology. A paradigm example is the 1967 hit "Ode to Billie Joe."[28] So is the Carter Family's "Single Girl, Married Girl," and perhaps some of the other songs named here, too.

I hold out hope that you've experienced other examples of country music that challenge inauthenticity. I leave it open to you to ask which country songs have made possible this experience for you, confirming the possibility of authenticity and undercutting its own origins in technology and industry.

NOTES

1. Dyck, John. 2021. "The Aesthetics of Country Music." *Philosophy Compass* 16 (5), 1–19, at 7.

2. Jones, Brett; Clawson, Rodney. 2009. "Crazy Town." *Wide Open*. Aldean, Jason (rec. artist). Knox, Michael (prod.) Broken Bow Records.

3. Jennings, Waylon. 1975. "Are You Sure Hank Done It This Way." *Dreaming My Dreams*. Jennings, Waylon (rec. artist). Clement, Jack; Jennings, Waylon (prods.) RCA Records.

4. Stimeling, Travis D. 2013. "Recording Reviews: The Bristol Sessions, 1927–1928: The Big Bang of Country Music." *Journal of the Society for American Music*. Cambridge University Press, 219–222.

5. Mazor, Barry. 2015. *Ralph Peer and the Making of Popular Roots Music*. Chicago Review Press, 69–75.

6. Gracyk, Theodore. 2023. *Appropriation, Racism, and Art: Constructing American Identities*. Pressbooks. Chapter 7, section 9.

7. Killin, Anton. 2018. "Music and Human Evolution: Philosophical Aspects." *The Routledge Handbook of Evolution and Philosophy*. Joyce, Richard (ed.) Routledge, 372–86, at 373. Killin observes that these are so sophisticated that they represent a later stage of a longer history of making instruments from less durable materials (*Ibid.*, 374). At least one flute made from mammoth ivory may have been made by Neanderthals.

8. Heidegger, Martin. 1977. "The Question concerning Technology." *The Question Concerning Technology: And other Essays*. Lovitt, William (trans.). Garland Publishing, 4.

9. *Ibid.*, 12.

10. *Ibid.*, 17.

11. See Kara, Siddharth. 2018. "Is Your Phone Tainted by the Misery of the 35,000 Children in Congo's Mines?" *The Guardian*, October 12.

12. Granted, Heidegger speaks of "fine art," but there is no reason in principle to agree to the implicit elitism of his proposal. If the mass entertainment of ancient Greek theater qualifies, why not Hank Williams?

13. Skaggs, Ricky. 1981. "Don't Get Above Your Raising." *Waitin' for the Sun to Shine*. Skaggs, Ricky (rec. artist and prod.) Epic Records.

14. Traditional, arr. Carter, A.P. 1928. "Single Girl, Married Girl." 10" RPM. The Carter Family (rec. artist). Peer, Ralph (prod.) Victor Records.

15. Hajdu, David. 2016. *Love for Sale: Pop Music in America*. Farrar, Straus and Giroux, 88.

16. Clark, Brandy; Dillon, Jessie Jo; McAnally, Shane. 2016. "Girl Next Door." *Big Day in a Small Town*. Clark, Brandy (rec. artist). Joyce, Jay (prod.) Warner Bros. Nashville.

17. Hubbs, Nadine. 2014. *Rednecks, Queers, and Country Music*. University of California Press, 70.

18. *Ibid.*

19. Peterson, Richard A. 1997. *Creating Country Music: Fabricating Authenticity*. The University of Chicago Press, 5.

20. Cash, Rosanne. 1981. *Seven Year Ache*. Cash, Rosanne (rec. artist). Crowel, Rodney (prod.) Columbia Records.

21. Clark, Gene; McGuinn, Jim; Crosby, David. 1966. "Eight Miles High." *Fifth Dimension*. The Byrds (rec. artist). Stanton, Allen (prod.) Columbia Records.

22. Moore, Allan F. 2002. "Authenticity as Authentication." *Popular Music*. Cambridge University Press 21(2), 209–223.

23. Carlile, Brandi; Hanseroth, Phil; Hanseroth, Tim. 2018. "Party of One." *By the Way, I Forgive You*. Carlile, Brandi (rec. artist). Cobb, Dave; Jennings, Shooter (prods.) Epic Records.

24. Inwood, Michael. 2019. *Heidegger: A Very Short Introduction*. 2nd ed. Oxford University Press, 28.

25. Goodman, Steve; Prine, John. 1975. "You Never Even Called Me by My Name." *Once Upon a Rhyme*. Coe, David Allan (rec. artist). Bledsoe, Ron (prod.) Columbia Records.

26. Heidegger, Martin. 1962. *Being and Time*. Macquarrie, John; Robinson, Edward (trans.) Oxford University Press, 220.

27. Heidegger, Martin. 1968. *What Is Called Thinking?* Gray, J.G. (trans.) Harper & Row, 14.

28. Gentry, Bobbie. "Ode to Billie Joe." *Ode to Billie Joe*. Gentry, Bobbie (rec. artist). Gordon, Kelly; Paris, Bobby (prods.) Capitol Records.

Three Chords
and the (Existential) Truth

Kristina Gehrman

"Country music is three chords and the truth,"[1] so said renowned songwriter Harlan Howard. Maybe he was right, but in Ken Burns' multi-part documentary, *Country Music,* singer-songwriter Rodney Crowell added, "'It's about the truth, even when it's a big, fat lie.'"[2] Howard's legendary spin and Crowell's rejoinder capture something at the heart of country music: it is deeply invested in its own *authenticity.* As historian Charles Hughes puts it,

> From the beginning, country music has been made and marketed around the idea of a particular vision of identity—it's not just about whether something *sounds* country, but how the artist *is* or *isn't* country. This plays out through the music itself, but also through the imagery and cultural associations [of the genre].[3]

The question is, who (or what) determines which country music and country musicians count as "real" country? What separates the authentic country truths from the "big fat lies"? As country music fans know well, these debates can be contentious.

With all of this in mind, philosopher Emmie Malone has argued that "given the way in which some country audiences and artists use the distinction between mere country music and so-called 'real' or 'authentic' country music, we might worry that the notion of authenticity employed in discussions of the genre is nothing but a cudgel used for a problematic kind of gatekeeping."[4] And, perhaps unsurprisingly, country artists themselves have weighed in on the issue. In a 2022 interview, country singer Luke Bryan (a performer who's had his own country credibility called into question)[5] claimed that "if you sing about hunting and fishing and drinking and trucks and s—, and I get you on my farm ... in one minute I can tell if you're a poseur ... or if you're not legit."[6] So, as we can see, those who produce, consume, and analyze country music all seem to have a concern for the concept of real or authentic country.

But all of this again raises some fairly obvious questions. How should thoughtful people understand the debate over authenticity in country music? And *why* is country music so invested in its own authenticity? Fortunately, authenticity is something that existentialist philosophers have had a lot to say about (though not always in precisely those terms). So, in what follows, I'll draw on the work of the existentialist philosophers Søren Kierkegaard and Simone de Beauvoir to introduce a set of connected ideas: *authenticity*, *bad faith*, and *existential truth*, and we can use these ideas to explain country's peculiarly strong investment in its own authenticity.

Existential Truth, Authenticity, and Bad Faith

Colloquially, "authentic" and "genuine" are often used interchangeably, as in "an authentic Rolex" or "an authentic smile." But existential authenticity goes beyond being genuine. After all, people can be shallow, or oblivious, and still be perfectly *genuine* about it. A truly authentic person dares to ask difficult, fundamental questions about our human condition. Questions like: What are we humans, anyway? Is a good life possible for me, given the conditions of my existence? And it's perhaps these very questions they have in mind when the country band Pirates of the Mississippi sings, "What we are and what we ain't / What we can and what we can't / *Does it really matter*?"[7] In a similar vein, Johnny Cash seems to ask, what's the point in living when "I'm a double first cousin to a dad blamed mole / Never get rich for to save my soul"?[8] The authentic person bravely poses questions such as these, searches for answers to them, and then lives their life with unblinking awareness of what they discover—no matter how daunting that reality turns out to be.

Of course, if we misunderstand our existential condition, we'll wind up striving toward the wrong thing altogether! So, authenticity requires that we grasp *existential truth(s)*: bedrock, fundamental truths about the human condition—both in general and in regard to our "specific life situations." Existential truths have deeply ethical and practical implications that go beyond just "knowing what's true." Human mortality, for example, is a natural fact that is also an existential truth we all have to grapple with to live authentically. On the other hand, it might be a fact that you really need a bang trim, but that truth's not existential (unless maybe you're Taylor Swift).

Finally, *bad faith* is the opposite of authenticity: running from, denying, or obscuring the existential truth *even though we know it's there.* That might mean failing to show up authentically for your own life, or it might mean undermining the existential struggle of others, or both, as in the case of Lefty's betrayal of Pancho. "All the federales say / they could have had him any day," but we know better. Does Lefty know? Does he *let* himself know? We can picture him, alone, far from the borderlands where he chose to play the villain in the central drama of his own life, having to live with himself, comforting himself with an empty lie: "I just did what he had to do [but] now he's growing old."[9]

So how do we avoid bad faith and come to know the existential truths of our own human condition? Our own and others' testaments to those truths, rooted in our undeniable immediate experiences, contribute incrementally to our "ongoing consciousness of [our own] existence,"[10] and thus to authenticity. We find such testaments in existentialist philosophy. We also find them everywhere in country music. Let's now look very briefly at two existentialist philosophers and their connection to country music, beginning with the Danish philosopher Søren Kierkegaard.

Kierkegaardian Faith "In Your Love"

Kierkegaard understood existential authenticity in terms of the difficulty of *faith*—understandably since he and everyone he knew were devout Christians. But Kierkegaard accused his fellow believers of failing to grasp the "prodigious paradox" of faith, "a paradox that is capable of making murder into a holy act well pleasing to God."[11] In the biblical story of Abraham and Isaac, God asks Abraham to sacrifice his son Isaac as a test of Abraham's faith. Kierkegaard would like us to stop and really think about that for a moment. "What is left out of Abraham's story is the anxiety, for … to the son the father has the highest and most sacred duty."[12]

How could God the Father ask this terrible, unspeakable thing of his son, Abraham? And how could Father Abraham do such a terrible thing to his truly beloved son, Isaac? "There were countless generations who knew the story of Abraham word for word by heart, but how many did it make sleepless?"[13] Kierkegaard asks. *Not enough of you* is the implied answer. Is it safer to avoid "faith" and stick to moral principles? No, that would be a form of bad faith, because none of us actually has the luxury of a clear, unproblematic moral code that we can follow without further thought.

In his lectures on existentialism, Hubert Dreyfus would sometimes illustrate this point with the case of a person daring to embrace their own non-heterosexual identity and deep loves, from within a social context that gave them no way to see themselves as good and right in so doing.[14]

Tyler Childers' "In Your Love" presents an example of precisely this kind of existential authenticity—a secular, modern-day case of having faith like Abraham's.[15] Childers released the single "In Your Love," a ballad passionately testifying to undying love and steadfast commitment, in 2023. But he waited until the song had gained in popularity and visibility before he released the music video, which depicts that powerful, undying love occurring in the 1950s between two coal mining men. As Childers sings "Honey I will wait for you / I will work for you / I will stand my ground," one man dies young, in the tender embrace of his life's love, felled by black lung disease.[16] The instrumental conclusion plays over footage of the survivor, now old, but still true to his love. Like Abraham's faith that sacrificing Isaac is righteous, the miners' conviction that their love for one another is right, good, and sacred is inexpressible in the moral terms of their mid-century, Protestant, Appalachian world. To truly love, for them, required a leap away from the logic of conventional morality; it required faith. For them, as for Abraham, "the movement of faith must constantly be made by virtue of the absurd."[17]

Bad Faith and Identity in Beauvoir

For Kierkegaard, the inexpressible struggle of faith necessarily takes place alone, deep inside the mind and heart. Consequently, he says very little about the existential importance of social identity and social context. In contrast, French existentialist Simone de Beauvoir was keenly aware of the social constraints she faced in virtue of being a woman. In *The Second Sex,* Beauvoir makes the case:

> If we accept, even temporarily, that there are women on the earth, we then have to ask: What is a woman? ... It would never occur to a man to write a book on the singular situation of males in humanity. [Whereas] if I want to define myself, I first have to say, "I am a woman"; all other assertions will arise from this basic truth.[18]

But defining one's womanly self is not straightforward in patriarchal societies like Beauvoir's, where merely b*eing a subject of experience* (being someone who has thoughts and experiences of one's own) is understood as a "guy thing"; it is at least somewhat male-gendered.

Thirty years later, Dolly Parton was testifying to the same existential predicament as she was just barely making ends meet despite working "9 to 5": "Barely gettin' by, it's all takin' and no givin' / They just use your mind and they never give you credit / It's enough to drive you crazy if you let it...."[19] For Parton, as for Beauvoir, to be a woman is to be a particular kind of social being whose mind is thought of primarily in terms of its usefulness to others, rather than being thought of primarily as the subject of experiences and actions of its own. Authenticity for women in social conditions like Beauvoir's and Parton's thus requires forging a sense of self-as-subject where one *also* still understands oneself as a woman. That achievement turns out to be just as paradoxical as Abraham's willing sacrifice or the coal miners' pursuit of their true love.[20] We can now distinguish two different ways in which bad faith can undermine the struggle for authenticity. One form of bad faith is to recoil from the intolerable existential truth yourself. In the conditions faced by Abraham, Beauvoir, Parton, or Childers' miners, this recoil might take the form of self-loathing, false consciousness, self-deception, and so on.[21] If your society presents you with a picture of yourself that you can't recognize as *you*, you might, as a matter of sheer survival, do your best to pretend it's not there *or* do your best to become what you see. In so doing, however, you are denying your own existence and burying the existential truth.

The other way bad faith crops up is in inauthentic *narratives* that are socially imposed and perpetuated. A bad-faith conception of self or other tells a story that squashes the pursuit of authenticity, by denying or silencing relevant existential truths (such as, "I am a woman-who-thinks-my-own-free-thoughts"). Society told a suffocating story about women to Beauvoir and Parton; a suffocating story about faithful romantic bonds to Childers' miners. These people *recognized* and *struggled against* the imposition of that bad-faith conception of themselves even while the conception remained part of "the long-term constraints and possibilities [of their] specific life situations."[22]

Bad Faith, Bad Country

Let's now return to Childers' "In Your Love." The mining couple illustrates the fact that the Kierkegaardian paradox of faith is part of the human condition. But the real example of existential truth-telling here is not the video's story *per se*; it is Childers' choice to force his country music audience to grapple with these characters' authenticity by producing it. *This is us too*, the video says. These men are also a part of the culture, the history, and the story of the coal-mining Appalachian communities that gave birth to country music. They share the integrity, the tirelessness, the commitment that defines those communities. And coal buried them just as surely as if they too had died in a shaft collapse.[23] Their realness (Childers implies) deserves mention among the existential truths that are narrated by country music.

Childers' statement of existential truth with "In Your Love" made some country music fans uncomfortable because it brought them face to face with their own bad-faith conception of country. *Baptist News* reported that "listeners, having heard audio of the song originally, were shocked that what they imagined happening in the song is not what the artist imagined happening... 'We lost Tyler,'" one fan proclaimed, while another griped that he didn't have to "shove it down our throats."[24] (This tacit admission that gay true love exists in the space of country is a gesture of deliberate bad faith right up there with Lefty's self-deceit.)

Childers' was not the first controversial country music video of 2023. In May of that year, pop country singer Jason Aldean released a single called "Try That in a Small Town."[25] The Hot Country charts hit celebrates rural White American men responding to random acts of violence, armed robbery, public civil rights demonstrations, and flag burning—all by violently taking the law into their own hands.[26] National controversy did not erupt, however, until Aldean also released the music video, which blatantly connected violence and White supremacist motifs of the song to particular historical instances of White supremacist, anti-black violence, including a 1933 lynching in Columbia, Tennessee.[27] Aldean, the song, and video were sharply criticized, and CMT pulled the video, but the song became a huge hit, and the video has been viewed over 66 million times on YouTube.[28] When Aldean announced the single's release, he said:

> To me, this song summarizes the way a lot of people feel about the world right now. It seems like there are bad things happening on a daily basis.... This song sheds some light on that.[29]

Here, Aldean implies that the song depicts things that are actually happening in small towns "on a daily basis," and he implies that the song explains *why* these things are happening. The existential truth the song invokes is thus perhaps something like "small town people proudly take care of one another in the face of constant hardship, and they tirelessly struggle together against the degradation of their communities by outside corrosive forces."

A song that testifies to the existential struggle of small-town America sure sounds like it should be authentic country. A central, poignant thread in country music testifies to this truth, from Merle Travis's 1946 "16 Tons" to Iris DeMent's 1992 "Our Town" to Tyler Childers' 2017 "Nose on the Grindstone" among countless others.[30] And no doubt "Try That in a Small Town" worked in part because listeners think of this theme when they hear it, and they identify with and approve of the values and ways of life that the song invokes.

But country singer-songwriter Jason Isbell invoked Harlan Howard when he weighed in to contradict a reading of the song as authentic:

> A lot of people are missing the fact that all the instances in Jason Aldean's song [of socially threatening violence supposedly calling for outlaw violence] are just paranoia. …a lot of people think "What's wrong with this! He's just saying don't do bad things to people!" But … none of *those* things are really a true danger to small-town America. They're a danger to this concept of masculine Whiteness. And that's the thing that's being traded on here. And I don't think that's okay. I think that country music should be three chords and the truth. And that's not the truth.[31]

The problem Isbell points out is twofold. First, the song and the video misrepresent the *sources* of small-town hardship, identifying Black Americans, protesters against police brutality, and flag burners as the enemy while saying nothing about, say, fentanyl, or the brutal economic disenfranchisement perpetrated on rural communities by coal monopolies and factory farms. Second, the song and the video present a fantasy of White supremacist violence against strangers as the ideal, authentic way to respond to the existential threats facing small towns. The fantasy of easy vigilante justice enacted on strangers obscures and demeans the bleak, unglamorous stoicism with which real people meet the hardships endemic to American small towns: getting up every day and living with diabetes, opioid addiction, bankruptcy, credit card debt collectors, the tedium of two part-time call center jobs … and on and on.

With this pair of strategic falsehoods, "Try That in a Small Town" asserts the insidious and toxic lie that rural White masculine authenticity is achieved through White supremacist violence. And it does so precisely by falsely equating White supremacist violence with the real enduring existential truths it *invokes* but does not honor. In so doing, "Try That in a Small Town" obscures the existential truth it claims to disclose. This is, in every respect, bad-faith country.

Telling the (Existential) Truth

If country music *is* a distinctive form of existential truth-telling, testifying to the existential condition of poor and disenfranchised communities of the American South, then bad-faith country is more than just a lie; it's a betrayal. It hides the very existential truths it claims to disclose.

And there's good reason to think that people see country music as having the quasi-sacred role of existential testament. Consider Rosanne Cash's tender reflection on the Carter family recordings:

> The Carter family were *elemental* … the building blocks for the rest of us. And those first recordings, and those songs—they were *captured*, rather than written. They were in the hills, like *rock* formations. So, in 1927, those first Bristol

recordings, these songs that were in the collective unconscious were gathered together, documented forever, with these plaintive voices and these elemental guitars, [and] the bedrock was formed for the rest of us.[32]

Cash describes these recordings, widely considered to be a (if not the) primary origin of country music, as a distilled record of the existential circumstances of the people in the hills. But who was tucked away in those hills, giving birth to those germinal songs?

The hills of Appalachia were, and are, home to all sorts of poor people: White coal miners and Black coal miners, Cherokee people (both before and after Removal),[33] White indentured servants and Black slaves, queer people and straight people, and women from every community doing the gendered labor of farming and foraging often while raising children and helping one another give birth ... and on and on. The banjo is an African American instrument.[34] The steel-string guitar was developed in the mid–1800s in America by German immigrant C.F. Martin, but why? "While the classical guitar was already a popular instrument at the time, it wasn't able to compete with the banjo or violin in terms of volume."[35] That is, *country* music needed the guitar to be a little noisier.

If those songs captured in Bristol were in the collective consciousness, it was the consciousness of *these* people from which they came. And from the standpoint of existential authenticity, what's striking is both what the people "in the hills" had in common, and what they didn't. They did not share a national origin, race, language, or even mutual respect. Instead, they had in common their poverty, their disenfranchisement, and their *place*—a place marked by a dramatic lack of infrastructure where an incredible array of endangered cultures mingled, producing what eventually became known as "country" music.[36]

These considerations point to a way in which country music may be uniquely vulnerable to the "big fat lie" of bad faith. If country is a kind of existential testament, and if people both inside and outside the community see the power of existential truth-telling, they can seek to manipulate that power in ways that amount to bad faith: perhaps to maintain false consciousness, to make a buck, or for other disingenuous purposes that trade on the claim to authenticity that's inherent in the genre. In fact, some would argue that this tradition of bad-faith appropriation is as old as the moment the Carter family brought their songs forth from the hills.[37]

Letting the Mystery Be

When a song, an artist, a music video, or some other element of country music discloses existential truth in a way that draws on or speaks through the cultural and musical roots, traditions, and resources of the American South, especially *but not exclusively* Southern Appalachia—that's "authentic" country. This kind of authenticity can come in degrees, and it can be realized in parts of a whole that itself fails to achieve it. (For example, it might be that the same song sung by two different artists strikes us very differently against this measure or that three out of four stanzas speak truth while the last misses the mark.)

And what if a country song, artist, etc., obscures, distorts or otherwise betrays existential truth? Well, if the way that it achieves this lie is *precisely by claiming to be engaged in the above, distinctively "country" kind of authentic testimonial truth-telling*, that's "bad-faith" country. That's just a con; a con that works by being an ironic antithesis to the straight talk it purports to be. Bad-faith country can still be catchy, popular, or instrumentally impressive, or emotionally moving. But it will always have a certain underlying *ick* factor that existentialism can help us to pinpoint and appreciate. Doing so is one way to affirm, acknowledge, and give fitting attention to the existentially authentic country music whose existential truths are co-opted and traded on by bad-faith country.

The distinction between authentic and bad-faith country that I'm describing here does not speak to every single thing separating the good from the bad from the ugly in this vast and varied genre. But I do think it merits three chords of its own.

NOTES

1. This remark is attributed to Harlan Howard, but where and when he said it is not clear. It may be apocryphal. Dansby, Andrew. 2022. "Country Scribe Harlan Howard Dies." *Rolling Stone.*

2. Lewis, Randy. 2019. "In 2019, country music has a raging identity crisis. For Ken Burns, that's a 100-year-old story." *LA Times.*

3. Faison, Anna, and Charles Hughes. 2019. "Author Interview: Charles L. Hughes on 'Country Music: A Film by Ken Burns.'" The University of North Carolina Press Blog, September 20.

4. Malone, Emmie. 2023. "Country Music and the Problem of Authenticity." *British Journal of Aesthetics*, Vol. 63, Issue 1, 75–90.

5. Gillick, Leo. 2024. "Luke Bryan Says He's Surprised at How Much Hate He Gets for His Tight Jeans." *Wide Open Country.*

6. Shots Podcast Network. 2022. "Luke Bryan Reveals What Katy Perry Is Really Like and Calls Out Fake Country Artists!" *Full Send Podcast.*

7. Mayo, Danny. 1991. "Feed Jake." *Pirates of the Mississippi.* Pirates of the Mississippi (rec. artist). Alves, Rich; Stroud, James. Capitol Records.

8. Travis, Merle. 1960. "Loading Coal." *Ride This Train.* Johnny Cash (rec. artist). Law, Don; Quaglieri, Al (prods.) Columbia Records.

9. Van Zandt, Townes. 1972. "Pancho and Lefty." *The Late Great Townes Van Zandt.* Clement, Jack; Eggers, Kevin (prod.) Tomato.

10. Henry, Paget. 1997. "African and Afro-Caribbean Existential Philosophies."

Existence in Black: An Anthology of Black Existential Philosophy. Gordon, Lewis (ed.) Routledge, 11.

11. Kierkegaard, Søren. 2006. *Fear and Trembling. Cambridge Texts in the History of Philosophy.* Cambridge University Press, 46.

12. *Ibid.,* 22–23.

13. *Ibid.*

14. Dreyfus, Hubert. 2006. "Phil 7: Existentialism in Literature and Film." *Internet Archive.* Audio of the lectures can be found here; they are in the public domain and they are an excellent resource for anyone seeking an introduction to existentialism.

15. Childers, Tyler; Seale, Geno. 2023. "In Your Love." *Rustin' in the Rain.* Tyler Childers (rec. artist). Hickman Holler/RCA Nashville.

16. Childers, Tyler. 2023. "In Your Love" Video. Story by Silas House and Jason Kyle Howard. Written by Silas House. Directed by Bryan Schlam.

17. Kierkegaard, 31.

18. Beauvoir, Simone de. 2011. "Introduction." *The Second Sex.* Translated by Borde, Constance, and Malovany-Chevallier, Sheila. Vintage Books.

19. Parton, Dolly. 1980. "9 to 5." *9 to 5 and Odd Jobs.* Perry, Gregg (prod.) RCA Nashville.

20. Beauvoir's work on the existential condition of women was informed and inspired by that of her existentialist predecessor, the African American pan-intellectual W.E.B. Du Bois (1868–1963). For the sake of brevity I do not discuss Du Bois here but I recommend his collection of essays: W.E.B. Du Bois. *The Souls of Black Folk.* 1903/2009. *Project Gutenberg.* There is also an excellent audiobook version of this public domain text available on librivox.org.

21. Frantz Fanon (1925–1961) is the existentialist to read on this kind of response to oppressive social impositions of identity. See *Black Skin, White Masks.* 1967. Markmann, Charles (trans.). Grove Press.

22. Henry, Paget. "African and Afro-Caribbean Existential Philosophies," in *Existence in Black: An Anthology of Black Existential Philosophy,* edited by Lewis Gordon, Routledge, New York, 1997.

23. Childers, Tyler. 2011. "Coal." *Bottles and Bibles.* "We coulda made something of ourselves out there / if we'd listened to the folks that knew / that coal is gonna bury you."

24. Challis, Mallory. 2023. "Why Tyler Childers' New Outlaw Country Music Video Is Dividing Fans." *Baptist News.*

25. Lovelace, Kelley; Allison, Kurt; Thrasher, Neil; Kennedy, Tully. 2023. "Try That in a Small Town." *Highway Desperado.* Jason Aldean (rec. artist). Knox, Michael. (prod.) Broken Bow Records.

26. Trust, Gary. 2023. "Jason Aldean's 'Try That in a Small Town' Tops Hot 100, as Country Hits Rank at Nos. 1, 2 & 3 for First Time." *Billboard.*

27. Zemler, Emily. 2023. "Sheryl Crow Slams Jason Aldean's 'Try That in a Small Town': 'It's Just Lame.'" *Rolling Stone.*

28. Rutherford, Kevin. 2023. "Here's How Much Jason Aldean's 'Try That in a Small Town' Video Factored Into Its Hot 100 Coronation." *Billboard.*

29. Aldean, Jason. May 18, 2023. Press Release: "New Single, 'Try That in a Small Town' Out Now." *Jasonaldean.com.*

30. DeMent, Iris. 1992. "Our Town." *Infamous Angel*; Childers, Tyler. 2017. "Nose on the Grindstone." *Our Vinyl Sessions.*

31. Isbell, Jason. 2023. "Jason Isbell: As a musician, I'm trying to let people know they're not alone." *Morning Joe, MSNBC.*

32. Burns, Ken. 2019. *Country Music.* Episode 1, 58:54. Florentine Films and WETA Washington, D.C. (prod.)

33. "The Eastern Band of the Cherokee Indians." *Indigenous Appalachia: An Exhibition by WVU Art in the Libraries in Partnership with the WVU Native American Studies Program.* Western Virginia University.

34. For a history of the banjo see Giddens, Rhiannon. 2019. "Uncovering the History of the Banjo with Rhiannon Giddens: From African Roots to American Music." *The Great Courses.*

35. Banner. "Who Invented the Acoustic Guitar?" *Acoustic Guitarist.*

36. Burns, 14, 30, "Country music is the music of the working class, is the music of people who don't have a lot of power. We like to talk about the founding fathers. But the people who built this country, that's the people where country and blues come from."

37. Charles L. Hughes' history of the "industry's" power in this regard is detailed and comprehensive. Hughes, Charles L. 2015. *Country Soul: Making Music and Making Race in the American South.* University of North Carolina Press.

(A)I Did My Part

CHRISTOPHER DOLL

Although the concept of artificial intelligence (AI) has been around for centuries and has been popularized in fiction ranging from *Frankenstein* to *The Matrix*, technological advances over the past decade have recently rendered AI a practical tool for the masses. So-called "generative" AI, which allows users to enter simple prompts to create text, images, and music, is now available worldwide, online, in the form of dozens of computer programs like ChatGPT, ImagineArt, and Soundraw.

As impressive as this technology is, higher-level use of AI can yield some truly astonishing results.[1] One particularly fascinating application is the impersonation of famous singers, a practice flourishing among content creators working outside the mainstream music industry. Some of the most prominent examples have mimicked pop and hip-hop artists like The Weeknd and Drake,[2] but country-music fans can also enjoy many AI impressions of their favorite artists, several of which are rendered by Texas social-media musician Dustin Ballard, who posts under the moniker There I Ruined It.[3] For instance, we can hear Hank Williams singing lyrics to N.W.A.'s gangsta-rap classic "Straight Outta Compton" over the music of "Settin' the Woods on Fire."[4] Johnny Cash can be heard introducing himself with a new signature line, "Hello, I'm not Johnny Cash," before breaking into "Folsom Prison Blues" but with lyrics from Aqua's bubblegum-pop hit "Barbie Girl."[5] Conway Twitty sings lyrics to 50 Cent's "In da Club" over "Tight Fittin' Jeans,"[6] George Strait croons Metallica's "Enter Sandman" backed by "Amarillo by Morning," and Elvis Presley performs Sir Mix-a-Lot's "Baby Got Back" to the tune of "Don't Be Cruel."[7] The list goes on.

Lawyers and legislators in the United States, driven by music-industry interests, have been busy working to silence these virtual voices. Country music has been at the forefront here. In 2024, the state legislature of Tennessee unanimously passed a first-in-the-nation bill, the ELVIS Act (i.e., the Ensuring Likeness, Voice, and Image Security Act) which bans the unsanctioned AI recreation of a singer's sound.[8] The original uploads of two of the tracks just mentioned, of AI Johnny Cash and AI Elvis, have already been (as of the writing of this essay) forcibly removed on copyright grounds—before the ELVIS Act even became effective.

And yet, just as corporations have attempted to slow the spread of unofficial AI that apes famous artists, they've simultaneously promoted their own version of it. Elvis Evolution is an authorized show developed by the London-based company Layered Reality, which promised an AI Elvis performing onstage by way of the 19th-century illusion technique known as "Pepper's ghost"—the same mirror-image trick used in Disney's Haunted Mansion ride to create a party of ghosts waltzing through a ballroom.[9] While we might not be surprised to learn that multimillion-dollar companies are eyeing AI as a way to resurrect dead talent in order to cash in on nostalgic fans, what should we think (and what are the artistic and ethical ramifications) when living performers use AI on *themselves*? Randy Travis's 2024 song "Where That Came From" was recorded while Travis was (is) still alive and with his permission, and yet the song was never actually sung by him, as a stroke in 2013 permanently ended Travis's ability to sing. When musicians themselves release AI performances as their own, we can't so easily dismiss them as cynical cash grabs; we would appear compelled to at least consider the possibility that artistic expression is among the motivating factors.

With all these cases, we're witnessing the earliest moments of a fascinating collision of technology with tradition, artificiality with authenticity. The situation seems particularly fraught in country music, where tradition and authenticity are so highly prized. While we have only begun to experience the potential of what AI can bring to country and other musical styles, its use in creating these virtual voices—sanctioned and unsanctioned—already raises a variety of questions. In this essay, I explore three of these seemingly simple yet philosophically challenging questions: Who is the *author*? Who, if anyone, *owns* the performance? And are these performances *authentic*?

Authorship

Artistic authorship is often romanticized as an individual endeavor, whereby lone artists bring forth new works from the depths of their souls. Writer James Baldwin represented this view when he wrote that artists "must actively cultivate ... the state of being alone."[10] In reality, contemporary song creation—within and without country music—is usually a collaborative process involving composers, lyricists, arrangers, producers, engineers, and (of course) performers.[11] Performers, including singers, as authors of their own performance, create elements that can be crucial to the identity and meaning of a song that might otherwise not exist (in the hands of different performers). Add to this mix the inherited constraints and formulas that styles and genres impose on all these musical roles, and we arrive at an intricate notion of authorship that's far from the tortured expression of lone genius.

But even granting a thoroughly collaborative conception of authorship, we can see that the incorporation of AI makes matters more complicated still. Within the confines of current technology (which will almost assuredly loosen in coming years), a convincing AI singing impression is realized by altering a human performance of the song. For example, Dustin Ballard of There I Ruined It first sings the lyrics himself, doing his own imperfect impression of Hank Williams or Johnny Cash or whomever, before applying AI to his rendition. In "Where That Came From," Randy Travis's voice is actually an AI-transformed version of a performance by country singer James Dupré.[12] In the Elvis Evolution show, AI was presumably used to alter original Elvis performances (so that each new performance can be distinct). The AI component in all current cases is created by a computer analyzing ("training on") past performances of the impersonated singer and then re-rendering a particular performance—usually a new one by a surrogate singer—to achieve the final impression. So, in addition to the human author of the altered performance, there's a kind of distant, indirect, second human author we can acknowledge: the impersonated singer, whose signature sound is literally copied by the AI. I think it's fair to say the impersonated singer is an *indirect* author of all the AI's performances, just as a grandparent can be considered an indirect creator of a grandchild.

Yet it goes even further. It's not just that the timbre and the aural mannerisms of the celebrity are artificially mimicked. The AI must also, if it's to be successful as an impressionist, usurp the impersonated singer's identity. The virtual voice counts as an impression only to the extent it both *sounds like* and *is identifiable as* the original. It must create the illusion (however impermanently) that the impersonated singer is the *direct* author of the performance. This direct authorship is indeed an illusion, like Pepper's (or Elvis's) ghost, but it's an essential part of the enterprise. This is true even in examples of obvious parody, as when long-dead singers perform newer songs in contrasting styles. If we can't identify the voice singing "Straight Outta Compton" specifically as that of Hank Williams, the joke is largely lost; the performance becomes just another cross-stylistic cover, its AI component a mere novelty with no relevance to the song's expressive content. The impersonated human singer, thus, isn't just an actual indirect author of her AI impression; she's a fictional direct author as well.

An easy objection to raise here is that an AI impression is a forged (fake) performance, and forgeries are, by definition, not created by the author in question. In those simple terms, it would be hard to disagree. That said, I think the concept of forgery here leans heavily on a notion of authorship as an individualistic endeavor. If, by contrast, we bring collaboration into the mix, then there's more space to explore regarding types and extents of authorship, and thus more ways to talk about the nature of authorship with respect to impersonators. By employing some basic distinctions like direct versus indirect authorship, and real versus fictional authorship, we can begin to articulate how an AI impression can be understood as being more than merely a product of a forger. In the right light, we might see it as a product of a group effort.[13]

Ownership

If we can think of AI impressions as having multiple authors, in different modes and degrees of directness, how then do we approach the question of ownership? How do we even define the thing owned? Philosophers disagree about contemporary musical *ontology* (i.e., the nature of the relationship between performances and recordings versus works and compositions and songs).[14] There is such a range of opinions on this topic that some of us might argue these terms are no longer usefully distinguished from each other if they ever were. This is no mere academic exercise; even the U.S. Register of Copyrights recognized in 1975 that "the lines between musical composition, musical performance, and musical recording have broken down almost completely."[15] Still, in current American federal law, music is defined as a type of ownable intellectual property (i.e., copyright) that's legally protected in two forms: as a sound recording (or its "master") and as a composition (or its "publishing"). (Terms like "work" and "song" tend to be used on the composition side, while "performance" is associated with the recording side.) In this system, the owner of a composition need not also be the owner of a recording of that composition, and vice versa.

How does this strict legal dichotomy square with a collaborative conception of musical authorship? The answer is that musical authorship has no fixed relationship with musical ownership. A "work for hire" contract often applies in the music industry, meaning that composers and lyricists may sell their labor on a song for a flat fee, and performers may (and usually do) play a session with no expectation of royalties. The same often goes for producers and engineers. This isn't even to mention the informal, unpaid contributions to songwriting, performing, and recording that happen all the time and go completely unrecognized. Copyrights may also be bought and sold, in part or in whole—and they don't last forever. One's own conception of authorship is largely irrelevant here; authors may be owners, and owners may be authors, but oftentimes these are distinct, non-overlapping roles.[16]

Given this legal reality, the introduction of AI into the performance side of the equation won't likely affect the ownership of an underlying composition/work/song.[17] It could potentially affect the ownership of a recording/performance, but even then, there's no reliable way to generalize how things would play out. Even in a hypothetical case where a preexisting copyright had been clearly violated by an AI recording, a pre-trial settlement might financially compensate the original owner without legally acknowledging the original owner as a partial owner of the AI recording; effectively, this would be an owner's equivalent of a "work for hire" arrangement.

While it's difficult to make sweeping statements about ownership of AI musical performances in general, AI *impressions* are another matter, because impressions raise the issue of the so-called "right of publicity," which can be understood as ownership over the indices of a person's identity. These indices include things like one's name, signature, visual likeness, and the sound of one's voice. This is a form of intellectual property distinct from a sound recording and musical composition, and although there's no federal protection of these indices in the United States, several individual states have their own applicable laws, such as Tennessee's AI-oriented ELVIS Act. If we acknowledge that an AI impression requires the evocation of the impersonated human's identity, then it can be legally legitimate (depending on the jurisdiction) to claim that the owner of that human identity has some degree of ownership over that impression. According to this view, the identity owner's rights can be violated when such an impression is released without the owner's consent. In one seminal case, Ford Motor Company was found to have misappropriated Bette Midler's protected identity when one of their commercials used an unauthorized vocal impression of her—and a mediocre impression at that.[18]

But advertising is one thing; parody is another. In the landmark decision *Hustler v. Falwell,* the U.S. Supreme Court held that parody of public figures is a fundamental right protected by the U.S. Constitution.[19] And Hank Williams performing "Straight Outta Compton," Johnny Cash performing "Barbie Girl," and the rest of Ballard's absurd unsanctioned AI impressions are, I think, obvious parodies. Still, given that the protection afforded by the label "parody" can have massive legal ramifications, we're obliged to articulate as clearly as possible the dividing line between, say, Ballard's mashups on the one hand and Ford's false Midler on the other.

Why is one parody and not the other? Both are impressions; both create the illusion of direct authorship by a particular human performer by leveraging that human's artistic identity. The crucial difference, to my mind, is that in a parody we *know* it's an illusion. Ford made no attempt to clarify that their singer wasn't Midler; on the contrary, their goal, it seemed, was to fool us. Ballard, by contrast, sometimes goes out of his way to include us in the joke; at the end of "Straight Outta Compton," we hear "my voice just don't quite belong … nothing good'll come from this AI"; in "Barbie Girl," the very first line is "Hello, I'm not Johnny Cash." Even when his forgery isn't explicit in the lyrics, the images of Ballard's videos make the AI component plain. Despite our recognition of the voices—or, rather, *because* of it—we know it's an illusion. We know Conway Twitty didn't try on hip hop and George Strait didn't attempt heavy metal, just as we know there aren't real ghosts waltzing through Disneyland. Part of the fun of these experiences is letting ourselves emotionally respond as though they were real, all the while knowing rationally they're fake—AI or otherwise. Ownership over the indices of identity doesn't change when AI gets involved, but if the impressions are parodies of public figures, then the Supreme Court says the legal power of that ownership becomes deliberately circumscribed. I think this is good policy.

And yet, some of Ballard's uploads have been forcibly removed. Is there a reasonable argument to be made for such action? To my mind, the only justification for withholding protection from an AI parody is if one denies its human authorship and ownership. "Robots should not be subject to free speech," said U.S. Congressman Matt Gaetz about Ballard's "Barbie Girl,"[20] the implication being that only humans—not AI—have rights under U.S. federal and state law, and a recording that features virtual voices is thus not a protected human endeavor, regardless of whether it's parody. As was explained earlier, however, the current state of AI technology can't produce a convincing singing impression without an underlying human performance, so human authorship of the performance still obtains, to some degree; presumably, then, so should human ownership. At least, it should for the time being. In the not-too-distant future, AIs may be able to produce other AIs, without direct human intervention; in such a world, a human's "right of publicity" might (at least conceivably) outweigh the latitude we grant parody.

Authenticity

At first blush, the question of whether an AI performance can be "authentic" might seem to have an obvious answer of "no." The word "artificial" of "artificial intelligence" can itself mean "inauthentic" in a certain context. And a moment ago, I emphatically argued that Ballard's virtual voices are "fake," and that our recognition of this is actually one of their essential features as parody. Still, the concept of authenticity in music is notoriously multifaceted. As musicologist Ralf von Appen has noted, it's an idea that "addresses different, sometimes contradictory values, which are also subject to historical change and therefore cannot be reduced to a fixed common denominator."[21] The question of whether an AI performance can ever be considered "authentic," therefore, is more complicated than it might first appear. It really depends on what we mean by the term itself.

I'll touch on three different meanings of "authentic" as they relate to performances and recordings (not compositions/works/songs), starting with the most literal. An authentic performance can be one that's genuinely (read: directly) by the performer it sounds like. In this sense, AI impressions (like all impressions) are obviously inauthentic, even when released by the artists themselves. "Where That Came From" is not an authentic Randy Travis performance.

And yet diehard Travis fans might insist that they *do* find the track "authentic." I myself am willing to say this, too—but authentic in a different way. In this second sense of the term, an authentic performance is one that conveys something emotionally compelling, a state of heightened experience which we viscerally empathize with and recognize from our own inner psychological worlds.[22] Is this possible with AI? Absolutely. While the AI itself has no emotion and—I must assume—no experience (heightened or not), our individual responses to a performance are not predicated on the performer's state of mind, or whether they even have a mind at all. Yes, an effective technique in crafting a compelling performance can be a so-called "method" approach, wherein an actor or singer attempts to create internally the emotional state she wishes to convey externally. But this isn't a requirement. What matters here, it seems to me, is the audience's reaction. "Authentic" in this context is more a description of our response to a performance, rather than of the performance itself. Consider the fact that even the king had his detractors: "ELVIS CAN'T SING," wrote journalist Herb Rau in bold capitals in a review of a 1956 concert.[23] But plenty of people thought he could, and could do so authentically, because of the way he made them feel. As Rau cuttingly put it: "two thousand idiots per show yelp every time [Elvis] opens his mouth." Were he alive today, Rau might say the same about fans of AI Elvis, but that wouldn't delegitimize their experience any more than it did in 1956. If we understand this embattled type of authenticity as residing not in performers or performances but in audiences' emotional responses to them, I see no reason why a virtual voice couldn't be considered authentic by a listener who finds it rousing or moving.[24]

The third and final meaning of "authentic" that I find relevant here is articulated by philosopher Emmie Malone as one that "demonstrat[es] and embod[ies] the core value commitments of the genre," especially a "commitment to tradition."[25] This version of authenticity is more obviously applicable to song *lyrics* (which is to say, the composition/work/song), but it's not entirely irrelevant to performance. If we take an "authentic" performance to mean one that embodies a commitment to tradition, then the tradition in question will be that of musical performance itself; in other words, the way to connect to tradition purely through one's performance is to perform in a traditional way. Even without any formal training in music, the average fan will likely be able to aurally distinguish traditional country singing from punk singing, or from heavy metal singing, or from hip-hop singing. Can an AI sing in a traditional country style? Of course, as long as the underlying (altered) human performance is sung that way.

Country Music and the Virtual Voice

Virtual voices are likely here to stay. As they continue to evolve, they'll no doubt present new challenges to our conventional notions of authorship, ownership, and authenticity, so much so that we may need to revise these notions in order to keep up. Some of this revision might be purely intellectual and social (will we form separate fan bases around pro–AI versus anti–AI sentiments?), but some surely will have significant, tangible consequences, as we've already started to witness in the form of laws like the ELVIS Act and in the exclusion of certain AI recordings from Grammy contention in 2024.[26] It may be that we'll become increasingly vigilant and effective in keeping human voices separate from AIs, but it's also possible such separation can't be sustained long-term. While parody, as I've argued, will always require a degree of recognition of the gap between the real and the impersonated, what will happen when singers start to follow Randy Travis's lead and release their own virtual voices? Will we always be able to tell the difference? The next time we hear Travis singing "I Did My Part," will we be so sure the "I" isn't "AI"?[27] And if not, will it matter?

NOTES

1. For a taxonomy of use cases of AI in popular music, see Galuszka, Patryk. 2024. "The Influence of Generative AI on Popular Music: Fan Productions and the Reimagination of Iconic Voices." *Media, Culture, and Society*, 47(3).

2. Coscarelli, Joe. 2023. "An A.I. Hit of Fake 'Drake' and 'The Weeknd' Rattles the Music World." *New York Times* April 19.

3. As of the writing of this essay, Ballard keeps a website at there-i-ruined-it.com. His content is distributed on TikTok, YouTube, and Instagram.

4. Rose, Fred; Nelson, Edward. 1952. "Settin' the Woods on Fire." Williams, Hank (rec. artist). Rose, Fred (prod.) MGM Records; Ice Cube; MC Ren; The D.O.C. 1988. "Straight Outta Compton." *Straight Outta Compton*. N.W.A. (rec. artist). Dr. Dre; Yella, DJ (prod.) Ruthless Records; There I Ruined It. 2023. "Hank Williams sings Straight Outta Compton (AI)."

5. Cash, Johnny. 1957. "Folsom Prison Blues." *Johnny Cash with His Hot and Blue Guitar!* Phillips, Sam (prod.) Sun Records; Raste, Soren; Noreen, Claus; Dif, Rene; Nystrom, Lene. 1997. "Barbie Girl." *Aquarium*. Aqua (rec. artist). Jam, Johnny; Rasted, Soren; Norreen, Claus (prod.) Universal Records; the original upload of the AI has been removed, but can be found elsewhere online.

6. Huffman, Michael. 1981. "Tight Fittin' Jeans." *Mr. T.* Twitty, Conway. (rec.artist). Chancey, Ron (prod.) MCA Records; Jackson, Curtis; Young, Andre; Elizondo, Mike. 2003. "In da Club." *Get Rich or Die Tryin'*. Dr. Dre; Elizondo, Mike (prods.) Aftermath Entertainment; There I Ruined It. 2024. "In Da Club (by 'Conway Fitty')."

7. Blackwell, Otis. 1956. "Don't Be Cruel." Presley, Elvis (rec. artist). Sholes, Stephen H. (prod.) RCA Victor; Sir Mix-a-Lot. 1992. "Baby Got Back." *Mack Daddy*. Rubin, Rick (prod.) Def American Recordings; the original upload of the AI has been removed, but can be found elsewhere online.

8. Tennessee Code Annotated, Title 47, Chapter 25, Parts 1101–1108. See also Cochrane, Emily. 2024. "Tennessee Makes A.I. an Outlaw to Protect Its Country Music and More." *New York Times* March 21.

9. Veltman, Chloe. 2024. "Just Because Your Favorite Singer Is Dead Doesn't Mean You Can't See Them 'Live.'" *NPR* March 15. The promised hologram was scrapped.

10. Baldwin, James. 1961. "The Creative Process." *Creative America*. Suehsdorf, Adolphe (ed.) Ridge Press.

11. See Jarrett, Michael. *Producing Country: The Inside Story of the Great Recordings*. Wesleyan University Press; and Bennett, Joe. 2011. "Collaborative Songwriting: The Ontology of Negotiated Creativity in Popular Music Studio Practice." *Journal on the Art of Record Production* 5. For a musicological take on the recording process, one not on country specifically but with applicability to it, see Zak, Albin. 2001. *The Poetics of Rock: Cutting Tracks, Making Records*. University of California Press.

12. Cowan, Lee. 2024 "More Than a Decade After a Stroke, Randy Travis Sings Again, Courtesy of AI." *Sunday Morning*.

13. On the philosophy of artistic forgeries, see Dutton, Denis. 1983. *The Forger's Art: Forgery and the Philosophy of Art*. University of California Press; and Janaway, Christopher. 1999. "What a Musical Forgery Isn't." *British Journal of Aesthetics* 39(1), 62–71.

14. For starters, see Gracyk, Theodore. 1996. *Rhythm and Noise: An Aesthetics of Rock*. Duke University Press; Davies, Stephen. 2001. *Musical Works and Performances: A Philosophical Exploration*. Oxford University Press; and Kania, Andrew. 2006. "Making Tracks: The Ontology of Rock Music." *Journal of Aesthetics and Art Criticism* 64(4), 401–14. Although these writers do not address country music specifically, virtually all their arguments about rock music apply equally well to country.

15. Ringer, Barbara A. 1975. Testimony. Register of Copyrights. *Performance Royalty, Hearing on S. 1111 Before the Subcommittee on Patents, Trademarks, and Copyrights of the United States Senate*. 94th Congress, 11.

16. The most bizarre example of this phenomenon is undoubtedly the 1997 rock hit "Bitter Sweet Symphony" by the Verve, the composition of which (after multiple lawsuits) was credited entirely to Mick Jagger and Keith Richards of the Rolling Stones, who personally played no part in the actual writing or recording of the song. Two decades (and many millions of dollars) later, in 2019, the Stones gave back authorship credit and ownership of the composition to the Verve's Richard Ashcroft.

17. To clarify, this essay isn't addressing AI generation of a composition, only AI singing. The former is its own can of worms.

18. *Midler v. Ford Motor Co. 849 F.2d 460. 1988.*

19. *Hustler v. Falwell. 485 U.S. 46. 1988.* The relevant protections were found in the free speech portion of the First Amendment and the equal protection portion of the Fourteenth Amendment.

20. U.S. House of Representatives Judiciary Committee Hearing on Artificial Intelligence and Intellectual Property. Part II. "Identity in the Age of AI."

21. von Appen, Ralf. 2020. "Feigning or Feeling? On the Staging of Authenticity on Stage." *SAMPLES* 18.

22. See Dibben, Nicola. 2009. "Vocal Performance and the Projection of Emotional Authenticity." *The Ashgate Research Companion to Popular Musicology.* Scott, Derek B. (ed.) Ashgate, 317–33; and McCarthy, E. Doyle. 2009. "Emotional Performances as Dramas of Authenticity." *Authenticity in Culture, Self, and Society.* Vannini, Phillip and Williams, J. Patrick (eds.) Ashgate, 241–55.

23. Actually, an unfortunate typo rendered the statement as "ELVIS CAN'S SING." Rau's intent is clear, however, as this is followed by "can't play the guitar, and can't dance." Rau, Herb. 1956. "Idiot's Delight." *Miami Daily News* (August 4), 6. Doubtless, Rau meant Elvis couldn't sing well at all, but I assume this includes a lack of emotional authenticity.

24. I don't mean to suggest that all emotional reactions to musical performance are usefully connected to "authenticity." Rau himself conveys an emotional response to Elvis, one of disgust. "Authenticity" is a positively valenced concept, and as such it's generally reserved for positive emotional responses to performance. (Note that this positivity is separate from the emotions conveyed in the performance itself. For instance, we may respond positively to a performance we find authentically angry or sad—i.e., emotionally negative. If we didn't, there'd be no emotionally authentic punk or heavy metal or sad country songs.)

25. Malone, Evan. 2022. "Country Music and the Problem of Authenticity." *British Journal of Aesthetics* 63(1), 76, 87.

26. Lamarre, Carl. 2023. "Recording Academy Says A.I.-Generated Drake & The Weeknd Song Isn't Grammy Eligible After All." *Billboard.*

27. Montgomery, Melba; Satcher, Leslie; Rouillier, Tim Ryan. 1998. "I Did My Part." *You and You Alone.* Travis, Randy (rec. artist). Gallimore, Byron; Stroud, James (prods.) DreamWorks Records.

All Your Rowdy Friends

Gordon P. **Barnes** is an associate professor of philosophy at SUNY Brockport. He is the author of *How Do You Know? A Dialogue*. He grew up fishing in Chickamauga Lake and listening to Alabama on the radio. His brother introduced him to Hank Williams, and his wife and sisters showed him the way to Brandi Carlile and The Chicks.

Walter **Barta** is a principal investigator at the Digital Research Commons at the M.D. Anderson Library at the University of Houston where he works on digital humanities projects. His country of origin is the Republic of Texas, and some of his favorite country artists include Lady A, Brooks & Dunn, and John Denver.

Eric C. **Brook** is a professor of history and humanities at California Baptist University. He has published articles in the *Journal of the Philosophy of History*, *Contemporary Aesthetics*, *Fides et Historia*, and *Bryn Mawr Classical Reviews*. His favorite country artists are the progenitors of Outlaw Country, known collectively as the Highwaymen: Johnny Cash, Waylon Jennings, Kris Kristofferson, and Willie Nelson.

Jeffrey Patrick **Colgan** is a Ph.D. candidate in the philosophy department at Tulane University. His research focuses on the limits of language, how such limits impact political and ethical thought, and the various forms of philosophical writing. He is partial to country artists from his home state of Texas, particularly Guy Clark, Townes Van Zandt, and Terry Allen.

Andrea **Conque** is an assistant professor of philosophy at the University of Louisiana at Lafayette. She is the author of *Heidegger, Levinas, and the Feminine* (2009) and "'To Be in One's Love': Heidegger, Love, & the Moral-Political Posture of Authentic Solicitude" (2021). She often listens to Willie Nelson or Loretta Lynn in her spare time.

Brett **Coppenger** is an associate professor of philosophy and the director of the Liberal Studies Program at Tuskegee University. He is the co-editor of *Intellectual Assurance* (Oxford University Press, 2016). His research interests include epistemology, philosophy of science, and philosophy of religion. Some of his favorite country artists include Johnny Cash and Hank Williams.

Alexander **Crist** is an assistant professor of philosophy at Pensacola State College. His research is in the field of philosophical hermeneutics and the works of

Hans-Georg Gadamer, and he has published in journals such as *Analecta Herme-neutica*, *Epoché*, and *Existenz*. His favorite country music singers include Waylon Jennings, Ernest Tubb, Kris Kristofferson, and Loretta Lynn.

Jeannie **DePoe** teaches Latin at Kingdom Preparatory Academy in Lubbock, Texas. She is married to her co-contributor, John. Together, they are raising three children and two dogs. Jeannie's favorite country music artists include Willie Nelson, Merle Haggard, Dwight Yoakam, Dolly Parton, and Johnny Horton.

John M. **DePoe** is head of school at Kingdom Preparatory Academy in Lubbock, Texas. He is married to his co-contributor, Jeannie. He teaches and researches mostly in metaphysics, epistemology, and philosophy of religion. His favorite country music artists include Dwight Yoakam, Johnny Cash, Asleep at the Wheel, Brooks & Dunn, and George Strait's older stuff.

Christopher **Doll** is an associate professor of music at Rutgers, the State University of New Jersey. He is the author of *Hearing Harmony: Toward a Tonal Theory for the Rock Era*. He enjoys a wide range of music, but when in the mood for country, he favors Bob Wills, Hank Williams, Tammy Wynette, Dolly Parton, and the young Esther Rose.

Ian J. **Drake** is an associate professor of political science and law at Montclair State University. He previously practiced law. Recent publications include "Free Speech Rights v. Property and Privacy Rights: 'Ag-gag' Laws and the Limits of Property Rights," *Independent Review* Vol. 25, No. 4 (Spring 2021). His favorite country artists include Waylon Jennings, Garth Brooks, George Jones, and Dwight Yoakam.

Heather Salter **Dromm** is an instructor of English at Northwestern State University in Louisiana. She is the author of "Sexist Barriers in Happy Valley" in *MAI: Feminism and Visual Culture* and "Authenticity in Save Me the Waltz" in *New Approaches to the Jazz Age*. Her favorite country music artists include Patsy Cline, Willie Nelson, Charley Crockett, Bella White, and Rhiannon Giddens.

Keith **Dromm** is a professor of philosophy in the Louisiana Scholars' College at Northwestern State University. He is the author of *Wittgenstein on Rules and Nature* and *Sexual Harassment: An Introduction to the Conceptual and Ethical Issues*, and he is the co-editor (with Heather Salter Dromm) of *The Catcher in the Rye and Philosophy*. Among his favorite country music artists are Willie Nelson, Charley Crockett, Sierra Ferrell, and Tyler Childers.

Catherine Villanueva **Gardner** is a professor of philosophy and women's and gender studies at the University of Massachusetts Dartmouth. Although she specializes in feminist philosophy, especially ethics, epistemology, and the retrieval of forgotten historical women philosophers, she enjoys writing about pop culture. Her favorite country artists are Guy Clark and Lil Nas X.

Zack **Garrett** is a high school philosophy teacher in North Carolina. He received his Ph.D. from the University of Nebraska–Lincoln. Despite writing an essay about Taylor Swift, Zack prefers listening to Johnny Cash. Having grown up in East Tennessee, Zack is obligated and happy to add Dolly Parton to his list of favorite country artists.

Kristina **Gehrman** is an associate professor of philosophy at the University of Tennessee, Knoxville. Her research focuses on ethics and theories of value, and she has written on practical wisdom, the nature of action, and character. She listens to Billy Strings almost every day and loves Iris Dement, Bonnie Raitt, Willie Nelson, The Drive-By Truckers, Jason Isbell, and Tyler Childers.

Jakob R. **Gibson** is a graduate of the Kinder Institute at the University of Missouri, where he earned a master's degree in Atlantic history and politics. He has written on enhanced interrogation and original intent in the Supreme Court, and he contributed to *Better Call Saul and Philosophy* (2022). Among his favorite country artists are Keith Whitley, John Anderson, Trace Adkins, and the Marshall Tucker Band.

Tobias T. **Gibson** is a professor of political science and security studies at Westminster College, in Fulton, Missouri. He is the co-editor of three books: *Contextualizing Security: A Reader*; *Red Reckoning: The Cold War and The Transformation of American Life*; and *International Security Studies and Technology: Approaches, Assessments, and Frontiers*. His first favorite song is Tom T. Hall's "Sneaky Snake."

Theodore **Gracyk** is the author of books and articles on the aesthetics of music and the history of aesthetics. His most recent book, *Making Meaning in Popular Song*, received the 2023 American Society for Aesthetics Prize for outstanding monograph in the philosophy of art. Two of his favorite-ever concerts have been George Jones and Loretta Lynn.

Joshua **Heter** is an associate professor of philosophy at Jefferson College in Hillsboro, Missouri. He is the co-editor of a number of books on popular culture and philosophy including *Punk Rock and Philosophy: Research and Destroy* and *Post-Punk and Philosophy: Rip It Up and Think Again*. Some of his favorite country artists include Hank Williams, Loretta Lynn, Waylon Jennings, and Lissie.

Benjamin **Hutchens** is a lecturer III in the philosophy department at Rutgers. His articles have appeared in *Psychoanalytic Review*, *Substance*, *Epoché*, *Labyrinth*, *Literature and Theology*, *Ricoeur Studies*, *Sartre Studies International*, and the *Journal for Continental Philosophy of Religion*. Some of his favorite country artists include Waylon Jennings, George Jones, Loretta Lynn, Jamey Johnson, Tyler Childers, and Sierra Ferrell.

S. Evan **Kreider** is a professor of philosophy at the University of Wisconsin Oshkosh. He earned his Ph.D. in philosophy from the University of Kansas. He has published a variety of essays on pop culture and philosophy, and he co-edited *The Philosophy of Joss Whedon*. His favorite country artists include Johnny Cash, Martina McBride, and Willie Nelson.

Jonathan **Reibsamen** is a professor of philosophy at Columbia International University. He received his Ph.D. in philosophy from Saint Louis University. He is the author of "Divine Goodness and the Efficacy of Petitionary Prayer" (*Religious Studies* 2019) as well as pieces on epistemology and moral theory. Some of his favorite country artists are Johnny Cash, Dolly Parton, and Emmylou Harris.

Casey **Rentmeester** is a professor of philosophy and associate dean of academic success at Bellin College. He is co-editor of *Heidegger and Music* and author of

Heidegger and the Environment as well as numerous peer-reviewed journal articles and essays on philosophy. His favorite country artists include Hank Williams, Waylon Jennings, Merle Haggard, Willie Nelson, and Johnny Cash.

Cindy Muenchrath **Spady** teaches philosophy at her alma mater, Simpson College. She received her doctorate from Drew University. She wrote about David Letterman (one of her popular culture heroes) in *Ethics in Comedy*, also published by McFarland. Besides Dolly Parton, Cindy appreciates other '80s country artists such as Kenny Rogers and groups like Alabama.

Anthony Petros **Spanakos** is a professor of political science and law at Montclair State University, where he teaches and writes about the politics of democratization in Latin America, international relations, and popular culture and political theory. His family's car was the only one in Brooklyn in the 1980s playing country music, and he still finds rest listening to Randy Travis and Rodney Crowell.

Jenna **Yuzwa** is a Ph.D. candidate at the University of British Columbia. Her research interests are primarily in ancient Greek philosophy. She is deeply passionate about music and its ability to heal, empower, and establish meaningful connections. Raised on country music, she counts Carrie Underwood, Erin Kinsey, Jo Dee Messina, Hunter Hayes, and Reba McIntyre among her favorite artists.

Index

www.ingramcontent.com/pod-product-compliance
Ingram Content Group UK Ltd.
Pitfield, Milton Keynes, MK11 3LW, UK
UKHW021913170526
5819IPUK00012B/84